Elizabeth Missing Sewell

History of the Early Church

From the First Preaching of the Gospel to the Council of Nicea

Elizabeth Missing Sewell

History of the Early Church
From the First Preaching of the Gospel to the Council of Nicea

ISBN/EAN: 9783744704595

Printed in Europe, USA, Canada, Australia, Japan

Cover: Foto ©Lupo / pixelio.de

More available books at **www.hansebooks.com**

HISTORY

OF

THE EARLY CHURCH

FROM THE FIRST PREACHING OF THE GOSPEL
TO THE COUNCIL OF NICEA.

FOR THE USE OF YOUNG PERSONS.

BY

THE AUTHOR OF "AMY HERBERT."

NEW YORK:
D. APPLETON AND COMPANY,
443 & 445 BROADWAY.
1860.

PREFACE.

THIS little history has been compiled solely from English authorities. The writer has no knowledge of the Greek and Latin languages, and would never have undertaken to write a Church History but for the urgent representations of persons whose judgment she valued, and who assured her that, deficient as her work must necessarily be in originality and depth of research, it might nevertheless prove useful to young persons not in a position to refer to the standard authorities. The writer gratefully acknowledges the assistance given her by the friends to whom reference has been made, and without which she would have felt it a presumption to place her history before the public.

BONCHURCH:
April 7th, 1859.

CONTENTS.

CHRONOLOGICAL TABLE.

First Century.

Roman Emperors.	A.D.	Ecclesiastical Affairs.	A.D.
Augustus Cæsar . .	1	Crucifixion of our Blessed Lord, and Descent of the Holy Ghost . . .	33
Tiberius . . .	14	Death of St. Stephen, and Conversson of St. Paul .	37
Caligula . . .	37		
Claudius . . .	41	Conversion of Cornelius .	41
		First Council at Jerusalem	48
		St. Paul at Athens . .	50
		St. Paul at Ephesus . .	53
Nero	54	St. Paul tried before Felix	56
		First Persecution of the Christians . . .	64
		Martyrdom of St. Paul .	67
Galba . . .	68		
Otho	69		
Vitellius . . .	69		
Vespasian . . .	69	Destruction of Jerusalem .	70
Titus	79		
Domitian . . .	81	Second Persecution . .	90
Nerva	96		
Trajan	98	Death of St. John . .	98

Second Century.

Roman Emperors.	A.D.	Ecclesiastical Affairs.	A.D.
		The Third Persecution, and the Martyrdom of St. Ignatius	107
		Pliny's appeal to Trajan .	111
Adrian	117	Fourth Persecution . .	118
Antoninus Pius . .	138	First Apology of Justin Martyr	150
Marcus Aurelius .	161	Fifth Persecution . .	162
		Death of Justin Martyr .	165
		Martyrdom of St. Polycarp	167
		Rise of Montanism . .	171
Commodus . . .	188	Victor, Bishop of Rome .	189
Pertinax . .	193	Clemens Alexandrinus .	194
Severus . . .	199		

Third Century.

Roman Emperors.	A.D.	Ecclesiastical Affairs.	A.D.
		Sixth Persecution	202
		Martyrdom of St. Irenæus	203
		Origen Head of the Catechetical School at Alexandria	203
		Tertullian made Presbyter at Carthage	207
Caracalla	211		
Elagabalus	218		
Alexander Severus	222		
		Origen ordained Presbyter at Cæsarea	230
		Gregory Thaumaturgus becomes a pupil of Origen	235
Maximin	235		
Gordias	238		
Philip	244		
		Cyprian chosen Bishop of Carthage	248
		Eighth Persecution under Decius	249
Decius	249		
Gallus	251	Anthony the Hermit born	251
		The Novatian Schism	252
Valerian	253		
		Death of Origen	254
		Controversy respecting Baptism between Cyprian, Bishop of Carthage, and Stephen, Bishop of Rome.	256
		Ninth Persecution	257
		Martyrdom of St. Cyprian	258
Gallianus	259	Martyrdom of Pope Sixtus and his deacon Laurentius	259
		Paul of Samosata made Bishop of Antioch	260
Claudius II.	268		
		The Council of Antioch condems and deposes Paul of Samosata	270
Aurelian	270		
Tacitus	276		
Probus	276		
		Manichæan Heresy springs up	277
Carus Carinus and Numerian	282		
Diocletian	284		
		The Tenth Persecution, under Diocletian	300

Fourth Century.

Roman Emperors.	A.D.	Ecclesiastical Affairs.	A.D.
Constantius Chlorus and Galerius	304		
Constantine the Great	311		
		Conversion of Constantine	312
		Constantine becomes sole Monarch	325
		Council of Nicea	325

HISTORY OF THE EARLY CHURCH.

CHAPTER I.

THE DESCENT OF THE HOLY GHOST.   A. D. 33.

THE history of the Christian Church is doubtless the most important which can be written; but it is also in many respects the most difficult. The early period of a nation's existence, obscure as in the generality of cases it must necessarily be, may be set aside with comparatively little notice. Its legends and traditions may amuse us, but the amount of belief which we bestow upon them involves no important consequences, and can safely be left to our own option. In the Christian Church, on the contrary, the whole strength and value of the completed history rests upon the foundation. The structure built upon it is so vast, and involves interests of such overwhelming greatness, that the inquiry as to how it was laid, and from what materials it was formed, becomes important above all others. Trifling incidents, accidentally related, prove the witness to truths of vital consequence; observations made apparently without reference to any but the subject under discussion, serve to illustrate and enforce doctrines which lie at the very root of Christian belief; and thus it becomes necessary to gather up every fragment of history, and search with the utmost care into every authentic record, in order to collect from the whole that knowledge which will enable us to feel that the Church to which we belong rests upon " the foundation of Apostles and Prophets," and is a portion of the Spiritual Building of which Christ, Himself, is the " Chief Corner Stone."

It may perhaps be said that with the New Testament in our hands,—the divinely inspired record to which all defer,—there can be no need of any further search into the early history of the Christian Church. But we must not forget that the New Testament, including the Acts of the Apostles and their Epistles, does not profess to give us any minute and regular account of the formation of the Church. Unquestionably such an account may in a great degree be gathered from it,—but only by a careful comparison of one part with another, and by the aid of other witnesses whose writings throw light upon expressions which would otherwise remain obscure. And thus the object of early Church History is, to a great extent, to serve as a comment on the Sacred Writings, and to show how the allusions made in them to certain institutions and forms of government were understood and acted upon by those who were either the contemporaries of the Apostles, or their immediate successors.

Yet there is another point of view, in which the History of the Universal Church is less perplexing than that of the nations of the world. Though it relates to a body of individuals collected out of many nations, and might therefore, at first sight, be supposed to be inextricably entangled with the records of those nations, and to require a separate narrative for each national Church, yet this is not so in reality :—the Christian Church was from the earliest days Catholic or Universal ; the same

in Africa as in Asia, the same in Jerusalem as in
Rome. The life of a Christian in Jerusalem was
that of a Jew ; and the life of a Christian in Rome,
that of a Roman ; but these were earthly differences.
In faith all were alike, worshipping the same God,
believing in the same Saviour, partaking of the
same Sacraments, and looking forward with joyful
hope to an inheritance in the same glorious Kingdom when the trial of earthly existence should
be ended. So it was then, over the known world,
wherever Christianity had spread ; so it is now
in those Churches which have preserved the pure
faith and practice of the first ages.

In the earliest ages of the world, the revelation of true religion was confided to one people,
the Jews ; and, strictly speaking, it is from them
that we must derive the origin of the Church ; but
our present object is to trace its course when the
Providence of God willed that His Name should be
known beyond the narrow precincts of Judea.
Although the Jewish and Christian Churches are
parts of the same whole, it is only the latter to
which our attention is now to be called. The Great
Completer of the Jewish Church and the Divine
Head of the Christian Church is our Lord Jesus
Christ, the Eternal, all Holy Son of God, who "for
us men and for our salvation " took upon him our
nature, and about four thousand years after the
sin of the first man, being " conceived by the Holy
Ghost, and born of the Virgin Mary, suffered under
Pontius Pilate, was crucified, dead, and buried, descended into Hell, rose again the third day, ascended
into heaven, and now sitteth at the Right Hand of
God." His wonderful History we all profess to
know ; we have read also of the events which immediately followed His Ascension ; we have heard

of the labours of St. Peter and St. Paul, of St. James and St. John; we have been told of the numbers converted to Christianity at one time, and we have an idea that this was the beginning of the Christian Church. But it is all so unlike anything which happens in our days that we can scarcely imagine any connection between those times and our own; between persons taught by Apostles, witnessing miracles, and liable to great danger on account of their faith; and ourselves, who are instructed by men in no way distinguished from others except by their office, and who live in a world of common sights and common events, and are able to profess our belief without any thought of peril. We read of the early Christians as of the dwellers in a foreign land, almost as of the inhabitants of another world.

Yet they were men,—beings of "like passions with ourselves," and subject to like influences. The government under which they lived, and the laws to which they were subject, must therefore have had a great influence upon their lives, and the early condition of Christianity cannot be understood without a reference to the political history of the period when it was first preached. The sun, we are told, never sets upon the dominions of the monarch of England. As it vanishes from our sight beneath the horizon, it rises upon other lands owning allegiance to the same sovereign. And thus in those early Christian days it was—in a still wider degree, so far as the world was then known—with the mighty emperors of Rome.

The civilised earth was their kingdom. Italy, Gaul, Britain, Spain, Egypt, Syria, Palestine, even to the confines of India—all was subject to them. The Romans were the lords of the earth.

When the Jews willed to crucify our Blessed Redeemer, they applied to a Roman governor, because Palestine was subject to Rome; and the Jews, although still retaining their own manners and customs and religion, were, it seems, forbidden to put any one to death, except by permission from their rulers.

St. Paul, born in Tarsus, a city of Cilicia, in Asia Minor, was a Roman citizen. Asia Minor was but a province of Rome, and laws made in Rome, extended over the whole of the vast empire.

The power of the Romans is brought before us continually in the New Testament, and we learn from it how the Providence of God has been pleased to order the affairs of men for the increase of His own kingdom, the Christian Church. Doubtless He could have caused Christianity to take root at any time, and under any circumstances; but He is pleased to work, for the most part, by what are called natural laws; and it must be acknowledged that the state of the world, at the foundation of the Christian Church, was especially favourable to its progress. The Roman empire was at peace, increasing in luxury, outward refinement, and civilisation. Communication between different places was comparatively easy; and the emperors, although many of them fearfully wicked, did not generally trouble themselves with the religion of their subjects, but were willing that all should worship the gods of their own nations, so long as they did not interfere with those which were especially reverenced by the Romans themselves.

We shall see this plainly as we examine into the history of the Christian Church from its commencement. Heathen persecution was unknown

1*

at first. It began only when the great doctrines of Christianity were spreading far and wide, and men were taught that they could not worship Christ without at the same time renouncing their false gods.

The earliest opposition to the Christians arose from the Jews, or, if at any time, as in the instance of the tumults at Ephesus mentioned in the Acts of the Apostles, the heathen population rose up against the professors of the new faith, the excitement was caused by peculiar circumstances in some one city or province, and was not the persecution of the government.

" Gallio cared for none of these things," is a true description of the feeling entertained by the rulers of the Roman empire, as they first watched the growth of that " grain of mustard seed " which was afterwards to " spring up and overshadow the earth, till the fowls of the air should come and lodge in the branches thereof." If we inquire, then, into the beginning of the Christian Church, we must look at it as it took its rise in Jerusalem, and amongst Jews.

The excitement consequent upon the crucifixion of our Blessed Lord was over, Jerusalem was at peace. Her rulers and priests had satisfied their cruel envy ; and, although startled by the tidings of Christ's Resurrection, had stopped the witness of the Roman soldiers by bribes. Amongst the thousands who dwelt within and around the city, not many more than five hundred had been permitted to see their risen Master, and but eleven— His chosen friends—were witnesses of His wonderful ascension. The rest—the multitude—thought not of Him ; or, if they did think, if the scenes of His dying agony still haunted them in the watches of the night, and the fearful cry, " His blood be on us, and on our children," still echoed in their ears, amidst the din of the world's business, they had the means within their reach for stifling the pangs of conscience. " Eating and drinking, marrying and giving in marriage," so they woke in the morning, and lay down to rest at night; and Pilate sat again upon his judgment seat, and Herod surrounded himself with his men of war, and the Chief Priests and Scribes followed their schemes of ambition and self-interest, and none probably deemed it worth their while to cast a thought upon the large upper room, (the same, it has been supposed by some, in which the Lord partook of His Last Supper,) where, obedient to the command of their Master not to depart from Jerusalem, but to wait for the fulfilment of His promise,—abode " Peter and James, and John, and Andrew, Philip and Thomas, Bartholomew, and Matthew, James, the son of Alpheus, and Simon Zelotes, and Judas, the brother of James."

Prayer and supplication, we are told, was their occupation, and in these prayers joined also " the women, and Mary the Mother of Jesus, and His brethren," with a small number of disciples, making in all about one hundred and twenty persons. It was a season of patient waiting and preparation; but one other duty was required of them. The number of the chosen apostles was broken. The vacant place of the traitor Judas was to be filled from amongst those who had " companied with them all the time that the Lord Jesus went in and out among them, and who had been witnesses with them of His resurrection."

St. Peter, first in zeal and energy now, as he had been when following his Lord, was the Apostle who proposed that this important step should be taken, and the rest of the disciples, agreeing with his opinion, two persons, between whom the choice was to be made, were selected;—"Joseph, called Barsabas, who was surnamed Justus, and Matthias. And they prayed and said, Thou Lord, which knowest the hearts of all men, show whether of these two Thou hast chosen, that he may take part of this ministry and apostleship, from which Judas by transgression fell, that he might go to his own place. And they gave forth their lots; and the lot fell upon Matthias; and he was numbered with the eleven apostles."

The first government of the Christian Church was now therefore established; but the Spirit which was to give it power was yet withheld. And still the Apostles and disciples assembled together in patient expectation, until "the day of Pentecost was fully come."

This festival was held seven weeks after the Passover, and appears to have been originally instituted as an acknowledgment of the goodness of God in securing to His people the fruits of the barley harvest, which was generally gathered in about that time. But the Jewish Rabbins also called it the day of the giving of the law, it being a received opinion amongst the Jews, that on this day—fifty days that is after the departure of the children of Israel from Egypt—the law was given from Mount Sinai.

A new law was now to be given, written not with "the finger of God upon tables of stone," but by the Spirit of God on the hearts of those who were admitted into the Kingdom of Christ.

On the festival of Pentecost then, the disciples, we are told, were "all with one accord in one place; and suddenly there came a sound from heaven as of a rushing mighty wind, and it filled all the house where they were sitting. And there appeared unto them cloven tongues, like as of fire, and it sat upon each of them. And they were all filled with the Holy Ghost, and began to speak with other tongues, as the Spirit gave them utterance." The place must, as it seems, have been one of public resort, for the knowledge of the wonderful event was quickly spread abroad, and the multitudes assembled in Jerusalem crowded to the spot to be witnesses themselves of the truth of the report.

Amongst them were persons gathered from various countries. Some Jews by descent, yet born in distant parts of the Roman empire; others, proselytes, or persons converted from heathenism to the knowledge of the true God, and joining therefore in the services of the Jewish religion. Many came from Asia Minor, others from Egypt and Arabia, others from Rome itself, yet each individual, whatever might be his native language, heard from the lips of those untaught, uneducated Galileans " the wonderful Works of God."

The effect of the miracle upon their minds differed according to their natural characters. It was not, as we might at first sight be inclined to think likely, so convincing as to convert them at once to a belief in the Apostles' divine mission. Those most religiously disposed were full of surprise and doubt as to the meaning of what they saw and heard; whilst others, turning the scene into mockery, accused the Apostles of having indulged in wine to a sinful excess, and having lost the use of their reason. Then Peter stood up in the midst of the assembly, and addressed the multitude in the first sermon delivered by a Christian minister to those whom he was sent to win to the service of Christ.

The words, as they have been handed down to us by a divinely inspired writer, are few, simple, and wonderfully calm, but they fell with an awful power upon the hearts of those who listened to them.

Touched by the sudden conviction that one whom they had rejected and crucified was indeed the Son of the Most High God, and that the offence committed against Him was heinous, and fearing probably that it was unpardonable, they exclaimed, addressing the Apostles: " Men and Brethren, what shall we do ? "

" Then Peter said unto them, Repent, and be baptized every one of you in the name of Jesus Christ, for the remission of sins, and ye shall receive the gift of the Holy Ghost."

Baptism then was the door whereby persons, on their repentance, and having made a profession of their belief, were admitted into the Christian Church.

For thus had our Lord commanded when, as He was about to ascend into heaven, He gave to His disciples that solemn injunction, " Go ye therefore and teach, or (as the words are more properly translated) make disciples of all nations, baptizing them in the Name of the Father, and of the Son, and of the Holy Ghost."

Then they that gladly received St. Peter's words were baptized ; " and the same day there were added unto them about three thousand souls."

It may be well to pause for a moment and consider the astonishing change which this event made in the position of the twelve Apostles, and the few disciples who had continued with them from the day of their Lord's Ascension.

On the morning of the Feast of Pentecost they had risen as usual unnoticed, uncared for, or, if observed at all, pointed at, probably, as the despised followers of that Jesus of Nazareth, who had endeavoured to mislead the people, and had suffered the death of a malefactor. Their small body was but as a drop in the vast ocean of human beings who were then crowding Jerusalem.

Before night the Apostles were the leaders and teachers of no less than three thousand followers, collected from various nations, bound to them by the most sacred of all ties, willing witnesses to the fact of the great miracle which gave them their power, and anxious only to follow their commands, and devote themselves to the service of their common Lord.

How did the Apostles act under such changed circumstances ?

When conversing with their Lord during His sojourn upon earth, they seem to have had continually in their minds the idea of an earthly dominion ; a power which was to free Judea from its subjection to the Romans, and establish its rule over the kingdoms of the world. Was there any such thought in their minds now ? Did they gather together their followers, and form schemes of worldly advancement, or plans of government for the increase of their own authority ?

Scripture gives us the answer when describing the lives of the first converts : " And they continued steadfastly in the Apostles' doctrine and fellowship, and in breaking of bread, and in prayers. And all that believed were together, and had all things common, and sold their possessions and goods, and parted them to all men, as every man had need, and they continuing daily with one accord in the Temple, and breaking bread from house to house, did eat their meat with gladness and singleness of heart, praising God, and having favour with all the people." Humility, faith, unselfishness, and charity towards each other, the observance of the Jewish worship in public, and in private, the celebration of the Sacrament of the Lord's supper—these were the distinguishing marks of the first Christians. And it was to form such characters that the divine energy conferred upon the Apostles was exerted. Many saw, and wondered, and reverenced, and at length joined them, "And the Lord added to the Church daily such as should be saved."

CHAPTER II.

THE DEATH OF ST. STEPHEN. A.D. 37.

THE spread of the new doctrines could not remain unnoticed. They caused a complete change in the lives of those who received them. With the feeling that all were brothers, the wealthier disciples were anxious to give up any particular claim to their worldly goods, and to share them with those who were in need.

But as the number of converts increased, it was felt desirable to distribute the alms more regularly. The money collected by the sale of lands and houses was therefore brought humbly to the Apostles and placed at their disposal.

The first person mentioned as adopting this

practice, was Joses, a Levite by descent, but a native of the island of Cyprus. He had relations living in Jerusalem, for his sister had a house there, but whether he was himself permanently settled in the city, or only resident for a time, we are not told. It is certain, however, that his benevolence and sympathy had already attracted the notice of the Apostles, for they had bestowed upon him the name of Barnabas, or the Son of Consolation. "He," we are informed, "having land, sold it, and brought the money, and laid it at the Apostles' feet." His example was followed by Ananias and Sapphira who,—attempting to practise a deception as to the amount which they had received for their property, and to offer a part for the whole, —were, after a solemn warning and prophecy from St. Peter, struck dead.

This was the first punishment inflicted by God through the Apostles, and its effects were extensive. Great fear fell upon all. If any had been tempted to profess themselves the followers of Christ merely for the sake of obtaining a share in the common property, they were now warned that they had to deal with persons whom they could not deceive; and the declaration made by St. Peter that Ananias in lying to men gifted with the Holy Ghost was lying unto God, must have been a fresh lesson even to the disciples as to the infinite Majesty of the wonderful Power which was working amongst them. Miracles were now constantly performed by the Apostles, and in the most public place— Solomon's Porch, under the colonnade of which was the common winter walk of the inhabitants of Jerusalem. Many persons even " brought forth the sick into the streets, and laid them on beds and couches that, at least, the shadow of Peter passing by might overshadow some of them." This was easily done, since the beds commonly used by the poorer classes among the Jews consisted only of mats or skins, with mattresses laid upon them; whilst their upper garment, which was a kind of loose blanket, served them for a coverlid. Multitudes also came out of the city around Jerusalem, bringing with them the sick, and persons vexed with unclean spirits, all of whom were healed.

That the influence of the Apostles should extend even beyond Jerusalem excited the envy of the High Priest to the utmost degree. He appears to have been inclined, himself, to hold the doctrines of the Sadducees, who denied the possibility of a resurrection, and must therefore have been especially indignant at the assertion of the resurrection of Christ, and they now joined in supporting his acts however unjust. The Apostles were suddenly seized and committed to the common prison, a place of confinement for the worst kind of offenders.

On the following morning the great council of the nation, the Sanhedrim, was assembled; together with the rulers collected from other Jewish cities who were in Jerusalem at that time.

As the Sanhedrim will be frequently mentioned in the history of the Apostles, it may be desirable to describe it more particularly.

It is supposed to have been instituted about sixty years before the birth of our Saviour, and was composed of seventy or seventy-two members. The High Priest presided over it, and under him were two vice presidents. One, called the father of the council, sat always on the right hand of the High Priest; the other was placed on the left hand. The remainder of the council consisted of the Chief Priests, the Elders, and the Scribes.

The Chief Priests were persons who had either

been high priests, or who were princes over the twenty-four classes into which the priests in general were divided. The Elders are supposed to have been the princes or heads of families, and the Scribes were persons learned in the law. But it does not appear that all the elders and scribes were members of the Sanhedrim; most probably those only belonged to it who were chosen to the office, or appointed by royal authority.

The Sanhedrim held its meetings in a council house close to the Temple, forming in fact part of it; for the Jews tell us that the room was of a circular shape, half built without the Temple and half within; and as it was never permitted to sit down in the Temple, this latter half was for those members of the council who stood up, whilst in the inner portion sat the judges.

It has been said that in particular emergencies the Sanhedrim was assembled in the High Priest's house, and thus it may have been in the instance of our Lord's trial. The power of the Sanhedrim was very great; but it had become less since the subjection of Judea to the Roman power. It could not now condemn a man to death.

The Jews had also other small councils, for judging cases of slight importance; two of these were established at Jerusalem, and there was one also in every city which contained 120 inhabitants. The heads of these smaller councils then present in Jerusalem were probably joined with the Sanhedrim on the day following the seizure of the Apostles, since they would of course be interested in inquiring into the spread of the Christian doctrines; and we are particularly told that besides the Council or Sanhedrim, "all the Senate of the children of Israel" were assembled on the occasion.

Great indeed must have been the astonishment of this large body of princes and rulers when, upon the return of the officers who were sent to bring the Apostles before them, they were told that the prison doors were shut, and the men whom they had so closely confined, were "standing in the Temple and teaching the people."

The captain of the guard went himself with the officers to the Temple, and, without violence, summoned the Apostles to the Council. On their appearance, the High Priest spoke to them, not so much angrily as reproachfully. He complained that they had neglected the command laid upon them, to desist from teaching the new doctrine, and insinuated that they were bringing upon the Council a false accusation, by suggesting to the people that the sentence of death pronounced against Jesus had been unjust. The reply of Peter and the other Apostles was bold and simple, as it had been when addressing the people. They openly repeated the charge of the murder of their Lord, and insisted upon the duty of obeying God rather than man. And the Council, cut to the heart by the accusation and the defiance, then began to consult together as to the possibility of silencing them by death.

The danger of the Apostles' situation was very great, but help was granted them from a quarter from whence they would have been little likely to expect it. Gamaliel, a Pharisee, and a member of the Sanhedrim, seeing the lengths to which the blind rage of his fellow-judges was likely to lead them, insisted upon the Apostles being taken aside whilst some more deliberate consultation was held respecting them.

Gamaliel was a man learned in the Jewish law,

a teacher and director of the most highly gifted young men of the day, and held in such reputation amongst the people that the title of Rabban—given only to seven persons—had been bestowed upon him. His opinion therefore was received with great deference. The Apostles were put forth, and Gamaliel then addressed the assembly in a cautious speech which showed the natural reverence of his mind, and a decided doubt whether the Christian doctrines were not indeed the Truth. This doubt must have been almost conviction, if it is true, as it has been stated, that he was the son of the aged Simeon who took our Saviour in his arms and blessed Him, and who would naturally have brought up his child in a confident belief in the speedy establishment of the Messiah's kingdom. The Council, he said, should take heed to themselves as to what they intended to do touching these men. In former days. persons had risen up in Judea and stirred up the people to insurrection; but their efforts had come to nought. If, therefore, this work of the Apostles was of men, they might naturally hope it would die away; but if it was of God, it could not be overthrown, and they themselves would be found to be fighting against God.

The opinion of Gamaliel checked the wrathful feelings of the Council; but they could not be prevailed upon to give up all thoughts of vengeance. The Apostles were therefore publicly beaten, again commanded " not to speak in the name of Jesus," and then once more released.

" And they departed from the presence of the Council, rejoicing that they were counted worthy to suffer shame for His Name;" whilst still, in the Temple and in private houses, they continued " to teach and to preach Jesus Christ."

2*

The whole management of the affairs of the Church was at this time entirely in the Apostles' hands; but as the number of Christians increased, the temporal or worldly business connected with them increased likewise, and something of a worldly spirit seems for the first time to show itself amongst them.

A complaint was made that the alms were not equally distributed. The murmurings arose amongst the Grecians, or Hellenistic Jews, so called because, although of Jewish origin, they were born, and generally lived, in foreign countries. A considerable difference of feeling had for many years existed between these two divisions of the Jewish people. The Jews born and educated in Judea, and speaking the language of their forefathers, were called Hebrews, and esteemed more honourable than the Hellenists. They considered themselves the especial keepers of the Law; and one cause of complaint against the Hellenistic Jews was that the Scriptures were read to them from the Septuagint, or Greek translation of the Old Testament.

It was natural that the Hellenists should regard with some suspicion the proceedings of persons who had long been taught to look down upon them; and even the feeling that they were all " one in Christ Jesus " does not seem entirely to have conquered their distrust.

A report was brought to the Apostles that the widows of the Hellenists were neglected in the daily division of alms. The disciples were immediately assembled, and a proposal was made to appoint an order of deacons, similar to one already known in the Jewish Church, whose particular duty it should be to attend to the wants of the poor; the Apostles declaring that it was not reasonable for them to give up their higher duty of praying and instructing the people, for the sake of superintending the tables at which the persons requiring alms were accustomed to receive their money.

The disciples were therefore desired to choose from amongst themselves seven men of " honest report," whom the Apostles might afterwards appoint to this work.   The suggestion was approved by every one, and seven persons were elected ; all of them, as it has been remarked*, probably Hellenists, since the names are Greek.

Stephen, " a man full of faith and of the Holy Ghost," was the most distinguished ; the others are named in Scripture, but only one of them is especially brought before us in the history of the Acts of the Apostles.   They were set apart for their office by solemn prayers and the laying on of the hands of the Apostles.

From the accounts afterwards given, they must have had authority also to teach and to baptize.

The Christian doctrines had by this time taken so deep a root, that a great company of the priests were obedient to the faith.   Probably the support given to the Apostles by Gamaliel had influenced them ; certainly it must have given them confidence by showing that one at least among the chief rulers in Jerusalem was disinclined to treat the new converts with severity.

The faith, wisdom, and energy of Stephen were especially instrumental in converting others to the truth, and his power of working miracles, which was very great, naturally attracted the people to him, and in the end excited a far fiercer persecution than had yet been endured by the Christians.

* See Blunt's " Scriptural Coincidences."

There were at this period in Jerusalem several synagogues intended for the use of foreign Jews. Amongst these were synagogues for the Cyrenians and Alexandrians, from Africa; and for others who were dwellers in Asia Minor; besides one for persons called Libertines, either the inhabitants of the city of Libertina in Africa, or, as is generally supposed, a body of Roman Jews or proselytes, who had been freed from slavery, and, a few years before, had been banished from Rome by the command of the Emperor Tiberius. These synagogues were not only places set apart for prayer and the reading of the law, but schools where young persons were instructed; and this circumstance gave occasion for public arguments concerning the new doctrines, to be held by persons belonging to them.

Stephen was the great upholder of Christian truth, and his opponents were not able to resist the " wisdom and the spirit by which he spoke." But instead of confessing themselves conquered they resolved to destroy him.

By working upon the minds of the people, who were jealous of everything likely to interfere with their old customs and traditions, they excited a tumult, in the midst of which Stephen was seized and carried before the Sanhedrim. Accusations were made against him by several witnesses, for it was contrary to the Jewish law to receive the evidence of one only. He was said to have spoken blasphemous words against the Temple and the Jewish law, and to have declared that Jesus of Nazareth would destroy the Temple and change the customs delivered to the Jews by Moses.

The same kind of accusation had been made against our Blessed Lord in a yet more fierce and enraged assembly, and doubtless, we may believe, that the remembrance stirred up the courage of Stephen to bear witness for his crucified and risen Master.

The eyes of all in the Council were fixed steadfastly on him, but he did not shrink. The glorious presence of God's Spirit filled his soul, and its brightness rested even on his outward form, and the proud judges of the Sanhedrim, as they gazed upon him, " saw his face as it had been the face of an angel."

His defence was long ; not confined only to the declaration of his innocence, but going back even to the very foundation of the Jewish religion, and showing that it was but a forerunner of the Christian dispensation. His feelings seem to have been more and more roused as he continued speaking ; and at length,—struck apparently by the similarity between the conduct of the ancient Jews in persecuting the prophets and that of·their descendants in murdering Christ,—he burst forth into an indignant expostulation, warning them against the indulgence of the same obdurate blindness which their forefathers had exhibited ; and reminding them that the law given immediately from heaven, had yet by the Jewish people been rejected.

Up to this point, Stephen had been heard patiently, but the keen reproof which now burst from him cut his hearers to the heart, and they gnashed upon him with their teeth. Calm, trustful, and filled with the Holy Ghost, Stephen turned from them and looked up steadfastly into heaven. A wonderful vision was revealed to him. He saw the glory of God, and Jesus standing on the Right Hand of God, and said, " Behold, I see the heavens open, and the Son of Man standing on the Right Hand of God."

His enemies would hear no more. In the mad-ness of their rage they stopped their ears, rushed upon him, and without waiting for any further examination, dragged him out of the city, and prepared to stone him.

Amongst those who followed in the tumult was a young man destined to become one of the most devoted followers of the Lord.   Saul (afterwards the Apostle Paul) was by descent a Hebrew of the tribe of Benjamin, though born in Tarsus, a large commerical city, the capital of Cilicia, in Asia Minor. He was also a Roman citizen, a dignity which conferred upon him many privileges that could only be obtained by others for a large sum of money. He had been early brought to Jerusalem, and instructed in the severe doctrines of the Pharisees, and he followed their customs with the utmost strictness. The teaching he received must in some respects have been good, for he was the pupil of the wise Gamaliel, whose character seems to have been both cautious and gentle. But Saul was by nature fiercely impetuous, though possessing warm affections and being personally self-denying.   He was zealous for his principles even to cruelty, and endued with a power of will which carried everything before it.

His intercourse with the Pharisees had aroused his zeal against the followers of Christ; and carried away by his strong feeling of indignation against the new doctrine, and probably also remembering the denunciation which Jesus had pronounced against those who had been his teachers and guides, he cast aside every feeling of justice, and joined in the fierce tumult which was to end in the death of Stephen.

By the Jewish law sentence against a criminal could never be carried into execution on the same day on which the trial was held. By the Roman law the punishment of death could only be pronounced by a Roman judge. Saul knew these things well. He had been versed in the Jewish law from his youth; and the power of Rome was dear to him as one of her noble citizens; but all was forgotten then. The savage cries of the multitude resounded in his ears, the witnesses, who, according to the Law, were the first to cast the stone at him whom their testimony had condemned, were preparing themselves for their fearful office, yet Saul stood by unmoved; so resolute indeed in his fierce determination that when the witnesses threw aside their loose outer garments, that they might be able with greater ease to fulfil their murderous task, they laid down their clothes at his feet, certain that he at least was heartily consenting to Stephen's death. " And they stoned Stephen." The words speak to us of horrible suffering, but the vision vouchsafed to Stephen might well wrap his soul in ecstasy, and steep in insensibility the quick sense of human anguish. As the heavy stones fell upon him with their crushing weight, he called upon God, saying, " Lord Jesus, receive my spirit. And he kneeled down, and cried with a loud voice, Lord, lay not this sin to their charge. And when he had said this he fell asleep."

CHAPTER III.

THE CONVERSION OF SAUL.　　A.D. 37.

Devout men carried Stephen to his burial; the first Martyr in the cause of Christ; the first who was laid to rest " in the sure and certain hope of joyful resurrection." Great were the lamentations over him, but far greater cause had those who bore him to lament for themselves. The persecution which had begun was not to cease as before with the first outbreak. The stormy passions excited by the murder of Stephen raged even after his death, and Saul especially, having joined publicly in expressing his enmity to Christianity, was carried on by his blind zeal and made havoc of the Church, " entering into every house, and haling men and women committed them to prison." In the trials that followed his voice was always in favour of the sentence of death, which was often passed against the disciples; and not satisfied with punishing them, he endeavoured to make them, from dread of suffering, blaspheme that Holy Name which was afterwards to be his only hope.

The disciples left Jerusalem, the Apostles only remaining behind. Many were scattered abroad in Judea, whilst Philip, one of the seven deacons, who had been appointed with Stephen to the especial charge of the poor, went to the city of Samaria.

The Samaritans, from their national enmity to the Jews, were perhaps less likely to have heard of the progress of Christianity than even the dwellers in more distant countries. Samaria had been inhabited now for many centuries by the descendants of the colonists, whom Shalmaneser, King of Assyria, placed in the country when the Israelites were carried away captive. The religion of the Samaritans was a corruption of Judaism. They rejected all the books of the Scriptures except the five written by Moses, but these were regarded with the same reverence by them as by the Jews.

But the chief question in dispute between the

two nations regarded the sacredness of the Temple of Jerusalem. When, in the days of Ezra and Nehemiah, the Jews were allowed to return and rebuild their Temple, the greatest opposition was made by the Samaritans, and ever since that time the enmity had continued. The Samaritans held that God might be worshipped on Mount Gerizim as well as on Mount Sion; their prejudices were less than those of the Jews, and they had not the same overweening idea of their own importance as the peculiar people of God. From these causes, probably, they were more prepared to receive Christianity, and when Philip, the deacon, fulfilling his office, preached the Christian doctrines, and performed many wonderful miracles, the Samaritans, we are told, heard him with joy, and consented to be baptized.

Tidings of this fact were carried to Jerusalem, and the Apostles, putting aside any prejudice which as Jews they might have entertained with regard to the Samaritans, immediately " sent unto them Peter and John, who, when they were come down, prayed for them, that they might receive the Holy Ghost, for as yet He was fallen upon none of them. Then laid they their hands on them, and they received the Holy Ghost."

The great gift then was only conferred through the Apostles. It is the earliest instance mentioned of the laying on of hands after Baptism, which is the origin of the rite of Confirmation; and with it is connected the first mention of one who afterwards caused many to turn from the faith, and whose name has been transmitted to us by the sin which after him has been termed Simony, or the endeavour to purchase spiritual power by money.

Simon Magus, or Simon the Sorcerer, who had for a long time deceived the people of Samaria by magical tricks, was so far convinced of the truth of the Gospel that he consented to be baptized. But the spirit of the world was still strong in him, and when he found that the Apostles, by laying their hands on the disciples, could impart to them the power of speaking with tongues and working miracles, " he offered them money, saying, Give me also the power that on whomsoever I lay hands he may receive the Holy Ghost."

Peter gave him a most stern rebuke, exhorting him to repent and " pray God, if perhaps the thought of his heart might be forgiven him," and Simon was for the moment awed; but we shall find from after circumstances, that his repentance had no reality, and was merely the effect of a momentary fear.

The Apostles returned to Jerusalem, preaching in several Samaritan villages on their way, whilst Philip, the deacon, was sent by a special command from God, delivered by an angel, to the south-west of Judea. There he met an Ethiopian eunuch, an officer in the service of the Queen of Ethiopia, and a proselyte to Judaism, who had visited Jerusalem for the purpose of joining in the public services. The eunuch was on his journey homewards, and as he travelled he studied the Hebrew Scriptures. Philip by divine direction joined him, and entering into conversation instructed him as to the facts and doctrines of Christianity. The eunuch professed his belief, was baptized, and went on his way rejoicing. Some say he was the first to plant the church in Ethiopia. Philip was caught away by the Spirit, and was found at Azotus, a town on the Mediterranean, about forty or fifty miles from Gaza, from whence he journeyed to Cæsarea preaching the Gospel.

Saul, in the mean time, was bending the whole force of his vehement will to the task of extirpating the Christians, not only from Judea, but from those more distant provinces of the Roman empire where they might have taken refuge. With this view he went to the High Priest, and entreated that he might be sent to Damascus, where at that period no less than ten thousand Jews were living, in order to make inquiries whether any professing the faith of Christ could be found amongst them. The suspected persons were to be brought bound to Jerusalem, there to be punished by the Sanhedrim; for that council had power in religious matters even over the Jews who were resident in foreign countries.

Letters to the heads of the synagogues in Damascus were accordingly given him, and Saul set forth accompanied by several other persons.

They had journeyed some days, and about noon had nearly reached Damascus, when suddenly, a light, dazzling and glorious above the brightness of the sun, burst upon them; and as they fell to the earth in exceeding terror, a voice from heaven was heard saying, in the Hebrew tongue: "Saul, Saul, why persecutest thou Me? It is hard for thee to kick against the pricks."

The words were understood by none but Saul. Fearful and conscience-stricken, he replied: "Who art Thou, Lord?" and again he was answered: "I am Jesus, whom thou persecutest. But rise, and stand upon thy feet; for I have appeared unto thee for this purpose, to make thee a minister, and a witness, both of these things which thou hast seen, and of those things in the which I will appear unto thee;

delivering thee from the people, and from the Gentiles unto whom now I send thee, to open their eyes and to turn them from darkness to light, and from the power of Satan unto God, that they may receive forgiveness of sins and inheritance among them which are sanctified by faith that is in Me."

And he trembling, and astonished, said, " Lord, what wilt thou have me to do?"   And the Lord said unto him, " Arise, and go into the city, and it shall be told thee what thou must do."

Saul obeyed ; and rose up from the earth blind, but in faith a Christian.

They led him into the city, and there for three days he remained in the house of Judas, (probably one of the disciples,) neither eating nor drinking, and in utter darkness.   Yet not hopeless, for he prayed.   At the expiration of those three days, God had mercy upon him, and sending to him a disciple named Ananias, who laid his hands upon him, restored him to sight.   And he " arose and was baptized."

The great persecutor of the faith was converted ; but it was long before the Apostles at Jerusalem were convinced of the fact.   For three years Saul remained in Arabia ; either in those parts of the country which were near Damascus, where he may have occupied himself in preaching the Gospel ; or else living a life of meditation in the most distant and solitary regions, as a preparation for his coming work.   Then, returning to the city of Damascus, he taught openly in the synagogues, to the great indignation of the Jews, who at length " took counsel to kill him."   Day and night they watched at the gates of the city, but the disciples having learnt ingenuity by danger, let him down by the wall in a basket, by which means he escaped and hastened to Jerusalem.

Here the difficulties and encouragements which were now to be his unceasing companions followed him. The disciples, knowing only what his former disposition towards them had been, shunned him. One friend, however, Barnabas, the Son of Consolation, was found to come forward in his support. Barnabas had known Saul before, and could vouch for the sincerity of his conversion. It is not unlikely, indeed, that they had been acquaintances from boyhood, for Barnabas was a native of Cyprus, an island forming part of that province of Cilicia of which Tarsus, Saul's native place, was the chief city. It would be natural, therefore, for Barnabas to have received his education in some one of the great schools in which Tarsus at that time abounded. There is a tradition also that he had been a fellow-pupil with Saul, in the school of Gamaliel, at Jerusalem. Either of these reasons would account for the interest in Saul which Barnabas displayed on this occasion, and which so satisfied St. Peter and St. James, who were the only Apostles then in Jerusalem to whom Saul had made himself known, that they at once received him with confidence, admitted him to their intimacy, and allowed him to preach, and especially to dispute with the Hellenistic Jews; and when his zeal had excited such indignation in Jerusalem as to cause his life to be in danger, they took measures for conveying him to Cæsarea, and sent him from thence to his native city Tarsus. The persecution which Saul had commenced was by this time stopped, and " the churches throughout all Judea, and Galilee, and Samaria, had rest, and

3*

walking in the fear of the Lord, and in the comfort of the Holy Ghost, were multiplied."

CHAPTER IV.

THE CONVERSION OF CORNELIUS.   A.D. 41.

THE events which have been described, including the season of peace, occupied about ten years from the crucifixion of our Lord.   During that period, many public changes had taken place, both in Rome and in Judea.   The Emperor Tiberius was dead, and Caligula, the youngest son of his nephew A.D. 87. Germanicus, had succeeded him.   Both these emperors were monsters of wickedness, and the Jews suffered from them some of the calamities which they had themselves inflicted upon the followers of Christ.

They had rejected their Lord, and owned no king but Cæsar, and Pilate brought the image of Cæsar into Jerusalem to be worshipped ; took the money which they put aside for the service of the Temple, and with it paid the cost of an aqueduct which he had built, and at last provoked them to open rebellion, and excited an insurrection in which very many were killed.

The Christians were then too inconsiderable to excite his anger.   It is even said that Pilate, looking upon our Lord's life and death merely as curious events in the history of the country which he governed, sent an account of them to Tiberius, who would have placed the statue of Christ amongst those of the Roman gods, but that the senate refused to permit it.   After Pilate had ruled over

Judea ten years, public accusations were brought against him, and the governor of Syria deprived him of his office, and sent him to Rome to answer the charges made against him. This was during the reign of Tiberius, whose death took place the following year. Caligula banished Pilate to Gaul, where we are told that he lived in misery, and at last died by his own hand. The story of his punishment and his fate still lingers amongst the mighty hills which separate France from Switzerland. The peasants of the district say that he cast himself from the summit of an inaccessible mountain, now called Mount Pilatus, and they point to its rocky peaks with awe, and shudder as they whisper that the lost spirit of the murderer of Jesus still haunts the spot where he sought his own destruction.

The reign of Caligula was one of peace for the followers of Christ, but for the Jewish nation it was marked by great troubles. The emperor, as insane as he was wicked, commanded the Jews to transfer their worship to him, and to dedicate their Temple to his honour. The Jews scoffed, as justly they might, at the idea of such a divinity, and when complaints were made against them to the emperor, sent the most learned man of their own nation, Philo, a nobleman of Alexandria, skilled in all the points of the Jewish religion as well as the Greek philosophy, to make their defence. This, however, only enraged the emperor the more against them, and cruelties were inflicted upon them, which were but the beginning of the calamities that, according to the prophecy of our Lord, were soon to end in their utter ruin.

A.D. 41.   Caligula died, and Claudius, his uncle, succeeded him. That was a memorable year for the Christian Church, the most memorable of all since the first outpouring of the Holy Spirit, for it was the beginning of the fulfilment of the great prophecy that Christ should be " a light to lighten the Gentiles" as well as " the glory of His people Israel."

Hitherto the Christian disciples had all been either Jews by birth, Samaritans, or proselytes to the Jewish religion. They observed the rites of Moses, kept the appointed festivals and fasts, assembled in the synagogues, and joined in the worship of the Temple. In all respects they were like their brethren, except that they believed the Messiah to be come, whilst the others looked forward to His future appearance. Even in name they were scarcely distinguished as a distinct people, for they were known only as the sect of the Nazarenes.

But the time was at hand when the glad tidings of salvation were to be made known not only to the children of Abraham, but to the farthest kingdoms of the earth.

For more than ten years salvation had been preached to the Jews. Some had embraced it, thousands had rejected it; now the Apostles were to turn to the Gentiles.

Saul was at Tarsus, preaching the faith of Christ in his native city; Peter was at Joppa, a city on the shores of the Mediterranean, where he had performed the miracle of raising the dead to life; and tarrying there many days, lodged in the house of " one " Simon, a tanner, whose house was by the sea-side.

It was the sixth hour of the day, an appointed hour for prayer, and Peter, who carefully observed all the outward rules of the Jewish religion, went up upon the flat roof of the house, overlooking the beautiful shores of the Mediterranean, to pray.

" And he became very hungry, and would have eaten, but while they made ready, he fell into a trance, and saw heaven opened, and a certain vessel descending unto him, as it had been a great sheet knit at the four corners, and let down to the earth: wherein were all manner of four-footed beasts of the earth, and wild beasts, and creeping things, and fowls of the air. And there came a voice to him saying, Rise, Peter, kill, and eat."

The command was strange indeed to a Jew, accustomed from his infancy to the most scrupulous distinctions as to food, clean and unclean. But when Peter hesitated, it was given a second time in the form of a reproof: " What God hath cleansed, that call not thou common." This was done thrice, and the vessel was received up again into heaven.

Whilst Peter was pondering upon the meaning of this vision, three men, strangers, had entered Joppa, and were inquiring for the house of Simon. Even then they stood before the gate.

Peter, directed by the Spirit of God, went down to them instantly, and demanded for what cause they had come. They had arrived from Cæsarea, an important city of Palestine, named by Herod the Great, in honour of the Emperor Augustus. A Roman centurion living there, a just and holy man, a worshipper of the true God, and " of good report among all the nation of the Jews," had been warned by an angel to send for Peter to his house, and to hear words of him. And this was the message brought by the strangers.

A few hours before, Peter might have doubted what answer to make. It was unlawful for a Jew to " keep company, or come unto one of another nation ; " unlawful, not according to the law of Moses, but according to the teaching of the Scribes and the customs of the country.   But the vision which he had seen bore a clear meaning.   God had showed him that he should not call any man common or unclean.

The men were received and lodged, for it was then too late to set out on the journey ; and on the following day Peter and several disciples from Joppa departed for Cæsarea.   They reached the city on the succeeding day.   Cornelius with his kinsmen and near friends were awaiting their arrival, and on Peter's approach, Cornelius, overcome with awe, and thinking him a heavenly messenger, fell at his feet and worshipped him.

Peter rejected in a moment the undue reverence, and declaring himself to be only a man, inquired further particulars of the reasons which had induced Cornelius to send for him.

The story was related in detail, and Peter then declared his conviction that God was no " respecter of persons," and turning to the persons assembled, spoke to them of the faith of Christ, and the promise of forgiveness of sins granted through Him. Whilst he was yet speaking, the Holy Ghost fell upon those who listened to him, enabling them to speak in other tongues.

No other proof was needed that God had willed that the Gentiles should be admitted to the same privileges as the Jews.   Even the Jewish disciples who had accompanied Peter were convinced.   And the new converts were forthwith baptized, and received as living members of that Holy Church which was now indeed to become Catholic.

So it has been considered by some that our Lord's

promise to St. Peter, "upon this rock I will build my Church," received its chief fulfilment. Through his means especially was the Church built upon its true foundation — faith in the Son of God. He had been the first to preach to the Jews on the day of Pentecost, and now he was appointed to open the gates of salvation to the Gentiles.

The tidings of the conversion of Cornelius were soon carried to Jerusalem, and although at first some of the strictest of the Jewish disciples objected to the admission of uncircumcised persons into the Church, yet St. Peter's account of the miraculous gift of the Holy Ghost convinced them at last that to reject them would be to reject the known will of God. But it was long before the Jews could fully overcome their early prejudice; and the first disputes which disturbed the peace of the Church were as to the necessity that the Gentile converts should adhere to the rites and ceremonies of the Jewish law.

The tranquillity of the Church was not again interrupted until about two years after the conversion of Cornelius. Up to that time the Gospel had continued to spread principally in Syria and the island of Cyprus, the birthplace of Barnabas. At Antioch in Syria, especially, the disciples were numerous, and both Barnabas and Saul dwelt there for a year to instruct the new converts, who were then for the first time called Christians.

The name is supposed to have been given them by the Gentiles, as the Jews were not likely to apply the sacred word Christ or Anointed to those whom they held to be the followers of a false Messiah.

The year 43 was marked by a terrible famine from which Judea especially suffered, and Saul and

Barnabas left Antioch and went up to Jerusalem, carrying with them the contributions which the disciples had collected for the relief of their brethren.   And in the same year another persecution was excited against the Christians, not, as before, by the Chief Priests and Scribes, but by Herod Agrippa, the king who then reigned over Judea.   This Herod Agrippa was a grandson of Herod the Great, in whose reign the Saviour of the world was born.   He had been much in favour with the Emperor Caligula, and was now still more so with Claudius, who, in addition to other gifts, had lately made him King of Judea. He was a prudent, clever, courteous, worldly-minded man, well aware that it was for his own interest to profess himself a zealous observer of the Jewish law.   No day, therefore, was suffered to pass without his being present at the sacrifice in the Temple; whilst, in order to gain the favour of the people, he resolved to persecute the Christians, as their doctrines were supposed to be entirely destructive of the law of Moses.   Herod's cruel zeal was first exercised upon the Apostle James, commonly called the Great, the son of Zebedee and Salome.   Salome is supposed to have been a first cousin of the Blessed Virgin, so that St. James was a near relation of our Lord.   He was apprehended and brought to trial, and a false accuser stood forth to witness against him; but the Apostle, supported by superhuman power, showed a courage and constancy which even his bitterest enemy could not look upon without wonder.   The very man who had publicly testified against him, became in heart his follower, and when, on the morning succeeding his trial, St. James was brought forth to the place of execution, his accuser threw himself at his feet, and entreated his forgiveness. The Apostle raised and embraced him. " Peace, my son," he said, " peace be to thee, and the pardon of thy faults." And the blessed words of reconciliation were followed by the only reward which could then have satisfied the heart of the Apostle ;—his enemy professed himself to be a Christian, and both were led away to be beheaded at the same time.

Neither baptism nor any other ordinance of the Church was required to testify the sincerity of such a convert, and no doubt could be entertained that God's Grace was with him. The early Christians, indeed, always looked upon martyrdom for the faith of Christ as fully admitting into the Church those who endured it, and were accustomed to call it the Baptism of Blood.

The anger of Herod Agrippa was not appeased by the murder of St. James. Peter also was thrown into prison, from whence he was released by the interposition of an angel ; and the king's wrath fell upon his keepers, who were put to death. But the punishment of Herod's crimes followed quickly upon their commission. Shortly after the death of St. James, he went down to Cæsarea for the purpose of holding a great festival in honour of the Emperor Claudius Cæsar. On the second day he came with great state into the theatre, to make an oration to the people. His robe, which was curiously worked in silver, shone with dazzling brightness, and the people, in their impious flattery, proclaimed him a god. Herod received their homage without any mark of displeasure, " and immediately the Angel of the Lord smote him, because he gave not God the glory : and he was eaten of worms, and gave up the Ghost."

4

CHAPTER V.

THE FIRST COUNCIL HELD AT JERUSALEM. A.D. 48.

THERE is a tradition (entitled to considerable respect) that our Lord commanded the Apostles not to leave Jerusalem till after twelve years from His ascension; and traces are to be found in the sacred history tending to support this opinion. It seems indeed to be in a manner confirmed by the fact already mentioned, that at the time of the persecution which followed the death of Stephen, all the Christians, except the Apostles, were " scattered abroad." A residence at Jerusalem did not, however, necessarily imply that they were always stationary in that city, but only that they made it their head-quarters, whilst visiting from time to time the churches established in Judea, Samaria, and Galilee. One great reason for this regulation has been suggested, namely, that our Saviour, in His infinite Wisdom, may have seen fit to establish the Gospel firmly in one place, and collect a great body of disciples united around one common centre, so as fully to draw attention to the excellence of the Christian Church, and cause its power to be known and felt, before any attempt was definitely made to spread it in distant lands. Certainly, there is every reason to think that up to this time none of the Apostles had left Palestine.

But the promise that in Christ Jesus " all families of the earth" were to be blessed, was now to be strictly fulfilled. Paul and Barnabas had returned to Antioch after their mission to Jerusalem, at the period of the famine, and were continuing their labours, assisted by several prophets and teachers; and amongst them Manaen, the fourth brother of Herod Agrippa, who had been brought up with him. They ministered, it is said, " unto the Lord and fasted "—words which imply some peculiarly solemn religious services; and whilst engaged in them a special intimation of God's Will was given. A great work was to be undertaken, and Saul and his faithful companion Barnabas were to be set apart for it.

Whether this communication was made by means of a voice from heaven, or by a vision to some of the prophets, we are not told, but it was instantly obeyed. A time of fasting and humiliation was observed, and the two friends, now publicly announced as the Apostles of Christ, were ordained by the laying on of hands, and sent forth on their first missionary journey. John, surnamed Mark, the nephew of Barnabas, accompanied them as their minister, or attendant, to assist them probably in their inferior and more mechanical duties, as we find before that there were " young men " ready to carry out the bodies of Ananias and Sapphira. The appointment of Saul and Barnabas is another proof that none took any office in the Church who were not regularly chosen; and that the laying on of hands was the form of ordination, as well as the means by which the gifts of the Holy Ghost were conferred.

The island of Cyprus and the South of Asia Minor were the regions first visited by the two Apostles; but at the very commencement of their labours they met with a grievous disappointment in their companion. John had, as it seems, gone with them willingly to Cyprus, where, probably, he had relations and friends, since his uncle was by birth a

Cypriote; but when they proceeded to Perga, in Pamphylia, his heart failed him. The journey before him was unknown, and likely to be full of perils, he could not summon up the courage necessary to encounter it, and he returned to Jerusalem, leaving the Apostles to pursue their way alone; cast down, doubtless, but not " in despair," at this instance of lukewarmness.

Wherever they went, they preached first in the Jewish Synagogue, and then, when persecution met them, turned to the Gentiles. Numbers were converted, and Christian congregations, always termed Churches, were formed in many cities; elders being appointed over them, who were ordained by the Apostles with prayer and fasting.

This journey seems to have occupied about a year, at the expiration of which time the Apostles returned to Antioch, and gathering the disciples around them, rehearsed all that God had done with them, and how He had " opened the door of faith" unto the Gentiles. It was during this journey that Saul is first mentioned in Scripture by the name of Paul. Some have supposed the change to have arisen from the conversion of the Proconsul, Sergius Paulus, in the island of Cyprus, and believe that the name of Paul was adopted by the Apostle in remembrance of the event : but it seems more probable that it was a second name borne by St. Paul from his childhood. Heathen appellations were often adopted by the Jews, sometimes from a special reason, and at others merely from a resemblance in the sound.

After this about three years went by, during which time the Christians remained undisturbed by persecution from without. But they were not so free from dissensions within. The reception of the Gentile converts into the Church had caused a controversy, which it required all the inspired wisdom of the Apostles to set at rest. The dispute was first made public at Antioch. Certain Jews came down from Judea and taught the Gentile converts that unless they observed all the laws of Moses they could not be saved.

This was a most important question, for the Mosaic law was full of rites and ceremonies, and minute regulations, which had in themselves a deep meaning, as referring to the sacrifice of Christ, and were sacred to the Jews as the token of their being the peculiar people of God; but the Gentiles knew nothing of them. They had no need of types and figures now that Christ had offered himself as the one atoning Sacrifice, and the customs which the Jews venerated were to them only burdensome.

Paul and Barnabas, taking part with the Gentiles, disputed the point warmly, but finding that it could not be settled satisfactorily, they determined to go up to Jerusalem to consult with the Apostles and elders.

Titus, afterwards bishop of Crete, went with them. Being a Gentile, he was uncircumcised. This fact was known to some of the Jewish Christians at Jerusalem, and excited considerable indignation amongst them. St. Paul, with the determination peculiar to his character, refused to yield for a moment to a clamour which he considered an encroachment upon the liberty of the Christian religion; and the differences between the two parties became more and more serious. Private conferences took place between St. Paul and the most important heads of the Church, St. James, St. Peter, and St. John, and at length it was resolved that a general council—the first council of the

4*

Christian Church—should be held to decide the point. (A. D. 48.)

James, commonly called St. James the Less, presided over it. Different opinions have been held as to the parentage of this Apostle. He is called in Scripture the Lord's brother. Several ancient historians say that he was the son of Joseph by a former wife; whilst others, finding that he is also called the Son of Alphæus, suppose that the word brother only implies that he was our Lord's near relation, probably His cousin, the appellation being often used by the Jews in that sense. The Jewish historian Josephus speaks of James, the brother of Jesus. Little is said of him in the Gospel, though we know from St. Paul that our Saviour vouchsafed to appear to him particularly after His resurrection. He was a man of singular piety, who had been educated in the strictest regard to his religious duties: but his humility was as great as his devotion; and although one of the twelve chosen Apostles, yet in speaking of himself in his Epistle he styles himself only, "the servant of the Lord Jesus." He was, we are told, consecrated to be a Nazarite from his birth, and always lived according to the strict rules given by Moses for those who wished thus to "separate themselves unto the Lord." He never ate meat nor drank wine, walked barefoot, and wore only linen garments. His reputation for sanctity was indeed so great that he was universally styled, James the Just. Many thought that the prosperity of their country depended upon his prayers, and gave him the title of Oblias, or Ozliam, " the defence and fortress of the people." Prayer was his business and delight; he continually resorted to the temple that he might pray alone; and we are informed that, from the habit of constantly kneeling, his knees became worn and hard as those of a camel.

St. James the Less is supposed to have been chosen Bishop of Jerusalem on account of his near relationship to our Blessed Lord; some have said that the dignity was conferred on him by Christ Himself, but this fact is doubtful. It is certain, however, that he was considered the head of the Church on the occasion of this first Council. The Apostles and Elders met together at the appointed time, and the discussions began irregularly; but " when there had been much disputing," Peter stood up to state the circumstances which had first proved it to be God's Will that the Gentiles should be admitted to Christianity; and strongly urged that they should not be called upon to submit to the yoke of ceremonies which neither the Jews themselves, nor their forefathers had been able to bear. He was followed by Paul and Barnabas, who gave their testimony as to the miracles which God had enabled them to work among the Gentiles, and which plainly showed that His blessing was upon their labours. The account must have been most interesting to those who had only known of these great events by hearsay. The multitude kept silence, listening attentively whilst the two missionary Apostles related the history of their wanderings and their success; and when at length they ceased, James, the presiding bishop, gave the decision which was to be from thenceforth the rule of the Christian Church.

The gentleness and consideration for the feelings and prejudices of both Jews and Gentiles, shown in the decree which was then set forth, is a most striking lesson to all in every age. Circumcision, as being only an outward rite, was at once declared unnecessary for the Gentiles, and the Apostle—speaking, as he himself said, by the inspiration of the Holy Ghost—declared that no greater burden was to be laid upon them than that of leading a life of purity, abstaining from meats offered in sacrifice to idols, and from things strangled, and from blood.

These latter orders were no doubt given out of consideration for the national feelings of the Jews. The laws of Moses strictly enjoined that the blood of animals used for food should be drained from them immediately after their death. The custom made a marked distinction between the Jewish feasts and those of the heathen. It formed somewhat of the same kind of barrier between them as that of caste does among the Hindoos. The Jews dwelt amongst the Gentiles, and bought and sold with them, but their family life was quite apart; and they would be the less willing to put an end to this separation, because it was well known that the grossest wickedness was practised at many of the feasts of the Gentiles, especially those connected with their idol worship; whilst the Law of Moses, read continually in the foreign synagogues, proved a perpetual protest against any connection with such guilty festivities.

In the same way the Jews felt an utter abhorrence of things sold for food after they had been offered to idols, whilst the Gentile converts had no such scruples. If, therefore, no regulation was made upon this subject, the Jewish Christians would be liable to be continually shocked by the conduct of their Gentile brethren. The laws laid down were necessary in those days, to preserve the peace of the Church, but they ceased to be requisite in after years, when idolatry was no longer prevalent throughout the world.

At the close of the Council, some other points, more particularly referring to St. Paul himself, were decided.   His conduct and that of St. Barnabas, as regarded the Gentiles, was fully approved; and it was settled, with the approbation of St. James, St. Peter, and St. John, that as God had so evidently appointed them to the work of preaching to the Gentiles, they should thenceforth devote themselves to it especially, while St. Peter laboured amongst the Jews.   St. Paul himself, when writing to the Galatians of the cordial unanimity of feeling shown on this occasion, says, " they gave to me and Barnabas the right hands of fellowship."   Words especially to be remarked because this occasion is the only one on which we know for certain that the gentle St. John, and the impetuous St. Paul, ever met, whilst it is the last mention made in Scripture of St. John, previous to his vision in the Isle of Patmos.

When the Council broke up, Paul and Barnabas returned to Antioch, accompanied by Judas, surnamed Barsabas, and Silas, " chief men among the brethren."   It has also been thought that Mark went with them, as he is soon afterwards spoken of as being at Antioch with his uncle Barnabas.   They carried with them letters from the Apostles and Elders, containing the decree which had just been made, and were charged also with a special mission to collect contributions from the Gentile and Jewish converts for their poor brethren in Jerusalem; a duty to which several allusions are made in the Epistles of St. Paul.

All differences of opinion upon the important question as to the necessity of observing the Jewish ordinances must now have appeared to be entirely set at rest; but religious prejudices are, of all others, the most difficult to be overcome. Some time after the decree of the Church was made known, a party of Jewish Christians came from Jerusalem to Antioch, and disregarding the opinion of the Council, still refused to eat with the Gentiles. The old feeling of distinction between the two parties was revived in consequence ; and St. Peter, who about the same time happened to be at Antioch, fearing to shock the Jews, not only yielded to their prejudice, although he had before mixed freely with all, but induced Barnabas likewise to dissemble his true sentiments, and separate himself from his Gentile brethren.   St. Paul only stood firm.

The circumstance affords an interesting illustration of the character of the different Apostles,— Peter, we are told, feared " them which were of the circumcision ; " so, in other days, had he feared the servants of the High Priest, and denied his Lord. Barnabas, the Son of Consolation, full of gentleness and affection, doubtless dreaded to provoke ill feeling, and yielded the point against the better suggestions of his reason and conscience,—whilst Paul, steadfast now in the cause of truth, as he had once been in that of error, boldly maintained his ground, declared that such doubleness of conduct was inconsistent with the uprightness of the Gospel ; and addressing Peter openly, before an assembly of their fellow-Christians, exclaimed, with all the ardour natural to him, " If thou, being a Jew, livest after the manner of the Gentiles, and not as do the Jews, why compellest thou the Gentiles to live as do the Jews ? "

St. Paul and St. Peter are, in this instance, strongly contrasted in character, and it may perhaps be interesting to remark that the scene to which allusion is here made, must also, according to the general impression handed down to us from tradition, have exhibited them as strikingly unlike also in personal appearance. St. Paul is said to have been of small stature, and to have suffered from lameness, or some other distortion. He is described likewise as having a bald head, and a beard which was long and thin, a complexion clear, and changing rapidly according to his feelings, bright grey eyes, with thickly overhanging eyebrows, and a manner cheerful and winning to all. He does not appear to have enjoyed very good health, and an ancient writer speaks of his being frequently afflicted with headache. St. Peter is represented as having been a much larger and harsher looking man, with a pale, sallow complexion, dark flashing eyes, and black hair curling thickly round his forehead and chin.

The result of the Apostles' disagreement at this time we are not directly told ; but if the excitable and unstable temperament of Peter led him, even after being strengthened with the Holy Ghost, into conduct inconsistent with the simplicity of Christ's religion, his generous affection and natural candour, doubtless, urged him to acknowledge it ; and when we read his reference, many years afterwards, to the " Epistles of his beloved brother Paul," we may find in it the proof of their mutual forgiveness and hearty reconciliation.

The tie which united Paul and Barnabas was probably of a yet more tender nature than that which linked together the two great Apostles of the Jewish and Gentile Churches. Barnabas had trusted and welcomed Paul when others had looked upon him with suspicion ; and the grateful, noble spirit of the converted Apostle must have clung to that of his earnest and gentle friend with a warmth increased perhaps by the very contrast in their natural dispositions.

One fault could not destroy a friendship so deeply rooted in the fellowship of Christian love. With a sad yet tender reproach, and offering, incidentally, an excuse for the error, St. Paul, in writing to the Galatians, alludes to the weakness of one whom he must have so dearly loved, " Barnabas also," he says, " was carried away by their dissimulation." It is but a passing mention required by truth, yet the uncompromising temper of St. Paul must have been sorely tried by the instability of his friend, not only in this instance, but in the circumstances which were shortly to follow.

CHAPTER VI.

ST. PAUL AT ATHENS. A.D. 50.

It has been said that before the Council at Jerusalem broke up, a division was made of the two great branches of the Christian Church; St. Paul and St. Barnabas being especially pointed out as the Apostles who were to labour amongst the heathen. The time was now come when this arrangement was to be carried into effect, and the missionary labours of the Church were again to commence. St. Paul applied to Barnabas, whom he evidently still considered his chosen companion. " Let us go again," he said, " and visit our brethren in every city where we have preached the word, and see how they do." The wish was in accordance with St. Paul's natural character, and the deep affection which he appears always to have felt for those who had been converted by his ministry. But the same human weakness which had induced Barnabas to yield to the prejudices of the Jews, rather than excite their ill will by opposition, now led him to insist upon carrying with them his nephew John, surnamed Mark, who had, on a previous occasion, left them at Perga.

A sharp contention followed. Paul could feel no trust in Mark, after his past conduct; Barnabas, probably, forgave everything from the consideration that he was his sister's son. Finding it impossible to agree, they at length determined to separate. Barnabas, taking Mark with him, proceeded to his native island, Cyprus; and Paul, accompanied by Silas, set forth on a journey through Syria and Cilicia, confirming the Churches, and delivering to them the decrees respecting the observance of the Jewish law, which had been ordained by the Apostles and Elders at Jerusalem.

At Lystra he was joined by Timothy, the son of a Greek who had married a Jewess. Eunice, the mother of Timothy, was remarkable for her unfeigned piety and the care which she had taken of her child's early education. Timothy had been instructed in the Scriptures from his youth, and his character stood very high with the Christians of Lystra and the neighbouring city of Iconium; but although well versed in the Jewish law he had never been circumcised. His father, being a Greek, probably did not consider it necessary. It is said that the parents of Timothy were converted to Christianity during St. Paul's first journey, when he came with Barnabas to Lystra and miraculously cured the impotent cripple; and we are further told that they received St. Paul into their house, entertained him hospitably, and gave up their son to his care.   Whether this was so or not, we know from the sacred writings that St. Paul's affection for Timothy was very great, and that it was his particular desire that his young convert should accompany him in his long and dangerous wanderings.   Previous to their setting forth, however, St. Paul required that Timothy should submit to the rite of circumcision.   There were many Jews dwelling in those quarters, and it must have appeared unwise to offend their preju- dices ; and although, at first sight, when we re- member how firmly St. Paul withstood the circum- cision of Titus, there may seem some inconsistency in this conduct, yet, when we look into the question carefully, we shall see that it was the same motive of Christian charity which actuated St. Paul in both instances.   The Jews demanded the circum- cision of Titus as necessary to his salvation; they said that unless the whole law of Moses was kept, a Christian could not be saved.   St. Paul denied this, and firmly refused to do anything which might be supposed to sanction the doctrine : therefore he would not allow Titus to be circum- cised.   But in the case of Timothy no such claim was made; only, as he was about to preach in places where there were many Jews, St. Paul, will- ing, as he says, to make himself " all things to all men," did not choose to shock them by introducing amongst them, as their teacher, a person who claimed to belong to their nation, and yet would not submit to the rites of their religion.

After their sójourn at Lystra, St. Paul and his two companions passed through Phrygia and Ga- latia,—turning aside from certain other provinces of Asia Minor by the express command of the Spirit of God,—and, journeying toward the sea-coast, reached Troas, a city of Mysia. Another friend was here added to their party,—Luke, commonly called the Evangelist, a physician by profession, and said to have been both a learned and accomplished man, and particularly skilful in painting. He is spoken of as a painter by ancient writers, and a very old inscription, found in a vault under a church at Rome, makes mention of a picture of the Blessed Virgin, as being one of the seven painted by St. Luke.

St. Luke was a native of Antioch in Syria, and, it is supposed, was converted by St. Paul during his residence in that city. His presence at Troas must have been no small comfort to the Apostle, himself a man of cultivated mind, and accustomed to associate with persons of learning and science ; and still greater must have been his satisfaction when he found that St. Luke, besides cheering him with his society during the short time that he remained at Troas, was also willing to accompany him into the distant regions where the Providence of God was calling him.

For the time was now come when the Gospel was to be preached in Europe.

We can scarcely realize the greatness of that fact. Europe is to us now more especially Christendom—the land of Christ. We can with difficulty carry back our thoughts to the time when temples thronged with the worshippers of Zeus and Aphrodite, Apollo and Athene, and the innumerable other deities whom the folly or the needs of men had invented, crowned the lofty hills, or lay sheltered in the quiet valleys of Greece. It is an effort to imagine the proud citizens of Rome bowing before the statue of Jupiter, and the noble Roman ladies devoting themselves to the service of Vesta. The histories of these deities seem to us too monstrous to be believed for a moment by beings on whom God has bestowed the gift of reason. Still less, perhaps, can we imagine the dreary darkness of the few wiser and better heathen, who felt in themselves that craving for perfection and immortality which God has left us as a part of our original nature, yet saw that the gods whom they professed to worship were, like themselves, sinful and miserable,— greater in wickedness as well as in power. Surely when they looked round upon the world lying in sin, and upwards to the heavens so silent, distant, and mysterious, it must have been with an intense longing to know the secret of their existence,—why they were born, whence they came, whither they were going. And the answer was now to be sent to them. In that sea-port town on the coast of Asia Minor, were the men now waiting whom God had destined to throw light upon the questions which sages had for centuries vainly endeavoured to solve.

They were sent forth by a special command from Heaven. A vision appeared to Paul in the night: " There stood a man of Macedonia, and prayed him, saying, Come over and help us. And after they had seen the vision, immediately they endeavoured to go into Macedonia ; assuredly gathering that the Lord had called them."

Neapolis, Philippi, Amphipolis, Apollonia, Thessalonica, Berœa, heard the word of God. Danger followed the footsteps of the preachers ; imprisonment from the Gentiles at Philippi, and the angry fury of a violent assault from the Jews at Thessalonica ; yet they went on their way rejoicing, for their labours were blessed. The humble-minded amongst the heathen, the pure-hearted and unprejudiced amongst the Jews, and the Greek worshippers of the True God, inquired into the doctrines taught by St. Paul, and believed them. Berœa especially was the dwelling-place of many Jews who "received the word with all readiness of mind, and searched the Scriptures daily whether those things were so;" and here the Apostle might for a while have found rest and sympathy, but that the Jews of Thessalonica, indignant at his success, followed him thither, stirred up the people against him, and at length compelled him to flee from the city under pretence of going towards the sea, but in reality with the intention of travelling to Athens. (A.D. 50.)

This journey was undertaken alone, or at least without the comforting society of the three friends who had accompanied him from Asia. St. Luke, it appears, had remained behind at Philippi, and Silas and Timothy were left at Berœa; perhaps because it was thought that the departure of the Apostle would in that case be the less marked. The separation from the latter, however, was not for long; St. Paul sent them an urgent message—by the friends who, after conveying him safely to his destination, returned to Berœa—begging them to join him with all speed; and in the mean time he waited for them at Athens.

No place on the face of the globe could have been found more likely to arouse the excitable temperament of St. Paul than this. It was the very metropolis of idolatry; crowded with magnificent temples; frequented by philosophers who prided themselves upon their human learning; inhabited by a people whose taste and refinement were the admiration of all the civilized world. If idolatry was ever exhibited in a form tempting to the better

5*

feelings of mankind, it must have been at Athens; where all that was gross and sensual was hidden beneath the solemnities of gorgeous ceremonies, and the splendour of buildings which, even to this day, have never been equalled.

But St. Paul did not at once and openly declaim against the worship he abhorred. Here, as elsewhere, he addressed himself first to the Jews in the Synagogue; and, when he did dispute in the market-place, directed his words to the few devout persons whom he daily met there. Yet it was impossible that he could remain unnoticed in a place where novelty was the great attraction for all.

His arguments were heard by certain philosophers, Epicureans and Stoics, persons who were accustomed to think and reason upon subjects connected with the destiny of mankind, and the government of the world, and who listened to the teaching of St. Paul with contemptuous unbelief! " What will this babbler say?" they exclaimed; " he seemeth to be a setter forth of strange gods."

Yet his startling words could not pass away and be forgotten. The tidings of One who had died, and risen again, and offered immortality to His followers, could not be heard without interest by men accustomed to ponder upon the deep mysteries of this present life. " And they took him and brought him to Areopagus,"—the great court where all questions of religious difficulty were determined, —and there entreated him to declare more clearly what this new doctrine whereof he spoke was. The judges of the Areopagus sat in the open air: their seats, hewn out of the solid rock, were on a platform forming the summit of a hill known by the name of Mars' Hill. Here it was that St. Paul stood, in the presence of the noblest and wisest of the Greeks, and entered without hesitation upon the subject of which his thoughts and his heart were full. " Ye men of Athens ! " he exclaimed, " I perceive that in all things ye are too superstitious. For as I passed by, and beheld your devotions, I found an altar with this inscription, TO THE UNKNOWN GOD. Whom, therefore, ye ignorantly worship, Him declare I unto you."

Strange that seems to us, accustomed from our infancy to address our petitions to the Great God, the Lord of Heaven and earth. Strange, that a people who could think, and talk, and write upon all other subjects so as to be the instructors of the world, should require to be taught the first, simplest truths of religion ! But so it was ; and St. Paul, following up his subject, spoke to the proud Athenians of Him in whom they lived, and moved, and had their being, even as we speak to the child kneeling to repeat his prayers, of God his Father, by whom he and all the world were made.

Still further the Apostle taught his hearers : he warned them of a judgment to come,—a Day in which God would " judge the world in righteousness by that Man whom He had ordained," and whom He had raised from the dead, to give assurance to all of the truth of this awful doctrine.

And then the Athenians would listen to him no longer. That there was a God who created the world, they could believe, for it was a fact set forth by every object in nature ; that the spirit might be conscious after death, they hoped, for God had implanted in their very nature the dread of utter destruction ; but that the body—the prey of corruption, the food for worms—should be restored, and again united to the soul, this was above the evidence of their natural senses : and some mocked, and others said, " We will hear thee again of this matter."

" So Paul departed from among them."

The preaching of the Apostle was not, however, without fruit. " Dionysius the Areopagite, and a woman named Damaris, and others with them," followed him. The former, especially, was a convert of great influence, for the members of the Areopagus were men of noble birth, wise, and prudent; and tradition tells us that Dionysius, especially, had travelled to Egypt, and studied philosophy and astronomy in the city of Heliopolis. He it was who was afterwards made the first bishop of the Church at Athens, and St. Paul himself is said to have consecrated him to that office.

CHAPTER VII.

ST. PAUL AT EPHESUS. A.D. 53.

CORINTH was the next place visited by St. Paul, and there, being joined by Silas and Timothy, he spent eighteen months, doubtless induced to remain by the fact that the city was one of the most important and luxurious in all Greece; and encouraged also by a special revelation assuring him that no man should set on him to hurt him, for that God had much people in the city.

But St. Paul's love for his new converts did not render him unmindful of those whom he had left behind him at Thessalonica. His two Epistles to the Thessalonians were written about this period. They contain many allusions to the crcumstances which had separated him from them, and which have already been mentioned. He speaks of his own sufferings at Philippi, and mentions a fact which is not named in the Acts of the Apostles; that he was so anxious to obtain tidings of their well doing, that he had consented to remain at Athens alone, in order to give Timothy an opportunity of going to Thessalonica to obtain tidings of them. This may perhaps account for the circumstance, that although St. Paul sent at first an urgent message to Silas and Timothy to join him at Athens, yet they did not do so until after his arrival at Corinth.

St. Paul probably stayed in Greece for more than a year. He then returned to Asia, and after a short stay at Ephesus, one of the wealthiest cities of Asia Minor, proceeded to Jerusalem, for the purpose of keeping the feast of Pentecost, and also of carrying to the poor Christians of Judea the contributions gathered from their brethren during his journey; and finally, about the end of the year 53, took up his abode at Ephesus. Here he remained for three or four years, occasionally visiting his converts in other parts of the country; and once, it is said, paying a short visit to Corinth.

The condition of this city seems to have caused him much anxiety. The first heretical or false doctrines respecting the nature of Christ had by this time sprung up, and the Church of Corinth was infected by them.

Simon Magus, the sorcerer, who had desired to purchase from St. Peter the gift of the Holy Ghost, was one of the earliest teachers of these errors. The punishment which had fallen upon him had not really touched his heart, and although declaring himself a believer in Christ, he turned aside from the faith of the Apostles, and mixed with it false opinions of his own, which he taught, and which spread widely in the countries where Christianity was preached.

Other false doctrines also, gathered from heathenism, were blended with those put forth by Simon Magus, and the whole formed a strange and perplexing creed, which, under the name of Gnosticism, was one of the greatest evils with which the early Christians had to contend.

It may be desirable to mention some of the leading features of this heresy, as it will enable us to understand the allusions which are made to it in the Epistles.

The Gnostics then taught that all which we call matter,—such as our bodies, and the things which we touch and feel and see,—was evil, and subject to an evil being. They believed that Christ our Lord proceeded from God, but they would not believe that He really took upon Him our nature; because, they said, that He, being pure and spiritual, could not dwell in a material or evil body; and therefore they declared that when He appeared among us a man, He was not really a man, but only bore the appearance of one.

So also they would not believe that the body would ever rise again. As they considered it to be in its very nature evil, they could not imagine that it would ever be reunited to a purified spirit. The souls of the good, they said, which were restored in baptism, would, after death, be gathered into the Bosom of God, and the souls of those not yet perfect would undergo a series of changes or transmigrations, until all the remains of evil had been purged away. The consequences of this doctrine differed with different persons. Those who were really in earnest in striving to become holy, endeavoured to live without any regard to the needs of the body, and practised the severest personal self-denial; whilst others took advantage of the idea that matter was in itself evil to indulge in every sinful excess, saying that the soul was so superior to the body that it could not be injured by anything done in the body.*

These false doctrines were not fully taught until the second century; but their origin may be traced back to the time of Simon Magus, and it is evident from the writings of St. Paul to the Corinthians that his converts in that city were in a degree infected by them. For instance, in the 15th Chapter of the First Epistle, he asks: "Now if Christ be preached that He rose from the dead; how say some among you that there is no resurrection of the dead?" And then he goes on to state the doctrine of the resurrection in the most solemn way, and to declare in the words which are a comfort and warning to us now, as they were to the Corinthian converts 1800 years ago, that "corruptible must put on incorruption, and mortal immortality;" and "then shall be brought to pass the saying that is written, Death is swallowed up in victory."

Again, in the 5th Chapter of his Second Epistle, he says; "We that are in this tabernacle do groan, being burdened: not that we would be unclothed," or deprived of our bodies, "but clothed upon;" or purified and sanctified, so, "that mortality might be swallowed up of life." And in his final exhortation he entreats them to examine themselves whether they were in the faith, evidently being aware

* The Gnostics had also many strange ideas regarding emanations from the Divine Being, to which they gave the name of Æons, but their theories were so fanciful and confused that it requires much study to understand them.

that error had crept in amongst them ; whilst the gross sins for which he reproves them were such as could scarcely in those early, and comparatively pure, days have been committed by persons calling themselves Christians, unless they had been taught to believe, according to the teaching of the Gnostics, that if the spirit was regenerated and united to Christ, the deeds of the body were of no consequence.

But there were other circumstances in the condition of the Church of Corinth to excite the anxiety of St. Paul. The converts had separated themselves into sects, calling themselves after their several leaders. This brought disunion and jealousy into the Church, and tended to set aside the all important truth that it had but one Head, even Christ Himself.

The miraculous gifts bestowed upon some individuals were also a source of dissension. The Apostles, we have seen, were able, through the immediate influence of the Holy Ghost, to speak in strange languages, and this power they conveyed to others, as an evidence to the heathen that they were inspired by God, and therefore that the doctrines taught by them were to be received as truth. Thus it was that some amongst the Corinthians were enabled to speak foreign tongues with ease, whilst to others was granted the privilege of understanding what was said, and explaining it. This was of course necessary, for it is evident that if none had been present to interpret when a man stood up in the assembly and addressed the people in a new language, the gift would have been useless. It would have been merely the utterance of sounds, and not the words of some language actually spoken in another land, though unknown to

the inhabitants of Corinth. The Corinthians, it
seems, took pleasure in the exercise of this new
power, and esteemed it more than the important
gifts of humility, charity, and purity. And St.
Paul hearing, whilst he was at Ephesus, of the
disordered state of the Church in consequence,
wrote to them strongly upon the subject, warning
them that although they were to speak " with the
tongues of men and of angels," yet if they had not
charity they would be but " as sounding brass or a
tinkling cymbal."

Another point of difficulty upon which St. Paul
gave his advice to the Corinthian converts, regarded the disputes as to matters of business which
might happen to arise amongst them. These could
not properly be decided by heathen courts of justice, because in that case the Christians would
have been obliged to take heathen oaths. The
Apostle's advice was given strongly that such differences should be settled amongst themselves.
" Dare any of you," he says, " having a matter
against another, go to law before the unjust, and not
before the saints ?" The word saints here meaning
Christians generally, who, because of their profession, were always considered holy.

These and other very important questions which
were also discussed by St. Paul in his First Epistle to the Corinthians, tend to prove that the Corinthian Church was in a state likely to cause the
Apostle much uneasiness; and therefore render it
the more probable that he visited them for a short
time during his stay at Ephesus. The visit is supposed to be referred to, when he says, in writing
to the Corinthians again : " This is the third time
that I am coming to you," implying that he had
been with them twice before.

In the conclusion of the Epistle to the Corinthians, St. Paul speaks of his intention of soon paying them a longer visit; possibly even of spending the winter amongst them ; but he adds, " I will tarry at Ephesus until Pentecost, for a great door and effectual is opened unto me, and there are many adversaries."

He did not then see how quickly he should be compelled to flee from Ephesus in order to escape from.persecution, though he was evidently aware of the many enemies whom he had made by his bold and persevering teaching. There was indeed no place in which the spread of Christianity could have interfered more with the habits and prejudices of the people than it did at Ephesus. The Ephesians were the worshippers of the great goddess Diana. The temple at Ephesus, dedicated to her, was one of the great wonders of those days.* One hundred and twenty pillars, sixty feet high, and each the gift of a king, formed the colonnades that surrounded the sanctuary in which the image of the goddess was kept. The folding doors were of cypress wood, a great portion of the building was roofed with cedar, and the staircase was formed of one single vine, the produce of the island of Cyprus. Moreover, this temple was the treasury in which a great portion of the wealth of Asia was kept. The image which gave to the building its peculiar sacredness in the eyes of the people, was indeed rough and uncouth, being formed of wood, and terminating at its lower extremity in a mere shapeless block ; but it was believed to have fallen from the sky, and the ig-

---

* See The Life and Epistles of St. Paul, by the Rev. W. Conybeare and the Rev. J. Howson.

norant multitude lavished all their treasures to do it honour.

There was also a more personal interest to excite the indignation of the Ephesians, when their worship was assailed. Many workmen in the city gained their daily bread by making silver shrines for the goddess Diana.

These shrines were miniature representations of the temple, in each of which, it is probable, a small image of the goddess was placed. They appear to have been purchased by strangers from curiosity, or used for purposes of devotion, the fame of the goddess and her image having spread throughout all Asia. But since the preaching of the Apostle, the traffic in silver shrines and the worship of Diana had visibly decreased. The glory of Ephesus was sinking day by day, for St. Paul had persuaded and turned away much people, saying that they were no gods which were made with hands ; and at length the workmen, excited by Demetrius, a silversmith, rose· up in insurrection.

" Great is Diana of the Ephesians," was the cry which resounded through the city, and even those who could not understand the reason of the tumult joined in it.

The town clerk, the chief magistrate of the city, interfered, and after a while, though with much difficulty, appeased the angry crowds ; but the feelings which had been aroused rendered Ephesus no longer a safe residence for St. Paul, and when the uproar ceased he took immediate measures for departure. His feelings as to the danger which he incurred on this occasion may be gathered from his own words, when afterwards writing to the Corinthians. " For we would not, brethren," he says, "have you ignorant of our trouble which came to us in Asia, that we were pressed out of measure, above strength, insomuch that we despaired even of life."

Europe was the country to which his interest and affections turned at this critical period. He had founded churches there in which he still felt the deepest interest, and after his long absence he might naturally feel anxious to assure himself of their welfare by personal inquiry.

In the Acts of the Apostles we read only that "he came into Greece, and there abode three months;" but by an examination of the Epistles we learn that he left Ephesus, accompanied probably by Tychicus and Trophimus, two of his Ephesian friends, sailed as before from Troas, and landing at Neapolis, proceeded to Philippi. The depression of his spirits at this time is very marked. Tidings had reached him of grievous sins committed amongst the Corinthians, and he had sent Titus to learn the truth of the reports, and expected to meet him at Troas. Titus did not however arrive, and St. Paul's distress was such that, to use his own expression, he had no "rest in his spirit." Even after his arrival at Philippi, "without," he says, "were fightings; within, were fears;" and there are allusions, also, to his bodily infirmity, which make us feel that his health must have been much shaken by all he had undergone. But Titus came at last to Philippi, and the whole tone of the Apostle's mind changed. Earnest desire for reformation, mourning for past sins, and fervent affection for St. Paul himself, filled the hearts of the Corinthians; and as he now assured them, in the Second Epistle which he addressed to them from Philippi, his confidence in them was restored.

Titus was the bearer of this second letter to Corinth, and at the same time he was commissioned to receive the contributions for the Christians in Judea, which St. Paul, according to the charge specially given him, was earnest in enforcing upon his converts. Besides the actual necessities of the inhabitants of Judea, who were at that time suffering greatly from the oppression of their rulers, and the disturbed state of the country, these subscriptions were a means of softening the prejudices of the Jewish and Gentile Christians, and making them feel that they had a material interest in each other.

St. Paul appears to have been most anxious that the offerings should be made liberally and without delay. After remaining in Greece about three months, the greater part of which time he is supposed to have spent at Corinth, he himself undertook to carry to Jerusalem the funds which had been collected.

Two Epistles, one to the Galatians, the other to the Romans, are said to have been written during this visit of St. Paul to Corinth. Galatia was the Asiatic Gaul, inhabited by the same race which afterwards overran France, and the peculiarities of national character which are remarkable in the French of the present day may clearly be traced in St. Paul's Epistle. The Galatians were quick but changeable, easily adopting impressions, easily giving them up. They had begun to run well, but they were soon hindered in the race. False teachers had appeared amongst them, insisting upon the necessity of circumcision, and an observance of the Jewish rites; and St. Paul, though he must have been well acquainted with their character, marvelled at the suddenness with which they

6*

had so soon shifted their ground; and wrote in the most vehement manner to warn them of the danger they were incurring by listening to the new doctrines.

To the Roman Church he was personally a stranger. Who first preached the Gospel in that great city, we do not know, but St. Paul was evidently well acquainted with many individual Christians resident there, as the salutations at the close of his letter are numerous. He expresses the most affectionate interest in the condition of the Church, whose faith, he says, is spoken of throughout all the world; and tells them that he wishes and hopes to visit them after he has transacted his business in Jerusalem, and to proceed from Italy to Spain.

But human plans, even those of an Apostle, are formed in ignorance, and St. Paul, though aware that " bonds and imprisonment" awaited him every where, and knowing that there were special reasons for dreading the enmity of the Jews, could scarcely have contemplated the lengthened trials both of body and mind which were to be the result of his journey to Jerusalem. He refers to it as to a short expedition for a special purpose, which when accomplished, would leave him free to follow the bent of his own inclinations. " Now," he says, " I go unto Jerusalem to minister unto the saints, for it hath pleased them of Macedonia and Achaia to make a certain contribution for the poor saints which are at Jerusalem. . . . . When therefore I have performed this, and have sealed to them this fruit, I will come by you into Spain."

The Epistle to the Romans was given in charge to Phebe, a Christian lady residing at Cenchrea, the eastern point of Corinth, and who was then about to sail to Rome upon some private business, supposed, from the terms made use of in referring to it, to have been connected with a lawsuit in which she was engaged. Phebe is spoken of as a servant, or deaconess, of the Church at Cenchrea. The persons who were appointed to this office were generally widows, who had been only once married; although sometimes the same employments were entrusted to those who were unmarried. Deaconesses assisted at the baptism of women, and catechised and instructed them previously. They were also accustomed to visit sick persons of their own sex, and perform other inferior offices which could not so well be entrusted to men. It is probable that they were blessed by the laying on of hands, but it is certain that they were not permitted to execute any priestly office.

CHAPTER VIII.

ST. PAUL TRIED BEFORE FELIX.   A.D. 56.

It would be needless to describe particularly the long and eventful journey which preceded the arrival of St. Paul for the last time at Jerusalem. We must often have dwelt upon its details, and imagined ourselves listening to the midnight sermon at Troas, which was followed by the miracle of restoring the dead to life; mingling with the Ephesian elders of the Church when they were summoned to Miletus to hear the last exhortation of the great Apostle whose face they were to behold no more; kneeling on the Tyrian shore with that loving company of friends, and wives, and children, who hallowed the farewells of earth by the prayers which whispered to their hearts of the eternal reunion in heaven; and at length, arriving with St. Paul at the doomed city, which was to prelude its own destruction by inflicting suffering upon all who would have saved it.

When St. Paul entered Jerusalem, at the time of the Feast of Pentecost, the hope which he had once entertained of being permitted after a short sojourn to return free to Europe must have vanished. Humanly speaking, indeed, there was no more reason than before to anticipate danger; but the forebodings which seem to have oppressed him from the very commencement of his journey were deepened towards its close by a special prediction, delivered at Cæsarea by Agabus, a prophet, that he should be bound by the Jews at Jerusalem, and delivered into the hands of the Gentiles. He could indeed, from his heart, exclaim, "I am ready not to be bound only, but also to die at Jerusalem, for the sake of the Lord Jesus." Yet he was keenly alive to the sorrow which his own trials would bring upon his friends. The sight of their tears broke the heart which would never have trembled for itself.

On his arrival at Jerusalem, St. Paul took up his abode at the house of Mnason, a Cyprian by birth, and an old disciple. His first evening was probably one of comfort. Several friends had accompanied him from Macedonia, and amongst them his favourite companion Timothy. Others also had joined him at Cæsarea, and the brethren at Jerusalem received them gladly. Yet the prophetic voice of Agabus must have been too present to his remembrance to allow him to look forward with any hope of permanent rest.

Even amongst the Jews professing Christianity there were many likely to regard him with suspicion, for in Judea, especially, the ceremonial law of Moses was strictly observed. St. James, who presided over the Church at Jerusalem as its bishop, was himself in outward respects a strict Jew; and the Jewish Christians would not be likely to understand why St. Paul, a Jew and an Apostle likewise, should reject what St. James thought fit to practise. They would not see that St. James, living amongst them, was willing to conform himself in all lawful ways to their habits and customs; whilst St. Paul, mingling continually with Gentiles, was equally called upon to show that he did not consider these observances of essential importance.

Not a day was lost by St. Paul in endeavouring to soften the prejudices of those whom he speaks of in his Epistle as " weak brethren." The morrow after his arrival he had an interview with St. James and the Elders of the Church, and in compliance with their advice agreed to take charge of four Jewish Christians, who had bound themselves by the vows of a Nazarite; to accompany them to the temple, and pay the expenses of the offering, required for the fulfilment of their vow. This, it was said, would satisfy the Jewish party that St. Paul himself was willing to keep the law of Moses, whilst it would in no way imply that similar observances were to be required of the Gentiles.

The suggestion was willingly followed. On the next day, which was the festival of Pentecost, St. Paul proceeded to the Temple, and with his four companions waited within its precincts until the necessary rites had been observed. These lasted for some time.   On the seventh day the Jews, imagining that St. Paul had taken with him into the sacred building Trophimus, an Ephesian and a Gentile, raised a tumult against him.   The Roman officer interfered to stop it.   St. Paul was seized and put under a close guard, and when it was discovered that the Jews had formed a plot against his life, he was sent to Cæsarea that he might be placed under the safer custody of Felix, the governor of the province of Judea.

A long captivity then commenced (A.D. 56). For two years St. Paul remained a prisoner under Felix, yet not shut out from his office as a preacher of the Gospel.   In an interview held with the proud and profligate Roman, he so reasoned with him upon righteousness, temperance, and judgment to come, that Felix trembled, and struck with awe, sent him from his presence until a more convenient season for repentance should be found.   Other interviews followed.   But delay had brought its natural consequences ; Felix no longer cared for truth, he wished only to discover some means by which the imprisonment of the Apostle might be turned to his own advantage, and imagining that St. Paul would be willing to purchase his freedom, communed with him often.

This is the only break in that wearisome imprisonment, of which we have any certain information, though it has been supposed, with some degree of probability, that St. Luke was with St. Paul, and occupied himself in writing his Gospel under the superintendence of the Apostle.

Portius Festus succeeded Felix in the government of Judea.   He appears to have been a man of a far nobler character than his predecessors, and anxious to fulfil his duties with impartiality.   The case of St. Paul was one of the first brought before him, for the Jews had by no means forgotten their enmity against the Apostle.

The same charges which had been alleged before Felix were repeated before Festus. St. Paul was said to be a ringleader of the sect of the Nazarenes, and to have excited disturbances amongst the Jews throughout the Roman empire. He was accused also of having profaned the temple at Jerusalem, and so insulted not only the religion of the Jews, but the authority of the Romans who authorised and protected it.

These charges involved questions of religious belief of which Festus, a foreigner and a worshipper of other gods, could have no knowledge. He proposed to decide the case at Jerusalem, where information would be more easily attained; and this idea would probably have been carried out had not St. Paul, to the surprise of all, and doubtless to the dismay of his enemies, fallen back upon his privileges as a Roman citizen, and insisted upon being heard before the Emperor Nero, the successor of Claudius.

The whole proceeding was at once stopped. The Procurator of Judea had full power in the province which he ruled; but an individual who claimed the honour of being a Roman citizen could at any time appeal from him to the emperor, before whom the cause was then of necessity brought.

The custom dated far back from the days when the Roman nobles oppressed the lower orders and drove them to rebellion, and when an officer called a Tribune was chosen from amongst the people, and entrusted with the special duty of protecting their interests and putting a stop to any law which might be enacted for their injury. The Roman emperors, when they seized the chief authority in the state, seized also the public offices. They were now the tribunes of the people, and an appeal to them made by a Roman citizen could frustrate the proceeding of any provincial court.

The immediate difficulty for Festus was thus removed, but another still remained. It was unreasonable to send a prisoner to Rome without fully stating his offence; yet how could this be done unless the charges were fully understood? An opportunity for a more thorough investigation and comprehension of St. Paul's position soon occurred. Herod Agrippa II., King of Chalcis, the son of that Herod whose horrible death took place at Cæsarea, was then in the neighbourhood, and came with his sister Bernice to pay a complimentary visit to the new governor. Agrippa had been from his youth familiar with the customs and feelings of the Jews, and was in some degree considered as their protector. He was the superintendent of the temple, and the power of appointing the high priest was also in his hands. His visit, therefore, was most opportune. Festus took advantage of it to confer with him upon the accusations brought against St. Paul, and interested the king so much by his account of the prisoner and his belief, that Agrippa expressed a desire to hear the statement of the Apostle's faith from his own lips.

The interview between Paul and Agrippa is the last great scene of the Apostle's life recorded in Scripture, and it seems scarcely possible to read it attentively without some feelings of awe and admiration. On the one side were the proud Jewish king and his sister, famed equally for her

beauty and her crimes, the upright Roman governor, the military officers and chief men of the
city, assembled with the pomp which became the
importance of the occasion; on the other, the
solitary Christian captive, bound ignominiously to
the soldier who guarded him, and waiting humbly
and silently till it was said, " Paul, thou art permitted to speak for thyself."

Even then dignity and influence must have been
on the side of the Apostle, as, stretching out his
hand, he addressed Agrippa with the graceful and
noble courtesy which marked the man educated
in the habits of refined life, and narrated the
circumstances of his conversion. It is a well-
known and often repeated history. Yet still,—
at this present day,—they are stirring words
which tell of the hope of the resurrection of the
dead, and the mission so solemnly given " to open
the eyes of the Gentiles, and turn them from
darkness to light, and from the power of Satan
unto God; " and we can feel little surprise at
Agrippa's exclamation when, having listened to
the declarations of the Apostle, made with the
calm but intense ernestness of truth, he professed
himself " *almost* " persuaded to be a Christian.

The interview over, Agrippa and Festus discussed the case in private. Both agreed that the
Apostle had done " nothing worthy of death or of
bonds ; " and Agrippa asserted positively that he
might have been set at liberty if he had not appealed to the emperor. This fact, however, prevented any interference on their part ; and nothing
remained but to take advantage of the first convenient opportunity for sending their prisoner to
Rome.

The voyage of St. Paul to Italy, interesting and

7

eventful though it was, is too well known to be minutely described.

Under the care of a Roman centurion, and accompanied by St. Luke and Aristarchus, a Macedonian, he, with other state prisoners, sailed, as it is supposed, in the month of August, in a ship of Adramyttium, a seaport town of Mysia; which, on their arrival at Lycia, was exchanged for a merchant ship, engaged in carrying corn from Alexandria to Italy, and probably a much larger vessel, as it was capable of accommodating two hundred and seventy persons. A violent storm caused the vessel to be wrecked on the shores of Melita or Malta, where St. Paul worked several miracles, especially restoring to health the governor's father; and after a delay of three months the centurion and his prisoners departed in another Alexandrian ship for Italy.

They were landed at Puteoli, on the northern shore of the Bay of Naples, and from thence proceeded to Rome, where the charge of the centurion ended, the prisoners being placed under the care of the prætorian prefect, whom we know, from different sources, to have been Burrhus, a man of great influence, the friend of Seneca, and the tutor of the reigning emperor Nero, the successor of Claudius.

A marked difference was made in the treatment of the Apostle, and that of his fellow-prisoners. He was suffered to dwell by himself, though the painful and ignominious restraint of chaining him by the hand to a soldier was still thought necessary. In this, his private lodging, after a rest of three days, St. Paul found means to assemble the chief Jews then resident in Rome; his object being to offer his own explanation of the charges of heresy and treason which had been brought against him by his countrymen, and at the same time to set before them the truths of the Gospel.

Christianity, as it has been before stated, was by no means a novelty in Rome; but the Jews seem to have regarded it with the same contemptuous suspicion there as elsewhere. In answer to St Paul's address, they replied that no accusation had been brought against him either by letter or by the brethren who had arrived from Judea, but they confessed that the opinion generally entertained of the Christians was unfavourable, and they desired, therefore, to hear St. Paul's own statement of his doctrines.

A day was fixed for the discussion, and numbers were present at it. St. Paul, under the impulse of deep earnestness, expounded, testified, persuaded, from morning till evening, endeavouring to convince the Jews that the Redeemer whom he preached to them was the same of whom Moses in the Law, and the Prophets had spoken. But ancient prejudice was too strong in the hearts of many of his hearers to be subdued, even by the teaching of an inspired Apostle. Some believed the words which were spoken and some believed not; and after much debate the unbelievers departed, carrying with them the solemn warning of St. Paul, gathered from their own prophet Esaias: "The heart of this people is waxed gross, and their ears are dull of hearing, and their eyes have they closed, lest they should see with their eyes, and hear with their ears, and understand with their hearts, and be converted, and I should heal them."

From that time St. Paul's mission in Rome was to the Gentiles.

CHAPTER IX.

MARTYRDOM OF ST. PAUL.   A.D. 67.

" AND Paul dwelt two whole years in his own hired house, and received all that came unto him, preaching the kingdom of God, and teaching those things which concern the Lord Jesus Christ, with all confidence, no man forbidding him."

How often must we have paused after these words, feeling, even if we did not express the feeling in language, a sense of wonder and disappointment at the sudden termination of the history of the great Apostle of the Gentiles, and of the book containing the inspired records of the early Christian Church ! Whatever information we may obtain from other sources must appear doubtful and insufficient after such testimony as we have hitherto followed ; but God, who governs all with unerring wisdom, must have seen, when directing the pen of the Evangelist, reasons far beyond our comprehension for placing this limit to our certain knowledge. It may be that we have in consequence learnt to look with greater reverence on the wonderful books thus standing apart,—separated as it were by a gulf of time, from all others ; and pleasant though it is to study them minutely, and by the help of profane history to throw light upon the manners and customs to which they allude, and to bring them down in a measure to our daily ordinary life, yet there can be little question that, as regards the greater part of mankind, the authority and influence of St. Paul and his fellow apostles, the founders of the Christian Church, is much stronger from the brief but most impressive witness of Scripture, which leaves so much for imagination to fill up, than it would have been from the lengthened details by which a common writer would have endeavoured to interest his readers in the life of a common man.

Why the Bible should be what it is,—why the book of the Acts of the Apostles should end where it does, are questions which can only be properly answered by those who have given up their hearts to the sacred influence of the Word of God, and who will be the first to allow that it contains all things necessary " for doctrine, for reproof, for correction, for instruction in righteousness."

Yet it is not forbidden, rather it is commanded, that we should search the Scriptures so thoroughly as to draw from them all the information which may reasonably be deduced from them ; and although the detailed narrative of St. Paul's life ends with the Acts of the Apostles, some further particulars respecting it may be gained from the letters written by him in after years to different churches.

St. Luke mentions the period of his imprisonment as lasting two years. This most probably was caused by the delay of his trial. His accusers were to be summoned from Judea, and witnesses would be brought from various parts of Asia Minor to testfy to the charge of sedition ; thus necessarily causing the postponement of the inquiry. The charge being a complicated one would also require a separate hearing for each point, and might be adjourned from time to time as best suited the emperor's convenience. These circumstances would naturally tend to prolong the Apostle's imprisonment, which,

7*

except for the degradation and annoyance of being chained by the hand, does not seem to have been rigorous.

His eagerness to proclaim the glad tidings of Christ must have been gratified by the opportunity afforded him of addressing those who visited him during his imprisonment. Tradition tells us that Pomponia Græcina, the wife of Plautius, the conqueror of Britain, was converted by the preaching of St. Paul; and it speaks also of Claudia, the daughter of Caractacus, as amongst his converts. Both these ladies are said to have been instrumental in introducing Christianity into Britain, but the foundation of the assertion is not to be depended upon.   We know, however, by St. Paul's own testimony, that amongst the rough soldiers of the prætorian guard, and in the palace of the emperor himself, were to be found those who had been, by his instrumentality, won over to the doctrines of Christ.

His friends appear to have been constantly with him. Timothy, who came to Rome about this time, served with him in the Gospel as a son with a father. Luke was his constant companion. Mark, sister's son to Barnabas, having repented of his former cowardice, was now looked upon as a faithful friend. Demas, for the time, sympathised with him. Aristarchus, a Macedonian, who had shared his travels in former days was now his fellow-worker, and, together with Justus, a comfort to him. Epaphras, a Colossian, and Tychicus, took part in his sorrows and his labours for a while, and left him only when they were entrusted with a letter to the Church at Colossæ, and with another, said to have been written to the Ephesians, but more probably addressed jointly to several churches in Asia Minor. These two epistles bear a great resemblance to each other, especially in the fervent wishes which St. Paul pours forth for the spiritual enlightening of his converts; a resemblance most natural when we consider that they must have been written very nearly at the same time.

Tychicus journeyed to Colossæ, accompanied by Onesimus, a runaway slave, converted by St. Paul during his imprisonment, and now sent back to his master, Philemon, with a letter containing an affectionate and most courteously expressed request that the slave, not now a slave, but "a brother beloved," might for the Apostle's sake be again received into favour. This request was no doubt granted, for tradition says that Onesimus became an influential person in the Church, and was made Bishop of Berœa, in Macedonia.

Epaphroditus, a dear friend and leading member of the Church of Philippi, arrived after the departure of Onesimus, bearing contributions from the Philippians, which had been liberally offered for the Apostle's support.

These tokens of affection were very characteristic of the Philippians, who seem to have been on all occasions foremost in liberality; and the evidence of their thoughtfulness for his comfort must have been very soothing to St. Paul, though the severe illness of Epaphroditus on his arrival at Rome caused him the greatest anxiety.

The Apostle's feelings as to the issue of the trial which was still pending may be gathered from the tone of the letter to the Philippians, which he entrusted to the care of Epaphroditus, who, having recovered from his illness, was anxious to return to Philippi. In it he intimates a wish to send Timothy to Philippi also, yet desires at the same time to keep him with him till he should see how it should go with him; and his thoughts evidently dwell upon what we are accustomed to call the chances of life or death; though he cheered the Philippians by the anticipation of his freedom and the prospect of being shortly able to visit them. "I trust in the Lord," he writes, "that I also myself shall come shortly."

St. Paul must, as we have seen, have had influential friends in the palace; and there are some circumstances which render it not improbable that he might have been acquainted with the only two persons who retained any influence for good over the mind of the wicked emperor. Burrhus, the tutor of Nero, was, as it has been said before, the chief of the prætorian guard, and as St. Paul was subject to military control he was very likely to have been visited by him. The acquaintance with Burrhus would naturally have led to that of Seneca, the philosopher, and the intimate friend of Burrhus, who had also taken part in Nero's education. There certainly was an idea in early times that St. Paul and Seneca knew each other personally: some have even stated that Seneca was secretly a Christian; but this is not to be believed, although there are remarkable resemblances between certain expressions to be found in his writings and in those of St. Paul. Seneca was the brother of Gallio, the deputy of Achaia, before whom St. Paul was brought whilst living at Corinth; this also adds in a slight degree to the probability that Seneca had at least heard of the Apostle, and so may have been willing to befriend him.

The result of St. Paul's appeal to the emperor is not told us in direct words in his own letters, neither is it distinctly mentioned in any other writings which have come down to us. But it was universally allowed by the early Church that the trial ended successfully, that St. Paul was acquitted of the charges brought against him, and that he was at liberty for several years previous to his final imprisonment and death. How those years were spent we cannot positively say, but we have reason to believe that he then fulfilled his intention, so long before expressed, of preaching the Gospel in Spain ; and afterwards revisited Asia Minor.

Clement, who was Bishop of Rome, and whom St. Paul mentions in the Epistle to the Philippians, expressly states that the Apostle preached the Gospel in the east and in the west ; that he had instructed the whole world (by which was then meant the Roman Empire), in righteousness, and that he had gone to the extremity of the west before his martyrdom.

In a list of the books of the New Testament compiled by an unknown Christian, about A.D. 170, it is also said in the account of the Acts of the Apostles, that "Luke relates to Theophilus events of which he was an eye-witness, but omits the journey of Paul from Rome to Spain."

Eusebius, the Church historian, and St. Chrysostom and St. Jerome (both reckoned among the fathers of the Church) allude to the same fact.

It is at this period, between the first and second imprisonment of the Apostle, that we have reason to believe the Epistles to the Hebrews, and to Titus, and the first Epistle to Timothy, to have been written.

The letter to the Hebrews speaks of Timothy as having been imprisoned, but states that he was then at liberty. St. Paul expresses his hope of being able, with him, to revisit Palestine shortly. It is imagined that this imprisonment of Timothy took place while St. Paul was in Spain. He had most probably been made Bishop of Ephesus some years before. We do not know the date of the appointment of Titus as Bishop of Crete, but it seems likely that it was made shortly before the letter addressed to him was written, and after St. Paul and Titus had been labouring together in the island. These letters to the two bishops — the Pastoral Epistles as they are called—form a most important part of the writings of St. Paul, as from them we learn what the government of the Church was in those early days, and what were the rules laid down for its guidance.

The Second Epistle to Timothy, the last written by St. Paul, gives us the only certain information we possess as to the situation and feelings of the Apostle at the close of his long life. From this we learn that, shortly before this letter was sent, he had visited Miletus, in company with Trophimus, and had sojourned for a while at Troas with his friend Carpus, who had charge of his cloak, books, and parchments. Corinth also is mentioned in a manner which gives us reason to believe that he had been there with Erastus, the chamberlain of the city. Now he was at Rome, in prison again, and in great danger, and his heart turned lovingly to the friend whose course he had traced from childhood, who had shared his sorrows and his joys, and to whom he had committed the care of the Ephesian Church. "Do thy diligence," he says, "to come shortly unto me, for Demas hath forsaken me, having loved this present world, and is departed unto Thessalonica, Crescens to Galatia, Titus unto Dalmatia." Luke, always devoted to

him, still cheered him with his company, and
Mark, esteemed as "profitable for the ministry,"
St. Paul entreats may accompany Timothy from
Ephesus.

It is this hoped-for meeting on which he anxiously dwells. Almost his closing words repeat
the earnest request that Timothy would come to
him; and the season specified—"before winter."
There was no time for delay. St. Paul knew
well the more than usual uncertainty of his life,
not only from his age,—he must have been then
nearly seventy—but from the peculiar circumstances of his position.

"Eubulus," he adds, "greeteth thee, and Pudens, and Linus, and Claudia, and all the brethren."
His friends, therefore, had access to him. Pudens,
the son of a Roman senator, and Claudia his wife,
the daughter of a British prince, were not ashamed
to visit the imprisoned Apostle. It may be — for
some records of those early days tell us that St.
Paul preached in Britain — that the British prin-
cess could cheer him with accounts of his converts
in those distant lands. Another is also mentioned,—
Onesiphorus,—a name on which the Apostle's grateful spirit dwells with a tender recollection of the
refreshment received from his friend's visits at
Rome, and in former days at Ephesus; and of the
noble unworldliness which made Onesiphorus not
ashamed to comfort him whilst subject to the
painful degradation accompanying his imprisonment. Onesiphorus appears to have died shortly
before St. Paul wrote. Human reward could not
reach him, but the Apostle prays that he may find
mercy in the Judgment Day; and his family are
affectionately remembered, together with Aquila
and Priscilla, who appear to have taken up their

abode at Ephesus, since the time when, as we learn from the Acts of the Apostles, they first visited it in company with St. Paul.

From his narrow prison the Apostle could travel in spirit through the greater part of the known world, and everywhere find friends and converts; and great indeed must have been the wonder and thankfulness with which he noted the astonishing success of the Gospel since the days when the small body of disciples, whom he, himself, looked upon with scorn, had assembled in the upper chamber at Jerusalem, waiting day by day for the coming of the Holy Ghost.

Asia Minor, Greece, Italy, Spain, Britain, Gaul, Africa, and, it is said, even the countries reaching to the confines of India, had heard the message of salvation. And he, " the persecutor and injurious," had been, perhaps, the chief earthly instrument of its progress.

Marvellous indeed was the Providence which had guided the events of his life. Marvellous to himself, and how much more to us who can trace the effects of his conversion through a course of more than eighteen hundred years.

At the time when St. Paul wrote to Timothy, he had already been once more brought to trial. An ancient writer asserts that he was not tried before the emperor; most probably, therefore, the presiding magistrate was the city prefect. Alexander the coppersmith, it appears, was one of his accusers, or a witness against him; but the charge brought forward is not mentioned. Most likely it was only one amongst many, it being the custom of Nero, and therefore, we may suppose, of his magistrates, to hear and decide each branch of the accusation separately.

On this occasion the Apostle seems to have been left without the support of his friends. "At my first answer," he says, "no man stood with me, but all men forsook me. I pray God that it may not be laid to their charge." Yet One, mighty to save, was near. "The Lord stood with him and strengthened him." Publicly before all the Gentiles he once more proclaimed the Gospel, and, contrary to all that might have been anticipated, was acquitted.

How little hope, however, he had of final escape may be seen from his own words: "I am now ready to be offered, and the time of my departure is at hand. Henceforth there is laid up for me a crown of righteousness, which the Lord the righteous Judge shall give me at that Day; and not to me only, but unto all them also that love His appearing."

Glorious was this expectation; calm and certain the confidence of its fulfilment. The Apostle had need of all the comfort which such a hope could give. He wrote those words most probably in the spring of A.D. 67. Before the summer was over, he had passed by a violent death to the land "where the wicked cease from troubling." His punishment was one of less lingering torture than that of St. Peter. As a Roman citizen, he was sentenced to be beheaded, and was led to execution beyond the walls of Rome, upon the road to the port of Ostia. The sword of the headsman ended his long toil. The traditions as to his burial are uncertain. Some say that his remains were carried to the subterranean labyrinths called catacombs, which the Christians had by that time begun to use as the place of rest for their dead. Others state that they were interred near the spot where he suffered, there to await the hour when corruptible shall put on incorruption, and mortal immortality. Nearly three hundred years afterwards, the Emperor Constantine built a stately church on the Ostian Way in memory of the great Apostle.

CHAPTER X.

THE DESTRUCTION OF JERUSALEM. A.D. 70.

OUR knowledge of the Apostolic Church is of course chiefly to be gathered from the Acts of the Apostles and the Epistles of St. Paul; but a few other events of the same period have been handed down to us by profane history, and, although for the most part merely legendary, it may be interesting to know them, as they are often alluded to an ecclesiastical history.

Two persons of great note are said to have died shortly before St. Paul closed his labours by the witness of martyrdom. The first of these was St. James, Bishop of Jerusalem; the other, Mark the Evangelist, often confounded with John surnamed Mark, the nephew of Barnabas.

St. James is brought prominently forward in the early history of the Church. The persecution against him arose in the short interval which preceded the government of Albinus, who succeeded Festus as procurator or governor of Judea. St. Paul having escaped from the malice of his Jewish enemies, it is not surprising that they should have turned their enmity against St. James who still resided amongst them, and had obtained great influence by his piety and self-denial. The Sadducees and Pharisees accordingly resolved, if possible, to rid themselves of him before another governor could arrive; and summoning a council, accused the Apostle of being a violator of the Mosaic law. This was at the time of the Feast of the Passover, when multitudes of strangers were assembled in Jerusalem. The High Priest and his friends, however, being willing, probably, to make a show of mercy and liberality, began the inquiry by flättering St. James, and assuring him that the whole nation looked up to him as a just and holy man; and then they entreated him to undeceive the people, and to make a public declaration that Jesus, whom they regarded as the Messiah, was in reality an impostor. Hoping that he would consent, they carried him to an elevated part of the temple, from whence he could be seen and heard by all. "Tell us," they exclaimed, "O Justus, whom we have every reason to believe; what is this doctrine of the crucified Jesus?" The Apostle made reply, in an audible voice, "Why do ye inquire of Jesus the Son of Man? He sits in Heaven on the Right Hand of the Majesty on High, and will come again in the clouds of Heaven." The testimony was heard below, and the response broke from the multitude, "Hosanna to the Son of David!"

The Apostle's doom was sealed. His enemies exclaimed that he himself was seduced and become an impostor, and, rushing upon him, threw him from the place on which he stood. The fall bruised, but did not kill him; he raised himself on his knees, and prayed for those who were murdering him, and whilst the petitions were yet lingering on his lips a shower of stones fell upon him, and a blow from a club released him from suffering for ever.

Even by his enemies his murder was looked upon as the forerunner of evil to the Jewish nation. The Jews, in their Talmud, make mention of him as a worker of miracles in the name of Jesus, his Master; and Josephus, the Jewish historian, regards his violent death as a crime which brought down the Divine vengeance upon his land and hastened the ruin of his people.

St. James wrote one Epistle; probably not long before his death, as there are passages in it which refer to the judgments coming upon the Jews. It was addressed to the Jewish converts dispersed in the countries of the East.

Less is known of St. Mark than of St. James. He was, we have reason to believe, a Jew by birth, and the constant companion of St. Peter, with whom he is said to have visited Italy, and at the request of the Christians of Rome to have written his Gospel under the immediate superintendence of the Apostle. This Gospel is frequently styled in ancient writings St. Peter's Gospel, and it is remarkable that it contains the fullest account of the Apostle's fall.

St. Mark, we are told, was sent by St. Peter to Alexandria and the eastern parts of Egypt, and from thence travelled into Lybia, preaching the Gospel to the barbarous nations of that country. The greater part of his time, however, was spent at Alexandria, and it was there that he died, about the time that St. Peter was enduring his second imprisonment at Rome.

The account of his death by martyrdom is given by ancient writers, but we cannot entirely depend upon their truth. It is believed to have taken place at the festival of Easter. St. Mark, we are told, was engaged in the celebration of the service suited to that holy season. The Alexandrians were also worshipping with peculiar solemnity their false god Serapis. The minds of the people were in a state of great excitement; and being resolved to assert the dignity of their idol they broke in upon the congregation of Christians, seized St. Mark, and binding his feet with cords, dragged him through the streets, and then thrust him into prison. A heavenly vision is said to have comforted him as he lay that night in his cell expecting death. The following morning his sufferings were renewed. He was again dragged mercilessly through the streets, till at length, worn and bruised, his flesh being torn from his body, he expired. His enemies are reported to have burnt his body, and it is added, that the Christians buried the bones and ashes near the place where he was accustomed to preach. Many years afterwards, the Venetians conveyed his remains with great pomp to Venice, where they dedicated a a most splendid church to his memory, and adopted him as the patron saint of their state.

The history of St. Peter's life must also be brought down to this same period. We hear little in Scripture of the labours of this Apostle after his visit to Cornelius and the opening of the door of the Church to the Gentiles; but we learn from other writings that he presided for several years over the Church at Antioch, and some have declared that he was the first bishop of that see. His imprisonment by Herod and his miraculous escape are related in the Acts of the Apostles. He is thought to have visited Rome soon afterwards in company with St. Mark, when he assisted

8*

in the writing of St. Mark's Gospel; and from thence to have returned to Jerusalem, where we know that he was present at the great council held to determine the necessity of circumcision for the Gentiles. The East, Africa, and Sicily, are said to have been the scenes of his labours afterwards, and it is probable that he visited Corinth and remained there some time, as Clemens Romanus, one of the earliest Christian writers, when addressing a letter to the Corinthians, recommends to them the example of St. Peter as of a person well known to them. About the latter end of Nero's reign, St. Peter returned to Rome. During this period he wrote two Epistles; the first is addressed to the Jewish Christians in Asia Minor, and the second is dated from Babylon. But this name is by some persons imagined to have been typically applied to the city of Rome, and the Epistle is supposed by them to have been written from thence shortly before his death. About the period of St. Peter's second visit to Rome the indignation of the Roman emperor Nero had been strongly excited against the Christians, and his vengeance was shown in the most cruel manner. A tremendous conflagration had broken out in Rome which destroyed almost half the city. Nero was accused of having caused it himself, and to avert the rage of the people he laid the blame upon the hated Christians. A violent persecution followed. Tacitus, a heathen historian, describes its horrors. Some, he says, were crucified; some disguised in the skins of beasts, and hunted to death with dogs; whilst others were clothed with inflammable dresses, and set on fire at night, that they might illuminate the Circus and the gardens of the emperor; Nero himself watching their agonies as he mingled

with the spectators disguised in the dress of a char-
ioteer.

A feeling of pity awoke in the hearts of the
Roman people at the sight of such suffering; but
the monster who had caused it seems to have had
no space in his heart for repentance, and when
St. Peter arrived at Rome, although the violence
of the persecution had abated, he must have known
that if Nero's attention were once drawn to him
there could be little hope of escaping a death of
torment.

Tradition tells us that the cause of St. Peter's
imprisonment was a contest with Simon Magus,
who was then at Rome professing to perform miracles. The emperor, it is said, upheld Simon, and
when the Apostle proved to the people that he was
an impostor, and performed himself the miracles
in which Simon had failed, Nero, in indignation,
commanded him to be apprehended, and thrown
into the great Mamertine prison together with St.
Paul. It is further stated that whilst in daily expectation of his death he was visited by his fellow
Christians, who earnestly entreated him to attempt
an escape, so that his life might be prolonged for
the service of the Church.

The advice was at first rejected; the bold spirit
of the Apostle shrinking from an act which might
be deemed cowardice, but the tears of his friends
at length prevailed.

Having prayed with his brethren, and taken his
farewell of them, he succeeded in making his way
to the city gate. But as he was about to pass it
he met One whom he knew to be his Saviour.
"Lord, whither art Thou going?" asked the Apostle. "I am come to Rome to be crucified a second
time," was the reply.

St. Peter's heart smote him. It was as though his Lord was warning him of the necessity of the suffering from which he was endeavouring to flee. He turned back, delivered himself up to the keeper of the prison, and patiently and cheerfully awaited death. The story is very beautiful, and fully in accordance with St. Peter's impetuous and affectionate character ; and we would willingly believe it although the testimony is acknowledged to be doubtful. So also it is a satisfaction to think of St. Peter and St. Paul as meeting in these last hours, and consoling and supporting each other. And this is the report of some of the ancient legends, which tell us likewise that the two Apostles suffered martyrdom on the same day. But a more careful examination has led others to place St. Peter's death about a year before that of St. Paul.

St. Peter, it is said, endured the agony of martyrdom, not only in his own person, but in the torture of his wife, who was led to execution before him. He it was who encouraged her in her hour of trial, bidding her to be mindful of her Lord, and rejoicing that she was admitted to so great honour, and called to her Eternal Home.

His own summons quickly followed. Like his Lord the punishment of a malefactor was assigned him, and he was condemned to be crucified. But the death which was a degradation in the sight of the world, was in the estimation of St. Peter an honour too great for one who had denied his Saviour. At his own request he was crucified with his head downwards.

His body having been taken from the cross, is stated to have been entombed after the Jewish manner and buried on the hill of the Vatican, where the magnificent church now stands which bears the record of his name.

The important question whether St. Peter was the first Bishop of Rome has long been a subject of dispute amongst the learned, and must still remain a matter of controversy. Some ancient writers speak of the Church as having been planted at Rome by the joint labours of St. Peter and St. Paul; and the fact of St. Peter having presided over the see is nowhere so distinctly asserted in early records, as to enable us to lay any stress upon it.

Linus, mentioned by St. Paul in his Second Epistle to Timothy, is the first Bishop of Rome whose name has been handed down to us by *universal testimony*, and he is said to have been appointed as early as the year 58, a considerable time before the death of St. Peter.

St. Luke the Evangelist, from whom the most important particulars of the lives of the Apostles is obtained, is declared by some writers to have survived St. Paul many years, and to have died at the advanced age of eighty-four; whether he suffered martyrdom is uncertain. He is supposed, as it has been before stated, to have written his Gospel with the assistance of St. Paul, and the Acts of the Apostles were doubtless compiled at Rome during St. Paul's imprisonment. St. Luke wrote in Greek, and when he quotes from the Old Testament always uses the Greek translation of the Scriptures, commonly called the Septuagint.

There are interesting traditions respecting St. Andrew and St. Thomas, but they must not be entirely relied upon.

It has been generally believed that the Apostles

agreed amongst themselves, probably not without the special guidance of the Holy Spirit, as to the countries they should visit; and Scythia is said to have been appointed for the labours of St. Andrew. On his way thither he is supposed to have preached the Gospel along the shores of the Black Sea; and at Sinope we are informed that he met with St. Peter, with whom he remained a considerable time. The author who states this circumstance adds that the chairs made of white stone in which the two Apostles were accustomed to sit when they taught the people were remaining in his time.

The inhabitants of Sinope, we are informed, were mostly Jews, very uncivilized and bigoted. The preaching of St. Andrew greatly exasperated them. They plotted together to burn the house in which he dwelt; and, not succeeding in this, treated him in the most cruel manner, throwing him to the ground, stamping upon him with their feet, beating, pelting him with stones, and at length actually biting off his flesh with their teeth. The Apostle was cast out of the town, and left for dead, but he is said to have recovered miraculously, and to have returned to the city, where he converted many by his wonderful deeds.

Leaving Sinope, he journeyed along the eastern shore of the Black Sea, and preached successfully to the inhabitants of Sebastopol, which even in those days was a place of note. He then proceeded to Scythia, and returning again to Sinope, founded a Church at Byzantium (since called Constantinople), and ordained Stachys (whom St. Paul calls his beloved Stachys) to be the first bishop of that place.

Thrace, Macedonia, Thessaly, and Achaia, are said to have been the scene of St. Andrew's later labour, and he is stated to have suffered martyrdom at Patræ, a town in Achaia. Ægeas, the Proconsul, alarmed at the spread of Christianity, endeavoured, we are told, by every means, to recall the people to their ancient idolatry, and threatened the Apostle that if he would not offer sacrifice to the gods he would cause him to suffer upon that cross which he so much extolled. The threat was carried into execution the next day.

St. Andrew was first scourged, and then ordered to be crucified; not however in the usual mode, by being nailed to the cross. His tormentors desired to make his death more lingering, and they commanded that he should be fastened to it with cords only. The Apostle went forth to meet death calmly and cheerfully; even the people who followed him declared that he was an innocent man unjustly condemned.

The instrument of his martyrdom, formed of two pieces of timber in the shape of the letter X, still bears his name. St. Andrew's cross has been the token of human honour, when given by kings to their nobles; it has been worn as an ornament by the thoughtless, and introduced as a beautiful figure in public decorations; but never again can it be so honourable or so worthy of admiration as it was on the day when the rough wood was made the means of testifying the love of the devoted Apostle to the Saviour who died for him.

" O Good Cross which hast received glory•from the Limbs of the Lord, long longed for, anxiously loved, unceasingly sought, and at last prepared for my longing soul, receive me from men and give me to my Master, that He, Who through thee redeemed me, may through thee receive me."

These are the words said to have been spoken by St. Andrew at the first sight of the instrument of his death.

For two days he hung upon it. Great entreaties were at length made to the Proconsul to spare his life. But the Apostle had only one wish for himself, that he might at this time depart, and seal the truth of his religion with his blood.

It was his earnest prayer, and it was granted as soon as offered. He expired, as it is said, on the last day of November, but the date of the year is uncertain.

The body of St. Andrew is stated to have been buried by Maximilla, the wife of the Proconsul, and afterwards to have been removed by Constantine the Great to Constantinople; and some hundred years after, in the time of the Emperor Justinian, the church being under repair, we are told that it was found in a wooden coffin.

The history of St. Thomas is still more uncertain. The province given to him was Parthia, and from thence he travelled, as it is said, through Persia to India. The Portuguese, when they first settled in India, found a body of Christians already in the country, who called themselves the descendants of the persons converted by St. Thomas, and related many traditions of the Apostle's life and labours. They declared that he came first to Socotora, an island in the Arabian Sea, travelled farther into the East, preaching successfully, and returned again to the kingdom of Coromandel, where he began to erect a place for divine worship. Sagamo, the prince of the country, was, they said, converted by the miracles which he witnessed, and many of his friends and subjects followed his example. This excited the fears of the Brahmins, and they resolved to stop the new doctrines by putting the Apostle to death.

St. Thomas was accustomed to retire to a tomb, not far from the city, for purposes of prayer and meditation. Thither the Brahmins followed him, and whilst he was intent upon his devotions, they cast a shower of darts at him, and at last struck him with a lance. His body was taken up by his disciples and buried in the church which he had himself built. It has also been stated, that during the government of a viceroy of India, in the time of John the Third King of Portugal, some brass tables were found containing certain inscriptions which could scarcely be read, but which were translated by a learned Jew, and declared to contain the record of a donation made by St. Thomas of a piece of ground for the building of a church. An inscription upon a famous cross was likewise, we are told, discovered in St. Thomas's Church at Malipur, and, being translated by a Brahmin, proved to be an account of the Apostle's martyrdom.

Whether these stories are true or not, it is quite certain that Christianity was known in India before the time of the European settlements. The Portuguese state that they found on their arrival as many as fifteen or sixteen thousand Christian families. The St. Thomas Christians, as they are sometimes called, are very poor, and their churches are generally mean, with no images of saints nor representations of any kind except that of the cross. They have always been under the government of a patriarch of their own, and have never been subject to the Bishop of Rome. They receive the Holy Communion in both kinds, and observe the seasons of Advent, and Lent, the festivals of our Lord, and of many of the Saints. The Sunday after Easter is especially kept sacred by them in memory of the famous confession made on that day, by St. Thomas, of his faith in our Blessed Lord. Their Bible, at least the New Testament, is in the Syriac language, and is allowed to be read by the people; their priests are permitted to marry once. In some of these respects a great resemblance may be traced to the customs of the English Church.

There are but few traditions of St. Matthew. He is stated to have preached in Parthia and the countries adjacent to India, sometimes called the Asiatic Ethiopia, and there he is supposed to have suffered martyrdom. His Gospel was written, it is said, in Hebrew, at the request of the Jewish converts, and afterwards translated into Greek during the lifetime of the Apostles. It is this Greek translation which has been always received as one of the sacred books of Scripture. St. Matthew is said to have been remarkable for his abstemiousness. Many writings besides the Gospel have been attributed to this Apostle, but all have been declared false.

St. Jude, sometimes called Thaddeus, and otherwise known as Judas, the brother of James, Bishop of Jerusalem, is reported to have preached the Gospel first in Judea and Arabia, and afterwards in Syria and Mesopotamia. The writers of the Latin Church say that he was martyred in Persia; but others declared that he survived most of the other Apostles, and died peaceably at Edessa. He was married, for his grandchildren are mentioned by Eusebius, the Church historian. St. Jude wrote a General or Catholic Epistle, in which he especially warns the Christians of those days against the errors of the Gnostics.

St. Simon, who is generally coupled with St. Jude, preached, we are told, in Africa; and there is a tradition, though a very uncertain one, that he even came to Britain, where he was martyred.

St. Matthias preached in Cappadocia, and was martyred probably about the year 61 or 64. The traditions of the Greek Church say that he was crucified. His body is declared to have been long kept at Jerusalem, and to have been translated to Rome by Helena, the mother of Constantine the Great.

St. Bartholomew, generally supposed to have been the same person as Nathanael, is said to have preached in the countries bordering upon Judea. The most interesting tradition respecting him is that he left behind him a copy of St. Matthew's Gospel written in Hebrew, which was found many years afterwards, when but few Christians remained in the country. Some of the latter years of his life were, we are told, spent in Phrygia, where he laboured in company with St. Philip, and narrowly escaped crucifixion. He was at last, it is supposed, martyred in Cilicia. Various accounts are given of his death. Some say that he was crucified with his head downwards, others that he was flayed.

St. Philip is thought to have preached in Upper Asia, and to have been martyred at Hierapolis, in Phrygia, at the time when St. Bartholomew escaped. The inhabitants of Hierapolis, were, it is said, devoted to heathen superstitions, and it was whilst endeavouring to turn them from the worship of a serpent or dragon, that St. Philip excited the indignation of the governors of the city, and after being imprisoned and scourged was put to death. Some declare that he was hung by the neck against a pillar, others that he was crucified. Mariamne, his sister, the constant companion of his travels, is reported to have buried him with the assistance of St. Bartholomew.

St. John, the only remaining Apostle, outlived all his companions, and saw before his death the fulfilment of his Saviour's prophecies concerning Jerusalem.

For several years after the death of our Blessed Lord Judea had been the scene of the greatest confusion and distress, the inhabitants being subject to Rome, yet in a continual state of rebellion In the year 66 open war broke out. Vespasian, the Roman general was soon afterwards sent to command the Roman armies. The Jews fought desperately. Town after town was taken, but still they were unsubdued. About three years afterwards, A.D. 70. Vespasian was made emperor, and the Roman armies were entrusted to his son Titus. By this time the Jews were reduced almost to despair. They shut themselves up in Jerusalem, abandoning the rest of the country to their enemies ; but instead of uniting in one common cause, they separated into parties, each hating the other more than they detested and dreaded their Roman foes.

Murder and famine followed. The condition of the city became almost too dreadful to be described ; and the words of Moses, uttered more than fifteen hundred years before, were strictly fulfilled : " Thou shalt eat the fruit of thine own body, the flesh of thy sons and of thy daughters, which the Lord thy God hath given thee, in the siege and in the straitness wherewith thine enemies shall distress thee," Deut. xxviii. 53. When Jerusalem was at length taken, the Romans could scarcely believe their own conquest. Titus, beholding the exceeding strength of the city, exclaimed : " We have carried on this war under the protection of God. It is God alone who has taken away the Jews from their stronghold; for of what service are human means and material engines against such towers?"

The Roman soldiers set fire to the houses, and levelled the wall with the ground. The unfortunate inhabitants were carried away captive. Ninety-seven thousand prisoners are said to have been made during the war, and eleven hundred thousand persons perished in the siege.

But in the midst of these calamities the Christians were comparatively safe. They had been warned by their Lord of the coming trials, and ordered to quit the city ere the siege began. Before Jerusalem was at all surrounded by armies they fled to Pella, a town on the eastern bank of the Jordan, which had long lost its former connection with Judea, and at that time formed part of the small dominions of Agrippa. Symeon, the brother of St. James, who had succeeded the Apostle as Bishop of Jerusalem, probably accompanied them. Many, it is supposed, left Palestine altogether, and their dispersion naturally increased the ill will so generally felt against them in heathen countries. Coming from Palestine, and being Jews by birth, they were considered to be of the same turbulent character as their fellow-countrymen, and their religion was in consequence looked upon with additional suspicion.

The residence of the Christians at Pella was followed by the rise of two sects, whose religious opinions have been the cause of much discussion. These were the Nazarenes and Ebionites. The name of Nazarene was at first a term of reproach given by the Jews to all who believed in Christ, but afterwards it was applied only to a sect whose

9*

doctrines were a compound of Judaism and Christianity.

The Nazarenes, being Jews by birth, were circumcised, and kept the Sabbath and other observances of the Mosaic law. At the same time they received the New Testament, acknowledged Jesus Christ to be the Messiah, practised Christian baptism, and honoured the Lord's Day. Afterwards they are said to have held heretical opinions to our Blessed Saviour's divinity.

Tertullus, when addressing Felix on the occasion of St. Paul's trial, accuses the Apostle of being a ringleader of the sect of the Nazarenes; but this only meant that he was a Christian, for the sect properly called Nazarenes was not then regularly formed.

The Ebionites were from the beginning more decidedly heretics. They were in fact a branch of the Gnostics, whose opinions have already been stated, but they observed the outward ceremonies of the Jewish law. There was always a danger lest the Jewish converts, from attachment to the law, should become either Nazarenes or Ebionites. But there were many who kept themselves in the true faith, and these seem chiefly to be found amongst the Christians, who after the destruction of Jerusalem returned to dwell in the ruined city. To them the downfall of their country, most mournful though it was, could not have been the utter destruction of all hope and interest that it was to the mere Jews. It was the fulfilment of a prophecy which only confirmed them the more strongly in their faith, and bade them turn their eyes from the earthly to the spiritual Jerusalem, — the City "not made with hands, eternal in the heavens." There alone could rest be found; and as the little company of

Christians gathered together amidst the wreck of their former happiness, they must have seen in the mercy which had guarded them amidst the dangers of that terrible war, the earnest of the Guiding Hand which was to lead them safely through the howling wilderness of life to the glorious land of immortality.

CHAPTER XI.

THE DEATH OF ST. JOHN. A.D. 98.

THE reign of the Emperor Vespasian and that of his son Titus were periods of peace for the Christian Church, during which religion must have made much progress. Jerusalem, Antioch, Rome, and Alexandria, had by this time become celebrated as the cities where the chief bishoprics were established. Jerusalem and Rome were called the Apostolical Sees, as having been founded by apostles; Jerusalem by St. James, Rome by St. Peter and St. Paul. Symeon, as it has been stated, succeeded St. James at Jerusalem; and Linus, Anacletus, and Clement, are mentioned as having been successively bishops of Rome. The name of Clement deserves particular mention, from the fact of his being called by St. Paul, in his Epistle to the Philippians, his fellow-labourer; and also from the letter which he left behind him, written in the name of the Christians at Rome to their brethren at Corinth.

This is the only document, except the Sacred Writings, which has been handed down to us as belonging to the first century of Christianity. It speaks of a persecution which the Roman Christians had lately endured; and from this some have supposed that it was written after the end of Nero's reign, when St. Peter and St. Paul had suffered martyrdom; but others imagine the expressions to allude to a later period of trial, which will presently be mentioned.

The Christians at Corinth appear to have been full of dissensions in the days of Clement, as they were in those of St. Paul; for the bishop earnestly exhorts them to peace. His letter was always held in great esteem, and was for many years publicly read, not only by the Corinthian Church but by many others.

There are several other books professing to belong to the first century of Christian history, but none of them are genuine. Many persons undertook to give accounts of our Lord and of the Apostles; but the stories which were related were evidently for the most part untrue. Some of them appear to have been written by Gnostics; and notwithstanding our natural desire to learn more particulars of lives so infinitely important to ourselves and to all mankind, we cannot but consider it a most merciful ordering of God's Providence which gave such honour to the true works of the Apostles and Evangelists, and has caused them to be handed down safely through so many ages; whilst those which contained imaginary stories, or were mixed up with false doctrine, are comparatively unknown.

Another person of great note living in the first century was Ignatius, who succeeded Euodius as Bishop of Antioch; but as his death did not take place till the second century, his history must for the present be deferred.

Towards the close of the first century the peace

of the Christian Church was greatly disturbed.
A.D. 81. The wicked Domitian, the half-brother of Titus, who succeeded him in the empire, set on foot a furious persecution, originally directed against the Jews, but falling heavily upon the Christians, who were often confounded with them.

After the destruction of Jerusalem, a tax had been demanded of the Jews by Titus, which was exacted by Domitian with great severity. A heathen historian mentions that some persons who professed the Jewish religion endeavoured to conceal the fact, in order to evade the tax. These, no doubt, were Christians, who spoke truly as regarded their religion, but were not believed. The general charge brought both against Jews and Christians was, however, that of atheism, or disbelief in the gods. Flavius Clemens, the uncle of Domitian, and whose son had been destined to succeed to the empire, was accused of this offence, or, in other words, was discovered to be a Christian, and was in consequence put to death : whilst his wife, Domitilla, was sent into an exile from which she never returned, even when Nerva, the emperor who reigned after Domitian, and who was famed for his clemency, recalled those who had been banished. But Domitian's enmity against the Christians was not merely on account of their religion. He suspected them of being disloyal to himself. They refused to worship him as a god, and he might naturally imagine that this implied unwillingness to acknowledge him as king. He had heard also of a report common amongst the Jews at the time of the destruction of Jerusalem, that a great prince was expected to appear in Judea, and that he was to come from the house of David. Upon inquiry, he found that some persons professing Christianity, and who were known as descendants of David, being the grandchildren of the Apostle Jude, were at that time residing in Palestine. He sent for them, and questioned them as to their condition and their belief; but they were poor men, labouring for their daily bread; and when Domitian saw their hard toil-stained hands, and heard them speak of their Lord as One who was not of this world and cared nothing for its pomp and its dominion, he foresaw no danger to himself, and allowed them to depart free; little imagining that the power which he thus despised was mighty to overturn the greatest empires of earth, and would one day shine forth triumphant in Heaven.

It seems probable from this circumstance that the Christians in Palestine escaped persecution. But the emperor's wrath was severely felt by those who were resident in Asia Minor; and the name of one martyr, Antipas of Pergamos, is mentioned to us in the Book of Revelation.

Ephesus, the chief city of Asia Minor, was the most celebrated for its Christian Church, and towards the close of the first century it became the residence of the last of the apostles, St. John, who is said to have shared in the sufferings inflicted upon his brethren by the cruelty of Domitian.

Of the life of St. John little is told us in Scripture, except in the early chapters of the Acts, where he is mentioned as being the companion of St. Peter, and assisting him in confirming and strengthening the Church in Samaria.

Asia fell to his share when the provinces were assigned to the Apostles; but he does not appear to have entered at once upon his charge. Probably he dwelt still in his own house at Jerusalem until after the death of the Blessed Virgin, which is sup-

posed to have taken place about fifteen years after
our Lord's ascension.

St. John's efforts in Asia were greatly prospered,
for he founded the Churches of Smyrna, Pergamos, Thyatira, Sardis, Philadelphia, Laodicea, and
others; and he is supposed to have extended his
labours still further to the east.   His chief residence
however was at Ephesus.

Some special incidents of his zeal for truth, and
the deep love for the souls of his converts which he
exhibited when living there, have been transmitted to
us.   Whilst visiting the churches near to Ephesus
he is said to have met with a young man who excited
his peculiar interest, and whom he gave in charge to
the bishop of the place to be educated.   The bishop
did not properly fulfil his office, and his pupil, as he
grew up, became in consequence very dissipated,
and at last joined a company of highwaymen.   St.
John, returning to the same place after a lapse of
time, was deeply grieved at the report which he
received, and, having sharply reproved the bishop,
expressed his determination to seek out the young
man and, if possible, bring him to repentance.

Unmindful of danger, he set out for the mountains, the haunt of the robbers.   He was taken
prisoner by their sentinel, and brought before their
commander.

In him he saw the youth whom he had so
dearly loved, and who now, conscience stricken at
his presence, fled from his sight.   The aged Apostle
followed, passionately entreating him to stay.
" My son," he exclaimed, " why dost thou flee
from thy father unarmed and old ?   Fear not; as
yet there remaineth hope of salvation.   Believe
me, Christ hath sent me."   The entreaties prevailed.   The young man stood still, trembling and

weeping bitterly. St. John prayed with him, exhorted him, and succeeded in bringing him to a full sense of his guilt. His repentance was sincere and lasting. He went through a course of penance as a proof of his sorrow for his crimes, and was then received again into the communion of the Church, continuing ever after a faithful disciple.

St. John's horror of any departure from the true faith is also said to have been exhibited in a memorable instance.

Whilst residing at Ephesus, he went one day to the public baths according to his usual custom, and inquired of the servant who waited there, who was within. He was informed that it was Cerinthus, a man of bad character, who professed himself a Christian, but held most dangerous and heretical opinions, denying the resurrection of our Lord, and declaring that he himself was an apostle, and had received revelations from heaven. St. John instantly turned to his companions, exclaiming, "Let us be gone, my brethren, and make haste from this place, lest the bath wherein there is such an heretic as Cerinthus, the great enemy of the truth, fall upon our heads."

The followers of Cerinthus were not the only heretics whom St. John opposed. In the Book of Revelation special mention is made of the Nicolaitanes, who professed to be the followers of Nicolas, one of the seven men chosen to assist the Apostles in the very first beginning of the Church. Nicolas was a man of most self-denying habits; but the sect which took his name were noted for wicked self-indulgence. The Nicolaitanes showed the weakness of their principles, by consenting in periods of persecution to eat meats which had been offered to idols.   This was now the test of the Christian when brought before heathen magistrates.

St. John was dwelling at Ephesus, when the enmity of Domitian is said to have overtaken him.

The proconsul of Asia, we are told, in obedience to the command of the emperor, sent him bound to Rome, where he was cast into a caldron of boiling oil, from the effects of which he was miraculously preserved. The circumstances of the story are not sufficiently attested to be received with positive certainty. We know, however, that the emperor ordered him to be banished, and that he was in consequence conveyed to Patmos, called by one of the writers of his life, "a disconsolate island in the Archipelago."

Such, doubtless, it was in the eye of man; but how different in the estimation of the holy Apostle! The Presence of God was with him, in that lonely exile, in a manner which has never been vouchsafed to any other mortal.. The Book of Revelation describes to us the series of stupendous visions which conveyed to him, in figure, the history of the Church throughout all the ages of the world, and placed him in the presence of the "great White Throne, and Him that sat upon it, before whose Face the earth and the heavens fled away;" bidding him rest at last in the vision of the glorious "City which shall have no need of the sun, neither of the moon to shine in it, for the glory of God shall lighten it, and the Lamb shall be the light thereof."

"Even so: come, Lord Jesus!" The words fall upon the ear as the fullest expression of the longing heart. After that sight of glory, what could earth have been to the mind of the sainted Apostle?

Yet many years of lingering trial were still before him. He was released from exile by the clemency
10

A.D. 96.   of the emperor Nerva, who succeeded Domitian, and he lived till the time of Trajan. Those latter years were spent, we have reason to believe, in the quiet superintendence of the Asiatic Churches, and in the writing of his Gospel and Epistles,—the First of the Epistles being catholic, or addressed to Christians generally; the Second, to a lady held in high honour in the Church; and the Third to Gaius, the kind friend and hospitable entertainer of the Christians, who had been baptized by St. Paul, and was his host at Corinth. Heresies were by this time abounding in the Church, and the bishops of Asia were earnest that the Apostle should give his own testimony to the true doctrine, received from Christ himself. We are told of the earnest entreaties of the ambassadors from various Churches, and of the great fast which was proclaimed before so solemn an undertaking as a record of the life and teaching of the Lord of Glory was begun; and, whatever may be the foundation of these traditions, no one can read the opening chapters of St. John's Gospel without feeling that he who indited them was favoured with a deep insight into the things of God, and a wonderful nearness to the spirit of Christ.

Love to God, and to men for His sake, are the distinguishing features of the writings of him who lay upon his Saviour's Breast, and was, of all the disciples, the closest to His Human Affections. And still, when too infirm to give lengthened instruction in the faith, St. John repeated the gentle exhortation, which had been the rule of his long life. "Little children, love one another!" were the words which he addressed to his disciples at Ephesus, when he was led to the church to join in the public assembly of the Christians.

There were those who were wearied with such constant repetition. They could not understand the depth of meaning which it conveyed. "Why," they said, "should they be told always one thing!" "Because nothing else is needed," replied the Apostle. And still he repeated, "Little children, love one another!" until the love of men on earth was exchanged for the communion of the saints in Paradise.

"He died in expectation of his blessedness." It is the expression used by an ancient writer.

Many were the legends concerning him current in the Church in after ages, founded upon those words of our Blessed Lord, "If I will that he tarry till I come, what is that to thee?" St. John himself seems to have foreseen the erroneous opinion which was to spring from them: for he adds: "Then went this saying abroad among the brethren, that that disciple should not die: yet Jesus said not unto him he shall not die, but, if I will that he tarry till I come, what is that to thee?" The words "till I come," meaning probably that coming of our Lord in vengeance upon the Jews which took place at the destruction of Jerusalem.

An early writer of St. John's life reports that only one of his disciples was present at his burial, and that he was strictly charged never to discover the sepulchre to any. Yet the Turks imagine him to have been buried in the confines of Lydia, and pay great honour to his supposed tomb.

The death of the last of the Apostles must have taken place very nearly at the close of the first century, about A.D. 98. He is supposed to have been ninety-nine years of age when he was summoned to his rest.

CHAPTER XII.

THE GOVERNMENT OF THE CHURCH.

WITH the death of St. John, the first remarkable epoch of Christianity ends: and here, therefore, it seems natural to pause, and dwell upon the astonishing progress made by the Church since its first foundation.

Perhaps the best mode of realising to ourselves its miraculous success is by comparing it with the efforts made to spread the Gospel among the heathen in our own days.

Who does not know how slow, how disheartening, how full of failure, is the work of the Christian missionary now,—though sent forth with all the advantages of learning and civilisation,—when he is called upon to battle with the prejudices of an ignorant and barbarous people? He may, indeed, be followed, and respected, and admired; he may be looked upon as a being of a higher sphere; he will find men willing to submit themselves to him, to be governed by him, to learn from him; but he cannot persuade them to worship with him. Only by slow degrees, by gaining their affections, watching for opportunities, working upon them through their children, can the minds of those who have grown up in heathen superstition be opened to receive the truths of Christianity. The real work is done by teaching the little ones, who have no knowledge of any other faith; and even with them it is a task of great difficulty, surrounded as they are by evil example, and with all the influence of their nearest and dearest relations leading them astray.

Human nature was not different in the time of

the Apostles from what it is now. The opposition to Christianity was not less, rather it was far greater, for the preachers were for the most part humble fishermen of Galilee, and the hearers were to be found amongst the enlightened citizens of the mightiest empire the world has ever known.

If an English missionary finds it so difficult to convert a Hindoo idolater, how did the followers of the crucified Jesus of Nazareth convert the Roman world? Many answers, drawn from the condition of heathen society, may be given to this inquiry, but they all relate to the progress of Christianity in after years. When we look at its first triumph there can be but one reply, found in the prayer made by the small company of faithful disciples who met together when the anger of the chief-priests had followed the healing of the lame man laid at the gate of the Temple, " And now, Lord, behold their threatenings : and grant unto thy servants, that with all boldness they may speak thy word. By stretching forth Thine Hand to heal : and that signs and wonders may be done by the Name of thy Holy Child Jesus."

If there had been no " signs and wonders," no Divine interposition, Christianity, though the purest, holiest religion the world has ever known, would have had the same difficulty in spreading itself then as it has now. And when we are inclined, as we sometimes may be, to wish that we had lived in the days of miracles, we shall do well to remember that God has given us one continually before our eyes, which only the hardness of our hearts prevents us from acknowledging.

The existence of Christianity is the greatest miracle which the world has ever seen.

But the new religion was not only intended to
10*

bring back individual men to the service of the true God; it was the establishment of a Divine kingdom. The Church had its own rulers, its own laws and discipline; its influence, humanly speaking, depended greatly on its authority; and the manner in which this authority was from the beginning regulated can be traced without difficulty. There is no doubt that at the first foundation of the Christian Church the Apostles themselves were its governors. The title of Apostle was probably first limited to the twelve chosen by our Lord, and to St. Matthias, who was elected in the place of Judas. But St. Paul claimed the same dignity, as being appointed to it by an immediate revelation from Heaven, and St. Luke applies the title to St. Barnabas. These then were the spritual rulers of the Church, who so far differed from the bishops of the present day that they were gifted with miraculous powers, and were not limited to any particular diocese, but were directed to preach the Gospel throughout the world.

Next in rank to the Apostles were the overseers or elders, often known also by the titles of bishops or presbyters. These are frequently mentioned in the Acts of the Apostles. We read that Paul and Barnabas, when proceeding on their missionary journey, ordained them elders in every church (Acts xiv. 23); and the decree respecting circumcision which was entrusted to them was given by the authority of the Apostles, elders, and brethren. The name "elder" was derived from an office common in the Jewish synagogues, and therefore adopted by the Christian Church in Judea; whilst, among the Gentiles, the title of bishop was more common.

The fact of these different titles having been applied at first to the same office, has caused many mistaken impressions respecting the government of the early Church. Persons who know the Bible only by our English translation, are apt to imagine, when they hear St. Paul's injunctions to Timothy, as to the conduct required of bishops, that these bishops held the same office as those in the present day. And thus they are accustomed, if they meet with persons who dispute the authority of bishops, to say that the office and its duties are mentioned in the Epistles of St Paul, and therefore must be upheld ; but this is a wrong argument, and easily disproved. A person acquainted with Greek, and having any knowledge of the history and the writings of the early Christians, can show at once that bishops, elders, and presbyters held originally the same office. The consequence of this is, that those who believe bishops to be necessary, only because they read of them in St Paul's epistles, are perplexed, and perhaps tempted to join some sect of Christians which has renounced Episcopacy, and will only allow the government of elders or presbyters. But all this is merely a question of words. If there is one fact more clearly proved than any other in the history of the Church, it is that in the times of the Apostles there were three distinct orders, answering to our Bishops, Priests, and Deacons ; and that the change made afterwards was not in the office but in the names attached to them. If we look at the Epistles to Timothy and Titus, we shall see clearly that the office conferred upon them was superior to that of the elders ; that in fact they held the same position in Ephesus and Crete which we now give to our bishops. St. Paul tells Timothy that he had left him in Ephesus that he might charge or command others not to teach false doctrine. He gives directions, which it is evident that Timothy is to carry out, respecting public worship, the character of bishops or elders, and deacons, the instruction of the Church generally, and the relief of widows. Timothy is told not to receive accusations against the elders unless there are two or three witnesses; to lay hands upon, or, in other words, to ordain no one suddenly; with many other warnings and exhortations of a similar kind, all of which are indisputable evidence that Timothy was called upon to act as the head of the Ephesian Church. So again the Apostle opens his letter to Titus, by stating that he had left him in Crete for the very purpose of ordaining elders in every city; and then he proceeds to describe the duties of such elders or bishops, or, as the Greek word would more correctly be translated, overseers.

Thus, then, from the Scriptures themselves we learn the fact that during the lifetime of the Apostles, Christian churches were governed by one person holding a position of authority like that of a bishop of the present day, and having a special charge to ordain elders or presbyters. The fact is confirmed by historical tradition. Dionysius, the Areopagite, converted by St. Paul, is declared to have been the first Head of the Church of Athens; whilst there is common testimony to the fact that Antioch was governed by Euodius, who had probably entered upon his office as early as A.D. 48. Epaphroditus is said to have been the Bishop of Philippi. St. Paul calls him " your messenger," but the word translated " messenger" is more strictly " apostle;" whilst Zacchæus, who after his call is believed to have attached himself to the Apostles, is declared to have been appointed Bishop of Cæsarea by St. Peter. If we wish for still further testimony, we must remember that, with the exception of the books of the New Testament, we have scarcely any writings of the first century after Christ. In the second century every church is spoken of as having its distinct ruler, and the title of bishop is then commonly given to the person holding that office.

The change in the name seems to have been made like many other changes which we read of in history, or even remark in our own day. For instance, in the later times of the Roman Republic, distinguished generals were called imperators or emperors. There might then be many imperators, all bearing the same rank; but when Augustus Cæsar took the supreme authority in the state he was called especially *the* imperator, as if there was no other. Thus the title became limited to him, and now we think of an emperor as of one having supreme authority, and quite forget that at first the title was shared in common with many. In the same way in the Christian Church, at first there were many bishops all subject to the Apostles; but when one of these was appointed to rule over the others he was called *the* bishop, as if there was no other, and so by degrees the titles of bishop and presbyter were separated; a bishop was understood to mean the ruler of the church, and the presbyter was the elder who acted under him.

We do not, therefore, rest the claims of Episcopacy upon the title given to certain persons in the Sacred Writings; but upon the facts which we may all see for ourselves,—that St. Paul unquestionably addresses Timothy and Titus as having authority over the presbyters;—that historical testimony alludes to other bishops in the first century after

Christ ;—and that for fifteen hundred years all great communities of Christians acknowledged the government of bishops, and the ordination of elders by them to be essential for the being of a church.

The third order, that of deacons, is supposed to have originated from the appointment of the seven " men of honest report," chosen to assist the Apostles in ministering to the poor, soon after the Day of Pentecost. The office of deacon, however, probably existed from the very first in the Church at Jerusalem. It is thought by some that the young men who assisted in the burial of Ananias and Sapphira were of the number ; and that the title of " young men " was given them in contrast with that of elders. In the Epistles to Timothy and Titus, direct mention is made of them, and their duties are clearly pointed out.

As regards the manner of ordination, we have no other record of the customs of those early times except the Scriptures. From them we learn that it was always performed by the laying on of hands ; and the first rulers of the Church appear to have been appointed according to some special declaration of God's will. Paul and Barnabas were separated for their work, by the command of the Holy Ghost ; and it is said of the governors of the Ephesian churches, who met at Miletus, that the Holy Ghost had made them bishops or overseers of the Church. St. Paul may probably allude to this miraculous appointment when, in writing to Timothy, he says, " This charge I commit unto thee, son Timothy, according to the prophecies which went before on thee, that thou by them mightest war a good warfare." This mode of election, according to a prophetic revelation, continued, at least, during the time of the Apostles,

We are expressly told by some early writers, that "the Apostles constituted their first-fruits to be the bishops and deacons of those who should believe, making trial of them by the Spirit:" and it is particularly reported of St. John, when visiting the churches near to Ephesus, that he ordained bishops, and such as were signified, or pointed out to him "by the Spirit."

Prophets and evangelists are also mentioned in the apostolic age, as assisting the Apostles in the work of instruction and guidance. Prophets were sometimes those to whom the will of God was distinctly revealed, and who were, therefore, able to foretell future events; but this was not necessarily the case with all who were called prophets. They were for the most part preachers of the Word of God, who declared and explained the Gospel to their brethren. Evangelists were missionaries, who went from place to place preaching to the heathen. We use the word when we speak of the persons who wrote the history of our Lord's Life, but this could not have been its original meaning, for those to whom the term is applied in Scripture were not the writers of the four Gospels. Philip, one of the seven, first chosen to assist the Apostles, is called an evangelist; so also is Timothy.

Whilst speaking of the government of the Church under the Apostles, it may be desirable at the same time to mention the Sacraments, which form so prominent a part of our Christian services. Baptism we find was considered so absolutely necessary, that it could not be omitted, even in the case of one, like St. Paul, converted by a miraculous interposition. Again and again, we find it required of the Christian converts, and St. Paul's mention of it in his Epistles is almost always accompanied by expressions which show its great dignity and importance.

There is great reason to believe that a public form of Baptism, including questions and answers such as are now common in the English Church, was used even in the Apostolic times, as it undoubtedly was afterwards. Many expressions in Scripture favour this idea, particularly Philip's questions to the Eunuch before he baptized him, and the allusion made in the first Epistle of St. Peter, to " the answer of a good conscience towards God," in connection with the sacrament of Baptism. That infants were baptized, appears certain, though it is not expressly mentioned. If it had not been so, there must have been some trace of the introduction of infant baptism in after ages, but there is none : the practice is immemoral. None, even in the earliest ages, could remember the time when it had not been. Baptism was administered by immersion, the convert being plunged beneath the water to represent his death to the life of sin, and then raised again as a sign that he had risen to the life of righteousness. This practice was discontinued as the Gospel spread in colder regions.

The Sacrament of the Lord's Supper appears to have been celebrated at first daily, and in connection with feasts called Agapæ, or Love Feasts, in which rich and poor, masters and slaves, met together as equals. This practice, however, was soon discontinued, on account of the abuses to which it led. St. Paul alludes to them in his First Epistle to the Corinthians, when he speaks of the excesses which were committed by those who came together into one place, to eat the Lord's Supper,—

or, as the expression is in that place supposed to mean, partake of the Love Feasts. " One," he says, is hungry, and another drunken," and then he proceeds to remind the Corinthians of the solemn manner in which the Sacrament which followed was first instituted, the sacred truths which it sets forth, the blessing it communicates, and the necessity of self-examination, before it can be received without danger. All these warnings being equally applicable to ourselves, and, indeed, adopted by the English Church in the exhortation used in the Communion Service.

It appears, upon examination, that the elements of bread and wine were consecrated in the days of the Apostles, as they are now: the consecration being accompanied by a solemn thanksgiving. This has caused the Sacrament of the Lord's Supper to be called also the Sacrament of the Eucharist, Eucharist meaning thanksgiving. St. Paul speaks of this consecration, when he says to the Corinthians, " When thou shalt *bless* with the Spirit, how shall he that occupies the room of the unlearned say, Amen, at the *giving of thanks*, seeing he understandeth not what thou sayest ? "—a passage which is thus explained by persons learned in the Greek language, in which the Epistle was first written : " If thou shalt bless the bread and wine in an unknown language, which has been given to thee by the Holy Spirit, how shall the layman say, Amen, so be it, at the end of thy thanksgiving or liturgy, seeing he understandeth not what thou sayest ? " It was customary also to symbolise the fellowship and affection of the Christian converts, by interchanging the kiss of peace before partaking of the Sacrament. St. Paul, in writing to the

11

Thessalonians, says, " Greet all the brethren with an holy kiss." A kiss, we must remember, was, in ancient times, as it is now in many foreign countries, the ordinary mode in which friends saluted each other.

The festivals of the Church in the Apostolic times, were at first, for the most part, the same with those of the Jews, although a higher and spiritual meaning was given to them. St. Paul says to the Corinthians, " I will tarry at Ephesus until Pentecost." He is speaking apparently of a festival, acknowledged and observed by Christians as well as Jews. So, again, he alludes to the Feast of the Passover, as one which they were in the habit of keeping, and warns them to " keep the feast, not with old leaven, neither with the leaven of malice and wickedness, but with the unleavened bread of sincerity and truth."

The first day of the week was also a festival in memory of our Lord's Resurrection, and was called for the same reason, the Lord's Day, a name which it has retained to the present time.

Meetings for public worship, did not, however, take place, only on the first day of the week. We gather from the Acts of the Apostles, that they were often held daily. The Christians in Jerusalem, at first resorted to the Courts of the Temple, and there the Apostles taught them ; but they are often spoken of as meeting in private houses. Very little is told us of the details of their worship. In many respects they must have differed widely from our own, owing to the miraculous gifts bestowed upon the new converts, and the power granted them of speaking in unknown tongues, interpreting, and prophesying. St. Paul gives directions to the Corinthians, which show that confusion was sometimes apt to arise from the manner in which these gifts were exercised. He desires that not more than two or three should prophesy in the same assembly; that persons having the gift of tongues should not exercise it, unless some one was present who could interpret what they said. He also orders that women should not attempt to teach in these public assemblies, and should appear veiled. All these directions point out a state of things wholly unlike that now existing.

Yet there are other allusions which bring back our thoughts to our own times. Prayer and thanksgiving, we know, formed a great part of the public service, and the mention of the Amen, uttered by the unlearned, or the laymen, shows that the people were accustomed to respond. Psalms, and hymns, and spiritual songs, also, we may believe, were used according to the Apostles' recommendations. The Jews chanted their psalms to simple melodies, which no doubt were dear to the hearts of the Christian converts, and which have, in all probability, been handed down to our own times, in the oldest chants now in use. The ministers of the Church were supported by the voluntary offerings of the people. St. Paul asserts their right to be thus maintained, in the very strongest terms. "They who preach the Gospel, have," he says, "a right to live of the Gospel." Yet he himself laboured with his own hands, at the occupation of tent-making, which he had been taught, according to the common custom of Jews of all ranks; being desirous to put his indifference to worldly interests beyond the reach of suspicion. Collections were made on the first day of the week, and out of the funds so raised, it is probable that a fixed stipend was paid to the clergy.

St. Paul seems to allude to this, when he says, that the elders who rule well are to be " accounted worthy of double honour,"—or pay, as the word used in the Greek not unfrequently means.

This, perhaps, is as much as can be gathered from the Books of the New Testament, as to the government and ordinances of the Church in the times of the Apostles, with the exception of the practice of anointing the sick with oil, which has given rise to the rite of Extreme Unction in the Roman Catholic Church. It appears evident from the manner in which this custom is mentioned in Scripture, that it accompanied the miraculous gift of healing. It was first practised by the Apostles when sent forth by our Lord. We are told that they anointed with oil many that were sick, and healed them. And St. James says, " Is any sick among you, let him call for the elders of the Church, and let them pray over him, anointing him with oil in the name of the Lord; and the prayer of faith shall save the sick, and the Lord shall raise him up, and if he have committed sins they shall be forgiven him." The miraculous gift of healing having ceased, the practice of anointing with oil has not been retained in the English Church.

CHAPTER XIV.

THE STATE OF SOCIETY AMONGST THE ROMANS.

THERE is something very dreary in turning from the records of sacred to those of profane history; yet the two arè so intermingled, that it is impossible thoroughly to understand either, when taken separately; and as we enter upon the second century of the Christian history, the first question which presents itself is, what was at that period the condition of the great empire in which the Church had taken root, and over which, in the ordering of God's providence, it was destined to triumph? The Roman world was heathen. What was a heathen world? What were the principles which guided the persons who composed it? Where did they find their happiness in life,—and what were their hopes in death? When these inquiries have been answered, we shall better understand the spirit with which the doctrines of Christianity were received by the Gentiles, to whom they were first preached.

Perhaps the most striking characteristic of that age was the unbelief of educated and thoughtful men. The old religion still kept its ground amongst the lower orders, but persons whose minds were cultivated had ceased to have faith in it. The stories of the gods and goddesses which are so shocking to us, were absurd, if not shocking to them. Even before the time of our Saviour, Lucilius, a clever, satirical writer, wrote an imaginary conversation between the deities, in which he described them as ridiculing amongst themselves the title of "father," which men were accustomed to give them; and at a later period, at the very time of our Lord's Human Life, the speeches and writings of the most distinguished Romans showed that they considered the monstrous fables of mythology totally unworthy of credit, except by the lowest of mankind. Yet they made no attempt to enlighten the ignorant people. They had learnt to disbelieve,—but they could not go farther. The best and wisest could

11*

only hope and conjecture; and what that state of mind must be, very few in the present day can imagine. Even the men who now say that they do not believe, prove by their anxiety to make others think like themselves, that the assertion is not strictly true. It is the fear that the Bible may be a revelation from heaven, which makes them take so much pains to overthrow it. But the clever Romans had no such feelings respecting the popular religion. They believed it to be a delusion; they scoffed at it, but they made no effort to uproot it. Rather, knowing that any religion was better than none, they encouraged the outward ceremonies, thinking them useful in keeping the lower orders under restraint. For themselves, they were compelled to live and die in darkness. A few listened to the teaching of their consciences, and tried to regulate their conduct accordingly; but the mass of the higher classes acted upon the proverb quoted by St. Paul—" Let us eat and drink, for to-morrow we die."

And who could expect it to be otherwise? The universe was to them without a God. Death was the end of their existence. What better could they do than strive to cast away care, and enjoy the few brief hours allotted to them, before they sank into nothingness?

But it is singular to observe that at this very time the ordinary life of a Roman was full of religious ceremonies, encouraged especially by the Emperor; since, in truth, religion was fast becoming not so much a worship of the gods as of the person who sat upon the throne of the Cæsars. Augustus, the first of the Roman emperors, allowed himself to be called a god. The princes who were in alliance to him erected altars to his honour.

In Athens a temple intended for Jupiter was dedicated to him; and after his death the infamous Tiberius offered him sacrifices. And this practice was continued with succeeding emperors in after years. Whilst the goddess Diana was represented on the stage and flogged publicly, and the imaginary will of the deceased god Jupiter was read aloud for public entertainment, the Romans worshipped the miserable monster, Caligula, during his lifetime, and even offered to him human victims. In such a religion there could be no faith. Temples, altars, sacrifices existed, but no reverence was felt for them. The empire was one vast scene of wicked mockery; and the consequences were too terrible to be described. Poets and philosophers tell us that the most atrocious vices were the common occupation of the chief men of their time; and were not hidden in secret, but published and spoken of as the known and remembered events of history. Cruelty naturally followed. Death was constantly mingled with the amusements of the Romans; men were thrown alive into the ponds in which fish were fattened; the pleasure of cutting off a man's head was purchased; and blood flowed at a feast as in the public games in which the gladiators fought. The lower orders were, if possible, even more depraved. They who professed a belief in the gods did not scruple to make use of that belief for the most shameful purposes. The prayers made in the temples were continually for help in the commission of crimes; the offerings brought to the gods were in order to obtain most disgraceful favours. And men's lives were like their prayers: they imitated the vices of the emperor in order to please him, and this without fear, for the idea of punishment in another world, following upon guilt, had ceased to exist amongst them. Even the little children, it is said, did not believe in it. Not that the Romans were without any consciousness of an unseen power. As they ceased to be religious they became superstitious. So it has always been, for the belief in a spiritual existence of some kind is a part of man's nature. Tiberius kept an astrologer by him, who pretended to foretell future events by observing the position of the stars. Tacitus, the great Roman historian, relates seriously the miracles of Vespasian. The world was full of predictions and marvels. Magic was considered a true science ; and yet crimes were committed in order to uphold it. A prophecy was often made that a particular person would die at a certain time, and then in order to fulfil it he was poisoned. Thus suspicion filled all hearts, and peace and safety were banished from the luxurious feasts of Rome.

Such was the state of society in the centre of the empire. Amongst the distant nations who formed its utmost limits, there would naturally be found considerable differences both in religion and habits. The Roman emperors, notwithstanding their cruelty, generally discouraged the barbarous rites of other lands. Each year a human offering was made to the god, Jupiter Latial, in Rome, but in Gaul, Britain, and Germany, such sacrifices were as much as possible prevented. Yet, as the Romans had no true religion to teach, they could never have effected any lasting change for the better even in this respect, if, at the time their power was spreading over the face of the earth, Christianity had not spread also ; and it is in order to bring out strongly the true condition, and dangers and difficulties of the early Christians that the gross corruptions of heathenism have now been alluded to.

For a Christian in those early days was a person obliged to separate himself from the habits and pleasures of the people amongst whom he dwelt, and to live a life apart.*   He did not send his children to the common schools, for there he knew they would be corrupted by heathen influence. He did not buy meat without first inquiring whether it was intended for the heathen altars; and if meat, which he knew had been offered to an idol, was set before him when he was dining with a heathen friend, he refused to partake of it.   He kept aloof from the public games and entertainments : for in the theatre immoral heathen stories were represented; and in the arena men fought to death for the amusement of their fellow-creatures. If his heathen acquaintances invited him to join in social festivities he was obliged often to refuse, lest he might in consequence find himself taking part in heathen rites. Ornaments sought for by others were forbidden to him. The crowns and chaplets, considered tokens of honour, were in his sight symbols of disgrace, for they were connected with the ceremonies of heathenism. He could scarcely borrow, or lend, or make bonds or contracts, because in case of any disagreement he might not appear before a heathen tribunal, to take a heathen oath. In these and in very many other ways the distinction was perceived daily and hourly ; even the ring which the Christian wore upon his finger, and the seal with which he secured his letter were marked with devices which had a secret meaning to him, though they were unintelligible to his heathen

* See "History of the Church," by the Rev. J. J. Blunt.

friends. And if we remember that these differences were felt, not merely amongst different families, but amongst the members of the same family, we shall understand more fully the meaning of our Blessed Lord's words, when He said, " I am come to set a man at variance against his father, and the daughter against her mother, and the daughter-in-law against her mother-in-law."

When the wife was a Christian and the husband a heathen ; when the child had given himself to the service of the Pure and Holy God, and the parent was sunk in all the wickedness of idolatry, there could be no union, no happiness.

It may easily be imagined with what dislike the heathens would look upon a body of persons who thus interfered with their ordinary habits. Whilst religion was only a matter of belief they did not trouble themselves about it ; it signified not to them whether the god in whom their relations and friends believed was a Grecian, an Egyptian, or a Roman deity ; but when their daily life was affected by the change of faith it became intolerable to them. We find this the case in some respects in our own day. Many there are who do not in the least trouble themselves about the religious creed of the persons with whom they live, whilst there are no outward differences of conduct ; but even a slight alteration in domestic habits becomes a grave offence. And the heathens were not without more decided cause of complaint against the Christians. The most false and horrible stories were told of them. When in consequence of the persecution raised against them, they were compelled to hold their assemblies at night, it was said that they met to commit atrocious crimes. Amongst other things it was stated that, on the occasion of the initiation of a convert, a child, sprinkled with flour, was presented to him, and that without knowing what he did he pierced it with a knife, after which the blood of the murdered infant was drunk, and the flesh eaten, as a token of union.

We can of course trace this story to the rite of the Holy Communion; but the heathens could not thus disprove it.

Again, Christians were considered dangerous citizens; they were heard to call Christ their King, and to sigh for His Kingdom. They objected to address the emperors by the title of Lord, when the word was used in a religious sense; and they would not swear by the Genius of the emperor — an oath which the heathens deemed so sacred that they built temples and offered sacrifices to this Genius, whom they reverenced as a deity. The lesser charge brought forward was that they were useless members of the state, because they sought to avoid public employments. Even the miracles which they worked were turned against them, for although not denied, they were attributed to magic.

That Christianity should ever have spread amongst a people so corrupted, and when so many difficulties stood in its way, may in itself be considered miraculous. Yet we must not forget that its doctrines, when thoroughly understood, were full of consolation for all persons who were disgusted with the wickedness around them, or who longed for a more settled creed and a firmer hope.

And there were such even amongst the Romans. Notwithstanding the gross corruptions of the mass, large classes of men were to be found, artizans, husbandmen, slaves, — the latter forming an immense proportion of the population, — who were removed from the temptations which beset the rich;

whilst the slaves especially were open to any influence which tended to raise them from their state of degradation, and open to them the prospect of equality and sympathy. The consciences of many of these persons were less blunted than those of their luxurious fellow-countrymen; they could understand somewhat of the guilt of the sins which idolatry permitted and encouraged; their minds were more prepared to receive the truth; and amongst them the religion which told of holiness in life and hope in death, made rapid progress.

And others there were, acquainted with all that the philosophy of paganism could teach, but unable to obtain rest for their minds, who were, for that reason ready to receive the instructions of Christianity. They inquired after God, but with Job they might have said "I go forward but He is not there, and backward but I cannot perceive Him, on the left hand where He doth work but I cannot behold Him, He hideth Himself on the right hand that I cannot see Him." And when they searched into the mysteries of their own existence, and, taught by conscience that they were sinners, asked how they could appease an offended Deity, no answer was returned. When such persons became Christians all these doubts were cleared up. They were instructed in the Nature of God, the Atonement made by Christ, the Hope brought to light through the Gospel. The promise of the Holy Spirit was confirmed to them by the lives of their fellow Christians and the miracles which they witnessed; and by faith and the sacred rites of Baptism and the Holy Communion they were made to realise that sacred and mysterious union with one All-Holy and All-Mighty, for which during their previous lives they had been continually thirsting.

That must have been a mighty change. We, who are Christians almost from our birth, can scarcely comprehend it. As a heathen, the Roman looked into futurity with doubt and terror. He longed to know his future destiny by observing the course of the stars, the flights of birds, or the entrails of animals offered in sacrifice. He was a slave to omens and dreams,—the cry of a mouse, or the crowing of a cock, was sufficient to fill him with terror. To have touched a dead body would have haunted his conscience more than the stain of the greatest crime. Now, he could trust himself to the love of an All-Wise God, without whose permission not even a hair could fall from his head. Fearing Him he knew no other fear. Life was full of hope, and death had lost its terror, for he could look upon it only as the entrance upon an existence of increasing and everlasting happiness.

Such were the effects of Christianity when fully taught and understood. But from the beginning it was injured by the corrupt doctrine of heretics, many of whom gave occasion, by their wicked lives, to the scandalous accusations which were brought forward against the truth, and thus increased the hatred of those who would of themselves have striven to uproot it.

Persecution indeed was—when the question is fully considered—the natural condition of the Christian Church. The Romans, though admitting the privilege of each nation to worship its own deities, allowed no interference with the state religion, and the first command of Christianity was the destruction of idolatry. It was, therefore, fundamentally opposed to the worship upheld by the government, and, as such, open to punishment.

12

From time to time this punishment was enforced by direct laws which were allowed to remain unrepealed, even when they were not acted upon; and thus the Christians were liable to be summoned before a magistrate at any moment; and whenever, from local causes, a prejudice was excited against them, it was easy for the rulers of provinces or cities to treat them with severity. Yet there were undoubtedly seasons when, in consequence of some stringent imperial edict, the laws were more rigorously executed, and the sufferings of the Christians increased, and these are more strictly called the times of persecution; ten of which are reckoned from the reign of Nero to the accession of Constantine the Great.

CHAPTER XV.

MARTYRDOM OF ST. IGNATIUS.   A.D. 107.

THERE was no public persecution of the Christians in the reign of the Emperor Nerva. His character was mild and forgiving, he was unwilling to punish even his enemies; and if his reign had been prolonged, the Church might have spread safely. After two years, however, he died, and was succeeded by Trajan, a clever, thoughtful man, and an excellent specimen of a heathen monarch, but who proved, A.D. 98. though almost unintentionally, a greater enemy to the Christians than many of his wicked predecessors. What amount of belief Trajan had in the gods and goddesses of Roman mythology no one can pretend to say, but he was too wise not to perceive that some kind of religion was necessary for the good of the people, and he therefore professed the utmost respect for the outward forms of it which were established in the empire. All changes were looked upon by him with suspicion, and in order to prevent any plans which might affect either religion or government, an order was sent to the magistrates in different parts of the empire to put a stop to all secret societies. This of course included the Christians, whose meetings were held in secret, and who were known to be united by laws and customs which were not revealed to heathens. But no direct measures were taken for their persecution for some time. The Emperor was engaged in distant wars, and the first accusation publicly brought forward against any distinguished Christian was made by some heretics against Symeon, Bishop of Jerusalem.

Symeon was now a very old man—it is said that he had reached the age of one hundred and twenty. His holy life left no room for any charge of actual crime, but being the son of Cleopas, he was, according to human relationship, the cousin of his Blessed Lord, and belonged to the family of David. This royal descent was sufficient to give rise to suspicion in the minds of the Romans; whilst the heretics hated him as a supporter of the true faith. When Symeon was brought before Atticus, governor of Syria, and accused of being a person dangerous to the state, the Roman magistrate, though he must have known how little a person of such a great age could in any way take part in political affairs, commanded him to be put to the torture. For several days the old man was racked with the most excruciating torments. The proconsul and all present marvelled to see his spirit of endurance, yet no mercy was shown him, and he was condemned and crucified. His successor in the See of Jerusalem was Justus.

But Symeon was not the only martyr at that period whose name was to be remembered in years to come. The Emperor had concluded a war with the Scythians and Dacians successfully. The Parthians and Armenians were, however, still unsubdued, and Trajan came to Antioch to make preparations for further conquests. Antioch was then the most renowned city of the east—a place of concourse for all kinds of people. By means of the Mediterranean Sea, its inhabitants carried on a trade with the west, whilst the caravans from Mesopotomia and Arabia, which made their way through the open country behind the mountains of Lebanon, brought them riches from the south and east. Seleucus, the son of Antiochus, one of the first kings of Syria, founded Antioch soon after the time of Alexander the Great, but since his days it had been much enlarged and increased. It was built on the banks of the river Orontes, at the foot of a hill called Mount Silphius, and the rugged bases of the mountains had been levelled for a magnificent street, which extended for four miles across the length of the city. The street was a continued succession of colonnades, through which the crowds, sheltered from the glare and heat, could pass from the eastern to the western suburb of the city. Gardens and houses ornamented the banks of the river. Beautiful buildings, groves, fountains, and aqueducts, were provided, for the gratification and comfort of the inhabitants. It was a place of singular enjoyment but also of singular wickedness.

The people of Antioch were noted for luxury and frivolity. They delighted in public amusements, especially the theatre and race course, and were devoted to magic and superstition; and it has been remarked, that under the climate of Syria, and the wealthy patronage of Rome, all that was beautiful in nature and art, had created a sanctuary for a perpetual festival of vice.*

Yet in this city of sin and self-indulgence, Christianity had from the beginning taken root, and now there ruled over the body of true believers who dwelt in it, a man, famed for steadfastness of purpose and purity of life; Ignatius, the friend and disciple of the beloved Apostle St. John. By himself and others he is often called Theophorus, or " one whose soul is full of God." It is certain that Ignatius had been intimately acquainted with the Apostles, that he had been educated and brought up amongst them, and was chosen by them to be Bishop of Antioch. For forty years he had retained this charge. They were stormy years, full of anxiety and danger. By prayer, and fasting, and preaching, Ignatius had kept his people together, and supported them under the terrors of persecution. For himself he had one longing—to be a marytr for his Master's cause.

He was now, however, an old man—" The days of the years of his pilgrimage" seemed to be nearly ended. It may have appeared likely that the aged bishop would be allowed to depart in peace. But the tempest was at hand. Trajan entered Antioch; —he passed through the city with all the pomp

* See Howson and Conybeare's Life and Epistles of St. Paul.

12*

and solemnity of a Roman triumphal procession. Religious ceremonies were parts of these public rejoicings, for Trajan never forgot the claims of the religion he professed. Doubtless the people applauded him, and praised his courage, and justice, and generosity. But there was one man to whom the Emperor's arrival was the signal of death. The shouts of the multitude as they followed their sovereign through the splendid street, were the prelude to the shouts which were soon to accompany the dying agonies of Ignatius. Trajan could be just and generous to all except those who opposed him in religion, and these times of public rejoicing necessarily brought to light the peculiar principles of the Christians; for they were called upon to join in paying honours to their monarchs which their faith forbade. So it appears to have been now. The citizens of Antioch were in a state of excitement when they found that the Christians did not unite with them, and the cause was soon made known to the Emperor; Ignatius also became aware of the danger to which he and his brethren were exposed, and without waiting to be accused, hastened to the presence of Trajan, and declared himself a Christian.

The interview which followed will be best told in the words of one who lived not long after the time of the holy bishop, and preserved the account for all succeeding generations.

As soon then as Ignatius stood in the presence of the Emperor Trajan, the Emperor said, "Who art thou, unhappy and deluded man, who art so active in transgressing our commands, and besides, persuadest others to their own destruction?" Ignatius replied, "No one ought to call (one who is properly styled) Theophorus, unhappy and deluded;

for the evil spirits (which delude me) are departed far from the servants of God. But if thou so callest me, because I am a trouble to those evil spirits and an enemy to their delusions, I confess the justice of the appellation. For having (within me) Christ the heavenly King, I loosen all their snares." Trajan replied, "And who is Theophorus?" Ignatius answered, "He that hath Christ in his heart." Then said Trajan, "Thinkest thou, therefore, that we have not the gods within us, who also assist us in our battles against our enemies?" "Thou dost err," Ignatius replied, "in calling the evil spirits of the heathens, gods. For there is but one God, who made the heaven and the earth, the sea, and all that are in them: and one Christ Jesus, the only begotten Son of God, whose kingdom may I enjoy." Trajan said, "Speakest thou of Him who was crucified under Pontius Pilate?" Ignatius answered, "(I speak of) Him who hath crucified my sin, with the inventor of it; and hath put all the deceit and malice of the devil under the feet of those who carry him in their hearts." Then asked Trajan, "Carriest thou, then, within thee him who was crucified?" "Yea," relied Ignatius; "for it is written, I will dwell in them, and walk in them." Then Trajan pronounced this sentence: "We decree that Ignatius, who hath confessed that he carries about within himself Him that was crucified, shall be carried in bonds by soldiers to the great Rome, there to be thrown to the beasts for the gratification of the people." When the holy martyr heard this sentence, he cried out with joy, "I thank Thee, O Lord, that Thou hast vouchsafed thus to punish me, out of Thy perfect love towards me, and hast made me to be put in iron bonds, with thine Apostle St. Paul." Having thus spoken he joyfully suffered his bonds to be put about him, and having first prayed for the Church, and commended it with tears unto the Lord, like a choice ram, the leader of a goodly flock, he was hurried away by the brutal and cruel soldiers, to be carried to Rome, and there to be devoured by blood-thirsty wild beasts.

The journey of Ignatius was long and very fatiguing. At Smyrna he was refreshed by an interview with his beloved friend Polycarp, the bishop of that city, to whom he commended the charge of his diocese. Polycarp had been his fellow disciple under St. John, and now rejoiced to receive and entertain him. Several neighbouring bishops, priests, and deacons, also visited him, greatly desiring his blessing and instruction. The affection shown him was, indeed, so great, that Ignatius feared it might, in some way, be the means of preventing the martyrdom, which he so earnestly desired. He therefore despatched a letter to Rome, to prepare the Christians in that place for his arrival, and his death. After having joined with his brethren at Smyrna, in most earnest prayer, and written epistles to several of the churches who had sent friends to meet him, he proceeded to Troas, and from thence to Italy; the soldiers also being very impatient for his journey, as it was feared he might otherwise arrive at Rome too late for the public shows in the amphitheatre, in which he was to suffer.

On arriving within sight of Puteoli, Ignatius wished to land, being desirous to follow the foot-steps of St. Paul, but a violent wind arising, it was found to be impossible, and the vessel sailed on with a favourable breeze. The friends of Ignatius mourned at the thought of the rapidly approaching separation; but the bishop only saw in all which furthered his journey, the accomplishment of his prayer that he might soon depart out of the world. As they approached Rome many of the Christians being prepared for his arrival, went out to meet him, some rejoicing in the opportunity afforded them, of beholding a man so venerated for his wisdom and piety; others only anxious for his safety, and desirous to take measures to calm the people, that they should not desire his death. Ignatius, however, soon put a stop to any such intentions. Expressing himself even more fully in his conversation than in his letter, he persuaded them not to hinder him who was "hastening to the Lord;" and kneeling down with them he prayed to his Saviour that He would cause the persecution of the Church to cease, and continue the love of the brethren towards each other.

The thirteenth of the calends of January, according to the Roman reckoning,—a day of peculiar solemnity,—had now arrived. The people were gathered in crowds and the games were nearly over. No further delay, therefore, was allowed. Ignatius was hurried to the amphitheatre, the wild beasts were let loose upon him, and death soon followed.

One of his chief wishes had been that he might not be burdensome to any of his brethren, by the gathering of his relics, but might be wholly devoured; and the desire was granted. Only the larger bones were left, and these were carefully collected, carried to Antioch, and there preserved. The martyrdom of Ignatius is said by some persons to have taken place on the 20th of December, 107; by others it is stated to have occurred in A.D. 116.

These details have been chiefly taken from the "Acts of Ignatius," written by Philo and Agathopus, who were the companions of the bishop's journey, and were present at his death. Their narrative is concluded in these words, " We ourselves were eye-witnesses of these events, with many tears. And as we watched all night in the house, and prayed God in many words, with bended knees, and supplication, that he would give us, weak men, some assurance of what was done, it happened, that having fallen into a slumber for a little while, some of us on a sudden, saw the blessed Ignatius standing by us, and embracing us, and others beheld him praying for us ; others saw him, as it were, dropping with sweat, as if he came out of great labour, and standing by the Lord. Having seen these things then with great joy, and comparing the visions of our dreams, we sang praises to God, the giver of all good things, and pronounced the saint blessed, and have now made known unto you both the day and the time : that being assembled together at the season of his martyrdom, we may communicate with the combatant and noble martyr of Christ, who trod under foot the Devil, and perfected the course which he had piously desired, in Jesus Christ our Lord, by Whom and with Whom, all glory and power be to the Father, with the Holy Spirit for ever. Amen."

The name of St. Ignatius has been handed down to us, not only by the memory of his martyrdom, but by the letters which he wrote, and which are perhaps the most important of all the early records of the Church. During the course of his long journey, his thoughts seem to have frequently turned to the condition of the different churches in Asia Minor, in which he was interested. When he rested at

Smyrna he took advantage of the opportunity, as it has been stated, to write to them. So again, when he paused at Troas, he wrote to the churches of Philadelphia and Smyrna, particularly addressing himself to St. Polycarp, Bishop of Smyrna, his great friend and fellow disciple.*

In these letters Ignatius gives particular warnings against the heresies which were then common, and strongly insists upon the duty of obedience to the Heads of the Church,—urging upon the persons whom he had addressed, that they should on no account separate themselves from them. " Without the bishops and presbyters," he says, " there is no Church. He that is within the altar is pure; but he that is without,—that is, who does anything without—the bishops, and presbyters, and deacons, is not pure in his conscience."

And again he adds in his letter to the Ephesians. " If the prayer of one or two has so much strength, how.much more that of the bishop and of the whole church. He who separates from it, is proud and condemns himself ; for it is written God resisteth the proud : let us study therefore obedience to the bishop, that we may be subject to God."

These and other similar expressions of Ignatius are so strong, and prove so clearly that immediately after the times of the Apostles it was considered essential for all Christians to be subject to the authority of duly appointed bishops, that many persons who have separated themselves from the Church, or who have not chosen to consider its form of government of much consequence, have striven to prove that the Epistles themselves were not really written by Ignatius. The attempt was first made

* History of the Church, by the Rev. J. J. Blunt.

many years ago. Bishop Pearson then searched very carefully into the evidence as to the truth of the Epistles, and finding them quoted by the earliest writers, and containing things which accorded entirely with the facts recorded of Ignatius, declared that there could be no doubt whatever, of their being the true letters of the martyred bishop. Almost every one who inquired into the case was satisfied, and it seemed that the question was entirely set at rest. Latterly, however, it has arisen again. A traveller on looking through some old manuscripts in a monastery in Egypt, discovered copies of three of the Epistles of Ignatius, written in the Syriac language—those before mentioned were in Greek. The Syriac letters were short; several passages were left out, especially those which spoke of the authority of the bishop; but some persons declared they were the only letters which Ignatius really wrote and that the Greek Epistles must have been the same, added to by some other person. The question was very interesting, and a great deal of discussion took place in consequence; but the evidence in favour of the Greek Epistles remains untouched. The three letters found in the Egyptian monastery appear to have been abridgments of the original writings. For what reason they were made no one can tell, but such abridgments were not uncommon in early days.

St. Polycarp, the friend of Ignatius, himself bears witness to the truth of the Greek letters. He quotes passages from them which are not to be found in the three short Syriac letters. The Greek letters were therefore in existence in his days, and as he was intimately acquainted with Ignatius, he must have known them to be genuine. Polycarp also alludes to several of the Greek Epistles not to be found in this Syriac version, and others of the Fathers do the same. It has been said that Syriac was the native language of Ignatius, and therefore he would surely have written in it. But the truth is, we do not know that Ignatius was a Syrian by birth; he was probably a Roman, and sent to Rome for execution because he was a Roman citizen.

Questions of this kind may, generally speaking, be left for learned men to settle, whilst other persons are not called upon to trouble themselves about them. But some knowledge of the truth is, in the present instance, desirable for the following reasons :—We are very likely, in these days of doubt and argument, to meet with persons who deny that the government of bishops descended from the Apostles is necessary for the Church; Presbyterians, Independents,—all Dissenters, in fact, would do so. Now one of the best proofs that the early Christians were subject to their bishops is to be found in these Epistles of St. Ignatius, which speak so strongly upon the subject. But if we were to say this, the person with whom we were arguing might perhaps reply, " You speak of the Epistles of Ignatius, but they have been lately proved not to be genuine ; the only Epistles he ever wrote were three written in Syriac, in which there are no passages relating to the authority of bishops."

This assertion might startle and disturb us,—and we should probably have no means of contradicting it. It is well, therefore, to know beforehand that the Syriac Epistles have been examined, and the arguments on both sides carefully pondered, the result being that they have been rejected as only abridgments of the Greek.

13

We have consequently as much cause as ever to rest on the authority of St. Ignatius, with regard to the obedience that should be paid to duly appointed bishops.

CHAPTER XV.

PLINY'S APPEAL TO TRAJAN. A.D. 111.

Up to this time, although Trajan, as we have seen, allowed the punishment of Christians, he does not appear to have issued any distinct orders to his magistrates concerning them; but the laws made by preceding emperors which remained unrepealed were quite sufficient to sanction persecution, and the sufferings of the Christians knew no permanent cessation during this and many subsequent reigns; the rage which burst forth against them from time to time being only, as it has before been remarked, a specimen on a larger scale of the enmity which was always at work.   In the year 111, the case of the Christians was especially brought to the notice of the Emperor by Pliny the younger, governor of Bithynia, in Asia Minor.   Pliny was presiding at a public festival held in honour of the Emperor, when some Christians were required to take part in the sacrifices, and to perform other acts in honour of the gods and of Trajan, which were forbidden by their religion.   They refused.   This was of course considered a proof that they were discontented with the government, and they were seized and brought before the governor.

Pliny was a kind and benevolent man, suffering much from ill health, and very fond of study, having been brought up by his uncle, Pliny the

Elder, a celebrated naturalist, who perished in an eruption of Mount Vesuvius. He was not likely to be very severe upon the Christians, especially as his uncle appears to have been equally indifferent to all religions. But he had a belief in Divine Power, and a respect for the pagan rites, and no doubt thought that it would be a great evil if the people were to be left without any restraint from religion. It startled him when he found that the temples were deserted, and that scarcely any one offered sacrifice; yet this was really the case. Men and women of all ages and of all ranks were fast becoming converts to Christianity. Pliny did not know how to put an end to this state of things; and although not naturally cruel, he could think of no remedy except persecution. The very obstinacy with which the Christians held to their opinions was in his eyes a crime. He consented to examine them three times, and if they did not renounce their faith he ordered them to execution.

Still Pliny was not satisfied. He felt that he ought to know more of the crimes alleged against those whom he thus punished; and in order to obtain this information, he had recourse to yet greater severity. Two female slaves, deaconnesses amongst the Christians, were seized, and in order to extract from them an account of what was called their superstition, they were tortured.

The following letter contains the result of this examination, and of other inquiries. It was sent by Pliny to the Emperor. The request for advice how to deal with the Christians for the future, shows that the conscience of the governor of Bithynia was ill at ease, and that he was anxious to throw off the responsibility of any further persecution.

Pliny to the Emperor Trajan.

" It is a rule, sir, which I inviolably observe, to refer myself to you in all my doubts; for who is more capable of removing my scruples or informing my ignorance?   Having never been present at any trials concerning those persons who are Christians, I am unacquainted not only with the nature of their crimes, or the measure of their punishment, but how far it is proper to enter into an examination concerning them.   Whether, therefore, any difference is usually made with respect to the ages of the guilty, or no distinction is to be observed between the young and the adult, whether repentance entitles them to a pardon ; or, if a man has been once a Christian, it avails nothing to desist from his error ; whether the very profession of Christianity, unattended with any criminal act, or only the crimes themselves inherent in the profession, are punishable ; in all these points I am greatly doubtful.   In the meanwhile, the method I have observed towards those who have been brought before me as Christians is this : I interrogated them whether they were Christians ; if they confessed, I repeated the question twice, adding threats at the same time ; and if they still persevered, I ordered them to be immediately punished. For I was persuaded, whatever the nature of their opinions might be, a contumacious and inflexible obstinacy certainly deserved correction.   There were others also brought before me possessed with the same infatuation ; but being citizens of Rome, I directed that they should be conveyed thither. But this crime spreading (as is usually the case) while it was actually under prosecution, several instances of the same nature occurred.   An information was presented to me without any name subscribed, containing a charge against several persons; these, upon examination, denied they were, or ever had been, Christians. They repeated after me an invocation to the gods, and offered religious rites with wine and frankincense before your statue, (which for that purpose I had ordered to be brought, together with those of the gods,) and even reviled the name of Christ; whereas there is no forcing, it is said, those who are really Christians, into any of these compliances. I thought it proper, therefore, to discharge them. Some among those who were accused by a witness in person, at first confessed themselves Christians, but immediately after denied it; the rest owned, indeed, they had been of that number formerly, but had now (some above three, others more, and a few above twenty years ago) renounced that error. They all worshipped your statue, and the images of the gods, uttering imprecations at the same time against the name of Christ. They affirmed the whole of their guilt, or their error was, that they met on a certain stated day before it was light, and addressed themselves in a form of prayer to Christ, as to some god, binding themselves by a solemn oath, not for the purposes of any wicked design, but never to commit any fraud, theft, or adultery, never to falsify their word, nor deny a trust when they should be called upon to deliver it up; after which, it was their custom to separate, and then reassemble, to eat in common a harmless meal. From this custom, however, they desisted after the publication of my edict, by which, according to your commands, I forbad the meeting of any assemblies. In consequence of this their declaration, I judged it the more necessary to en-

13*

deavour to extort the real truth, by putting two female slaves to the torture, who were said to officiate in their religious functions; but all I could discover was, that these people were actuated by an absurd and excessive superstition. I deemed it expedient, therefore, to adjourn all further proceedings in order to consult you. For it appears to be a matter highly deserving your consideration; more especially as great numbers must be involved in the danger of these prosecutions, which have already extended, and are still likely to extend, to persons of all ranks and ages, and even of both sexes. In fact, this contagious superstition is not confined to the cities only, but has spread its infection among the neighbouring villages and country. Nevertheless, it still seems possible to restrain its progress. The temples, at least, which were once almost deserted, begin now to be frequented; and the sacred solemnities, after a long intermission, are revived; to which I must add, there is again also a general demand for the victims, which for some time past had met with but few purchasers. From the circumstances I have mentioned, it is easy to conjecture what numbers might be reclaimed, if a general pardon were granted to those who shall repent of their error."

To this letter, Pliny received the following reply :—

" Trajan to Pliny.

" The method you have pursued, my dear Pliny, in the proceedings against those Christians which were brought before you, is extremely proper; as it is not possible to lay down any fixed rule by which to act in all cases of this nature. But I would not have you officiously enter into any inquiries concerning them. If indeed they should be brought before you, and the crime should be proved, they must be punished; with this restriction, however,—that where the party denies he is a Christian, and shall make it evident that he is not, by invoking our gods, let him (notwithstanding any former suspicion) be pardoned upon his repentance. Informations without the accuser's name subscribed ought not to be received in prosecutions of any sort; as it is introducing a very dangerous precedent, and is by no means agreeable to the equity of my government."

Trajan reigned for six years after the writing of this celebrated letter; but we know no further particulars which would show that he was personally inclined to persecute the Christians. His time was occupied by war. The Jews indeed suffered greatly, having risen in rebellion against the Roman power in several countries, and being in consequence slain in great numbers; but it does not appear that the Christians generally were mixed up with them. The chief circumstance which would lead us to think to the contrary, is the record of the number of bishops who, about this period, succeeded each other as rulers of the Church of Jerusalem. St. James was bishop for thirty years, and Symeon for forty-five years, but after that time we find seven bishops in the space of eighteen years. This seems as if their deaths must have been hastened by persecution.

One fact, however, is quite certain, that Christianity made great progress during the reign of Trajan. A season of war was always advantageous to the Church, because the minds of the heathens were then so occupied that they had less leisure to bestow upon questions of belief.

CHAPTER XVI.

INSURRECTION OF BAR-CHOCHAB. A.D. 135.

TRAJAN was succeeded by his nephew Hadrian, who was a clever man, kind-hearted, and A.D. 117. fond of learning, but extravagant and capricious. Like his uncle, he was zealous for the religion of his country; but he allowed the Christians to remain undisturbed for some time.

In the present day kings seldom travel far, but the Roman Emperors were continually traversing their vast dominions, and Hadrian especially seems to have taken pleasure in visiting distant lands. Only two years after he came to the throne he visited Judea, but his arrival was a signal of suffering to the Jews. They were still rebellious at heart, and constantly giving proof of their feeling. Hadrian came to triumph over them, and to show that he was their master. He erected a town with buildings after the Roman fashion on the site of the ancient Jerusalem, and ordered a temple to Jupiter to be built on the very spot where the glorious temple of the True God had once stood. The indignation of the Jews was roused to the utmost pitch; their hatred of the Emperor knew no bounds; and they waited only for a signal again to rise in every province.

From Jerusalem, Hadrian went to Alexandria, in Egypt, where the Jews had also caused great disturbance, quarrelling with the other inhabitants, and nearly causing the destruction of the city. Alexandria was a place likely above all others to be interesting to a thoughtful, clever, and inquiring prince. The race of the Ptolemies—

kings of Egypt in former generations—had made it their capital, and invited learned men to settle at their courts. They had also collected a magnificent library of upwards of 400,000 volumes, and founded an establishment in which persons devoted to study were maintained at the public cost. Though no longer the metropolis of a separate kingdom, but subject to the Emperor of Rome, Alexandria was still the most wealthy and splendid city of the known world, and the resort of distinguished persons from all countries, who came thither either to teach or be taught. Many and strange were the opinions set forth by the philosophers who resided there. Heathens, Jews, and professed Christians were to be found amongst them, reasoning, disputing, and giving instruction to others. But too many of those who had originally been baptized into the true faith of the Gospel, had mixed up with it the falsehoods of their own imagination. They had lived amongst men who prided themselves upon their talents, and from them they had learnt to seek after an explanation of the truths of Christianity, instead of humbly accepting them. Alexandria was the great source of heretical doctrine in those early days.

It would not, however, for that reason have been the less interesting to Hadrian. True doctrines and false were alike to him, for all religions except that which he professed, appear to have been equally indifferent to him as matters of belief. Yet he liked to inquire into them as we often take an interest in inquiring into the religious creed of Hindoos or Mahometans. The various doctrines taught in Alexandria must, therefore, have excited his curiosity, but he appears to have gained no fixed idea of the truths of Christianity. In a letter

written a few years later he confounds Christians
with the worshippers of Serapis, an Egyptian idol,
and seems to consider them, as well as the Jews
and Samaritans, to be impostors and mountebanks.
In all probability, therefore, his information must
have been gathered from the heretical teachers, one
of whom, Basilides, had some time before the Emperor's visit, become unfortunately notorious. It
would be painful and unnecessary to enter into
the fearful errors of this false teacher, or of those
who followed him; but it is good for us to observe
how the Providence of God, watching over His
Church, brought good out of evil. The wickedness of the heretics caused the true believers to
write works declaring their real faith; and thus
we have a clear idea of the doctrines handed down
from age to age, and can see how entirely they
were at the beginning the same in every church
and nation. Hadrian left Alexandria apparently
ignorant of the true nature of Christianity; but
the subject was again brought before him when he
visited Athens. There, as we know, the Gospel had first been preached by St. Paul. Since
his time, the body of Christians had increased.
Dionysius the Areopagite, said to have been the
first bishop, was dead; Publius, one of his successors, suffered martyrdom; and when Hadrian
arrived at Athens its bishop was Quadratus, a
man of great zeal, piety, and influence, not afraid
to bring himself before the Emperor's notice by a
written defence of the faith which he professed.
Many of these defences, or apologies, as they were
sometimes called, were written in the second
and third centuries; that of Quadratus, which, as
being the earliest, would have been peculiarly interesting, has unfortunately been lost. One passage

is, however, quoted by Eusebius, the Church Historian. In it Quadratus speaks of the miracles wrought by our Blessed Lord, which were declared by the heathen to have been the work of magic. "Those," he says, "who were healed by Him (that is by Jesus Christ) or raised from the dead, lived not only during the lifetime on earth of the Saviour, but for a long period after His departure, so that many of them have come down to my days." Quadratus himself is mentioned as possessing some of the supernatural gifts common in the age of the Apostles. A man with such personal knowledge of the facts he asserted must have been well fitted to bear witness to the truth before the Emperor; and Hadrian received also another testimony of the same kind, though probably in a different form, from Aristides, an Athenian philosopher, who had been converted to Christianity. But Christianity had no charms for the philosophic Emperor. It was put aside as one amongst the many false forms of belief with which he had no concern; while at the same time he could give credit to the most absurd lies of his own religion. When his favourite, Antinous, was drowned in the Nile, he ordered divine honours to be paid him, and placed him among the number of the gods. The Christians, of course, noticed this irrational impiety, but the Emperor was blind to his own folly. Yet he appears to have been influenced in some degree by the representations he received as to the character of the Christians, and the severity with which they were treated. The proconsul of Asia wrote to him saying that it seemed unreasonable to put the Christians to death without trial, and without any crime proved against them, merely to gratify the clamours of the people. The

Emperor's reply shows a considerable sense of justice. It is addressed, not to the governor who wrote upon the subject, and whose rule was apparently coming to an end, but to his successor.

" To Minucius Fundanus.

"I have received the letter written to me by the most renowned Serenius Granianus, whom you succeeded. It seems to me that the matter must not be left without inquiry; lest those men should be troubled, and a means of evil-doing should be opened to false accusers. If then the people in the provinces are able to advance so far in their accusations against the Christians as to answer before the seat of judgment, let them have recourse to these means alone, and not act by vague accusations or mere clamour. For it is far better, if any one wishes to bring an accusation, that you should examine it. If, therefore, any one accuses them, and proves that they have done any thing against the laws, dispose of the matter according to the severity of the offence. But I require you, if any man bring such a charge falsely, deal with him according to his deserts, and take care that you punish him."

If attention had been paid to this edict, the condition of the Christians under Hadrian would certainly have been much improved, but, unfortunately, there is good reason to believe that the Emperor's commands were disregarded in the provinces, and that many magistrates considered the mere belief in Christianity to be a violation of the law. Persecution therefore continued, and in its most dreadful form. The ancient lists of martyrs tell of thousands who suffered in Hadrian's reign.   Amongst these a husband and wife, with their two sons, are said to have been thrown to the lions at Rome, and when the savage animals had spared them, they were ordered to be burnt to death in the interior of a hollow brazen bull. Probably Hadrian's interest was not particularly aroused by those circumstances; another subject engrossed his attention. The Jews had never forgotten the insult shown to their city. Their resentment was for a while hidden, but it was not the less vehement because it smouldered, and at last it broke out in an open insurrection. Bar-chochab, or The Son of a Star—a man reckless and enthusiastic, and well fitted to become the leader of a desperate people, put himself forward as their head, and the Jews followed him as they would have followed their Messiah—for the expectation of that Mighty Deliverer had never died away.

It was a hopeless contest,—a scattered and conquered people rising against the most powerful of earthly monarchs. But the Jews still considered themselves the chosen of God, and forgot that by their own crimes they had withdrawn themselves from that Almighty Protection. For nearly four years the war was carried on. Jerusalem was not now the great fortress and citadel, upon the safety of which everything depended: it was soon in the hands of the Romans. The great struggle was at Bitthera,—a town lying between Jerusalem and the sea,—and for three years and a half the Jews at Bitthera held out against the Roman power. The town fell at length, and the war was ended A.D. 135. But 580,000 Jews are said to have perished during its continuance, and from that time the subjection of the Jewish people may be said to have been complete.

14

Jerusalem, " the holy and beautiful city," was no longer permitted to be their resort, even for a short time. Only on one day in the year—the anniversary of the taking of the city by Titus, was it lawful for them to approach it. Then for a single hour they were allowed to look upon the walls. Long years went by after that law was made, — years which brought changes of fortune and varied hopes and fears to other nations, but the harsh edict against the Jews still remained in force, — unless a special indulgence could be purchased by a large sum. All that was left to them of their ancient home, was the undying memory of its former greatness, clinging to them even as it does to this day. For still, although no law now forbids them to inhabit their city, the Jews meet at stated periods beneath the walls of Jerusalem, and their sorrowful wailings for its downfall are heard even as when the Psalmist exclaimed in the bitterness of his desolation, " If I forget thee, O Jerusalem, let my right hand forget her cunning."

Strange though it may seem, the Jewish Christians do not appear to have been involved in this misery. As Jews, they dearly loved the land of their fathers, and were little disposed to submit to the yoke of Rome ; but they could not follow an impostor like Bar-chochab, who required them to acknowledge him as a leader sent from Heaven, and sentenced them to horrible punishments if they refused to deny that Jesus was the Christ. They dreaded the Romans less than their unbelieving countrymen. Many sought refuge elsewhere; those who remained took no part in the war, and the Romans probably learnt at last the distinction between them and the Jews, and ceased to regard them as possessing the same rebellious spirit. We know at least that a Christian Church existed in Jerusalem after the reign of Hadrian as well as before it. It has been said that it consisted entirely of Gentiles, and that a Gentile bishop named Marcus, was the first who presided over it after the edict of Hadrian had been enforced; yet it is difficult to imagine that an entirely new body of Christians settled in Jerusalem at this period. One great change was made, however, in the name of the Church. Hadrian called Jerusalem Ælia Capitolina, and the Church of Ælia continued to hold a distinguished place amongst the Eastern Churches; its bishops being ranked in dignity with those of Antioch, Rome, and Alexandria.

Hadrian lived for three years after the Jewish war. Although his own feelings were not exactly unfavorable to the Christians, and he passed, as we have seen, some merciful laws respecting them, yet the heathen persecutions were undoubtedly increasing in severity under his rule. The Romans were attached to the pomp of their public worship, and many gained their livelihood by its maintenance. This alone would have induced them to look with dislike upon the simple rites of Christianity; but they were also becoming more and more addicted to the barbarous spectacles of the amphitheatre. They delighted in seeing men exposed to fight with wild beasts. The governor of a province knew no surer way of gaining the applause of the people than by condemning a constant succession of Christians to the lions, whilst the heathen priests upheld this cruelty as a tribute of reverence to the gods. This was the most obvious form of persecution. Another, which, but for the Providence of God, would have been more fatal to the cause of truth, arose from the attacks of the learned philosophers. These men, giving themselves little trouble to learn what Christianity really was, confounded it with the absurdities of Gnosticism and then argued against it. Celsus, who lived in the reign of Hadrian was one of the most noted amongst them. He wrote a book, called " The Word of Truth," a few fragments of which have been handed down to us by Origen, one of the early Christian writers, who in after years undertook to reply to it. The arguments of Celsus appear to have been chiefly such as infidels of the present day might use, but they bear witness to the fact, that the Divinity of Christ was an admitted doctrine of the Christians, and that His miracles were acknowledged even by His enemies, although they attributed them to magic.

CHAPTER XVII.

THE FIRST APOLOGY WRITTEN BY JUSTIN MARTYR.
A. D. 150.

THE death of Hadrian brought hope to the Christian Church. Antoninus Pius, his adopted son and successor, was less prejudiced in favour of heathenism, and strongly desirous of acting justly by all men ; and when he had reigned about three years, the claims of Christianity were forced upon him in a manner so striking, that although he remained unconvinced of its truth, he yet, as it appears, dared not punish its profession as a crime.

A. D. 138.

Justin Martyr was the person who thus ventured to stand forth in defence of the despised faith. His history is strange and interesting. The time had gone by when Christianity spread chiefly amongst the poor and ignorant. The power of working miracles which had attracted them, but had been scoffed at by the philosophers as the work of magic, had been permitted by the Wisdom of God to become less common ; and now reason and argument were used to bring before the minds of the educated classes the truth of which external signs had failed to convince them.

Amongst those whose conversion, by God's Grace, was effected through these means was Justin Martyr. He was born in Palestine, at Neapolis, the ancient Sichem, in the province of Samaria, it is supposed about the beginning of the second century ; his parents were heathens, and he was himself educated in the religion of the Greeks. God had bestowed upon him by nature a love of information, and a delight in the search after truth, and these inclinations were early gratified. He was yet young when he left Palestine, and set out on a journey into distant lands, in the certain expectation of finding in the great schools of philosophy, then so highly esteemed, some teacher who should instruct him in the mystery of man's existence, and the means by which he might raise himself to a life of uprightness and purity.

Alexandria as being at that time the most learned city in the world, was the place to which Justin repaired. The many heathen sects to be found there all professed to know the road to happiness, and were willing to give him instruction. He placed himself at first under the teaching of the Stoics, who appeared to him to hold the highest position, for they despised the pleasures of the world, and declared themselves superior to its temptations. They knew nothing, however, of the nature of the Deity, the knowledge for which above all other Justin pined ; they even pronounced it to

14*

be unnecessary, and the young man left them in disgust, and turned to another sect — the Peripatetics. But here a still greater disappointment awaited him. His instructor was mean and avaricious, and showed himself so anxious to settle the price of his lectures, that Justin was convinced truth was not to be found with him.

His next teacher, a Pythagorean philosopher, had a high reputation for deep thought, and refinement of feeling; but when Justin went to him, he launched out into the praises of music, geometry, and astronomy; an acquaintance with these sciences he declared to be absolutely necessary for a philosopher, and finding that his pupil did not understand them, he sent him away to study them. There was greater hope for Justin in the Platonic philosophy, to which he then turned. Plato, the founder of the sect, was one of the wisest of heathens. His doctrines approached wonderfully near to those of revealed religion. His disciples were, for the most part, earnest and inquiring men. Justin found great satisfaction in the teaching of the Platonists. He almost thought that they could solve all his difficulties. He gave himself up to thought and contemplation, and spent his time in retirement, meditating upon the deep mysteries of his own nature and the Being of the Unseen God.

A lonely spot on the sea shore was his accustomed resort; there undisturbed except by the rush of the waves, he was wont to walk, absorbed in thought. One day as he was thus employed, he happened to look back, and saw coming behind him an aged man, of gentle, venerable aspect. Justin did not wish for interruption, but he could not avoid the meeting, and he stopped till the stranger overtook him. The old man had come down to the beach to wait for some absent relations, whom he was anxiously expecting.   He told this to Justin, who in reply could not avoid explaining the reason of his own presence in that spot.   He had sought it, he said, for the purpose of private meditation, and speculation upon hidden truth.   "You are then a lover of discourse," observed the stranger, "but no lover of deeds, nor of truth; nor do you attempt to be a man of action so much as a clever disputant." This appeared an unfair judgment, and Justin answered, that in his opinion no emplyment could be more worthy than that of proving that intelligence was the presiding principle of all things; and teaching people, by means of this intelligence, to discern in every pursuit what was erroneous and undivine.   Philosophy, therefore, he thought, ought to be an object of universal attention.

"But does philosophy lead to happiness?" inquired the old man, "and how can you define it?"

"Philosophy," answered Justin, "is the science of being, and the knowledge of truth; and happiness is the reward of this knowledge and wisdom."

The reply was vague, and the stranger took occasion from it to enter more deeply into the subject. The knowledge of God, undoubtedly, was the most important that man could have, and the Platonists thought to attain it by their speculations; "but," argued the old man, "such knowledge cannot be acquired, like music, arithmetic, or astronomy, by any human means.   No one can really teach anything concerning the Deity who has not been favoured himself either with a view of the Divine Nature, or with the instructions of one who has enjoyed such a view.   Reason teaches us the existence of God, and gives us certain laws of duty to which we are bound to conform. but it can reveal nothing to us concerning the Essence of God." The doctrines of the Platonists, he declared, were therefore based upon false principles, and he entered into them at length, proving the unsatisfactoriness and uselessness of the whole system, until Justin, whose mind was naturally candid, felt his confidence in the opinions he had embraced painfully shaken.

"On what teacher can we rely?" he exclaimed bitterly, "or to what quarter can we look for aid, if these are not the doctrines which contain the truth?" The stranger knew well how to turn to good account the perplexity he had occasioned. He stated that "in remote ages there had appeared men called Prophets, distinguished above all the philosophers by their antiquity and holiness. Their divine mission," he said, "was proved by miracles and prophecies, and in their writings were to be found the choicest treasures of religious truth." Then, without entering into the deeper mysteries of Christianity, he set before Justin somewhat of its nature and evidences, adding, "Above all things, pray that the gates of light may be opened to you; for they are not discernible, nor to be understood by any one, unless God and his Christ enable a man to understand." "Many other things," relates Justin, in his account of this singular interview, "he spoke to the same effect. He then directed me to follow his advice, and he left me. I saw him no more—but immediately a fire was kindled in my soul. I felt a strong affection for the prophets, and for those men who are the friends of Christ. I weighed within myself the arguments of the aged stranger, and in the end I found the Divine Scriptures to be the only true philosophy."

Justin was now a convert to Christianity, persuaded not only by reason, but by the innocency of the lives of the Christians and their constancy in death. So he himself says, in giving an account of his own convictions, at this period of his life. "For my own part," he states, "being yet detained under the Platonic institutions, when I heard the Christians traduced and reproached, and yet saw them fearlessly running unto death, and venturing upon all those things that are accounted most dreadful and amazing to human nature, I concluded with myself it was impossible that these men should wallow in vice. For what man that is a slave to pleasure and intemperance can cheerfully bid death welcome, which he knows must put a period to all his pleasures and delights?" The courage which the philosopher thus admired he did not shrink from exhibiting in his life. He openly professed his change of faith, though, as he was still interested in literary pursuits, he continued to wear the mantle, or peculiar dress of the philosophers. Perhaps also he considered it wise to show that Christianity was not the superstitious creed of the ignorant only, but that it would bear the searching inquiry of the learned and thoughtful.

When his heathen friends, surprised and troubled at his sudden change, inquired into its cause, Justin wrote a discourse to them in explanation of the step he had taken : "Think not, O ye Greeks," he begins, "that I have rashly, and without any judgment or deliberation, departed from the rites of your religion, for I could find nothing in it really sacred, and worthy of the Divine acceptance. A man can no sooner apply himself even to the most learned among you for instruction, but he shall be entangled in a thousand difficulties."—And then, after exposing the absurdities of the creeds of Paganism, he adds : " Come hither, O ye Greeks, and partake of a most incomparable wisdom, and be instructed in a Divine religion, and acquaint yourselves with an immortal King. Become as I am, for I, sometime, was as you are. These are the arguments that prevailed with me; this is the efficacy and divinity of that doctrine which, like a skilful charm, expels all corrupt and poisonous affections from the soul.

The new faith became from this period the mainspring of Justin's life. All his powers were directed to the service of the Christian Church and the glory of the True God, for he felt, as he says himself, that " every one who is able to speak the truth, and does not speak it, will be condemned by God." His inclinations, as well as the circumstances of the times, led him to travel, and in every place which he visited he endeavoured to spread the knowledge of Christianity. At length he settled himself in Rome, and, it is said, opened a school there.

The condition of the Roman Church at this period was very unsatisfactory. Hitherto it had been singularly free from error. The heresies which had infested other places had taken no deep root amongst the Christians of Rome; but in the beginning of the reign of Antoninus, two heretical teachers, Valentinus and Cerdon, visited the capital, and were followed by Marcion, a native of Pontus, and the son of a Christian bishop. He had been guilty of a great crime, and having been expelled from the Church by his own father, was obliged to leave Asia. He went to Rome still calling himself a Christian; but many suspected him of heresy, and the Roman Church would not receive him. This made him indignant, and he then sided openly with

the heretics, and at length became their greatest
leader.

The Bishop of Rome at that time was Pius, who
is chiefly noted as being in all probability the brother of Hermas,—the author of a book called " The
Shepherd,"—one of the oldest Christian works remaining to us, and interesting for that reason, though
much that is weak and of little value is mixed up
with its devotional sentiments. We are not told
whether Pius strove particularly to stop the progress of heresy,—but when Justin Martyr visited
the city, a strong effort was made by him, both in
conversation and writing, to refute the erroneous
doctrines of Marcion. Not content with this endeavour to shield the truth from the attacks of heresies, he also ventured upon a more open defence of
Christianity against heathenism, set forth under the
form of a letter, or Apology, which he addressed
to the Emperor. This first Apology is said to
have been published about A.D. 150. In it Justin
complained of the unfairness with which the Christians were treated, refuted the charges of atheism,
immorality, and disaffection to the Emperor, which
were brought against them, proved the truth of
Christianity by the power of miracles and prophecies, and concluded with a description of the mode
in which proselytes were admitted into the Church,
and of other rites and customs common among
Christians.

This latter portion of the Apology contains the
clearest and most interesting account which has
been handed down to us, of the public services of
the primitive Christians.

" After the believer is baptized," writes Justin,
" we take him to the place where those who are
called brethren are assembled ; in order that we

may offer up prayers in common for ourselves, and for the baptized person, and for all others in every place ; that, having learned the truth, we may be deemed worthy to be found walking in good works, and keeping the commandments, so that we may attain to eternal salvation. Having ended our prayers, we salute each other with a kiss. Bread is then brought to that brother who presides, and a cup of wine mixed with water ; and he, taking them, gives praise and glory to the Father of the universe, through the name of the Son and of the Holy Spirit, and employs some time in offering up thanks to him for having deemed us worthy of these Gifts.

"The prayers and thanksgivings being ended, all the people present express their assent by saying, Amen. The president having given thanks, and the people having expressed their assent, they who are called by us *deacons* give to each of those present a portion of the bread and of the wine mixed with water, over which the thanksgiving was pronounced, and carry away a portion to those who are absent. And this food is called among us Eucharistica, of which no one is allowed to partake who does not believe that what we teach is true, and has not been washed with the laver (of baptism) for the remission of sins and unto regeneration, and does not live as Christ has enjoined. For we do not receive it as common bread and common drink ; but in the same manner as Jesus Christ our Saviour, being made flesh through the word of God, had both flesh and blood for our Salvation, so we are also taught that the food over which thanksgiving has been pronounced by the prayer of the word which came from Him (by which food, undergoing the necessary change, our flesh and blood are nourished), we are taught, I say, that this food, is the Flesh and Blood of the Incarnate Jesus. For the Apostles, in the memoirs composed by them, which are called Gospels, have declared that Jesus gave them this injunction; that having taken bread and given thanks, He said, *Do this in remembrance of Me, this is My Body ;* and that in like manner having taken the cup and given thanks, He said, *This is My Blood;* and that He distributed the bread and wine to them alone."

Justin then proceeds to give the following account of the meeting of the Christians on the Lord's Day. " On the day called Sunday," he says, " there is an assembling together of all who dwell in the cities and country : and the Memoirs of the Apostles and the writings of the Prophets are read as circumstances permit. Then when the reader has ceased, the president delivers a discourse, in which he admonishes and exhorts (all present) to the imitation of these good things. Then we all rise together and pray, and, as we before said, prayer being ended, bread and wine are brought, and the president offers prayer in like manner and thanksgivings, according to his ability, and the people express their assent by saying Amen ; and the distribution of that, over which the thanksgiving has been pronounced, takes place to each, and each partakes, and a portion is sent to the absentees by the deacons. And they who are wealthy, and choose, give as much as they respectively deem fit ; and whatever is collected is deposited with the president, who succours the orphans and widows, and those who through sickness or any other cause are in want, and those who are in bonds, and the strangers sojourning among us, and, in a word, takes care of all who are in need.

15

But we meet together on Sunday because it is the first day, in which God, having wrought the necessary change in darkness and matter, made the world; and because on this day, Jesus Christ, our Saviour, rose from the dead. For he was crucified on the day before that of Saturn; and on the day after that of Saturn, which is the day of the Sun, having appeared to the Apostles and disciples, he taught them the things which we now submit to your consideration."

Some defence of Christianity was at this period much required, for the general feeling against it was so strong as to put a stop to all sense of justice, and even calamities such as earthquakes common to all mankind, were ascribed to the vengeance of heaven against the followers of the new religion. The Emperor alone was inclined to view the case more impartially. Shortly after he had received the appeal of Justin Martyr, the Christians made a formal complaint to him of the grievances under which they laboured, and the following edict, addressed to the Common Council of the province of Asia, was issued by Antoninus in consequence.

"The Emperor Cæsar, Titus, Ælius, Adrian, Antoninus, Augustus, Pius, High Priest, the fifteenth time Tribune, thrice Consul, Father of the country, to the Common Assembly of Asia, greeting.

"I am well assured that the gods themselves will take care to discover such persons. For it much more concerns them, if they be able, to punish those who refuse to worship them, than it does you. But you harass and vex the Christians, and accuse them of atheism, and other crimes which you can by no means prove. To them it appears an advantage to die for their religion, and they gain their point, while they throw away their lives rather than comply with your injunctions. As to the earthquakes which have been in past times or lately, is it not proper to remind you of your own despondency, when they happen, and to desire you to compare your spirits with theirs, and observe how serenely they confide in God ?

" In such seasons you seem to be ignorant of the gods and to neglect their worship. You live in the practical ignorance of the Supreme God Himself, and you harass and persecute to death those who do worship Him. Concerning these same men, some others of the provincial governors wrote to our divine father Hadrian, to whom he returned answer, 'that they should not be molested, unless they appeared to attempt something against the Roman government.' Many also have signified to me concerning these men, to whom I have returned an answer agreeable to the maxims of my father. But if any person will still persist in accusing the Christians—merely as such—let the accused be acquitted, though he appear to be a Christian ; and let the accuser be punished—Set up at Ephesus, in the Common Council of Asia."

This was no empty edict, but was really put in execution, and it would seem therefore that Justin's clear and earnest explanation worked for good upon the Emperor's mind.

CHAPTER XVIII.

DEATH OF JUSTIN MARTYR. ABOUT 165.

NOT long after Justin's first Apology, he visited
Ephesus, and there became acquainted with Trypho,
a Jew of great note, said to have been a Rabbi,
who had fled from his country in the war caused
by the insurrection of Bar-chochab, and had since
lived in Greece, and interested himself much in philosophical studies. Justin entered into a controversy with Trypho, which was carried on for two
days. He has left an account of what passed in a
work called, " A Dialogue with Trypho the Jew."
Learned men have considered the arguments
brought forward to be wanting in force, but the
Dialogue is interesting from the many curious
particulars it gives as to the feelings with which
the Jews at that time regarded the Christians.
The Rabbis, we are told, forbade their hearers
to hold any intercourse with the Christians, they
pronounced curses against them in the synagogues,
and sent persons into every part of the civilized
world with directions to denounce Christianity as
a pestilent heresy, and to misrepresent the conduct
and morals of those who professed the faith of the
Gospel.

The Rabbi Trypho, however, declared himself
highly pleased with Justin's arguments, stating
that he found in them more than he could have expected, and wished he could enjoy such intercourse
oftener, as it would greatly conduce to the understanding of the Scriptures, adding that he begged
for Justin's friendship in whatever part of the
world he might be.

This wish was probably especially called forth

from the fact that Justin was then upon the point of departing, but whether with the intention of returning to Rome or visiting some other place is not known.

Rome, however, was the scene of his last labours and the place of his martyrdom. He was residing there when, after the death of Antoninus Pius, A.D. 161. Marcus Aurelius, the adopted son of Antoninus, reigned over the vast Roman Empire, with the assistance of Lucius Verres, whom he had taken as his partner in the government.

Marcus Aurelius is a singular instance of the virtues which a man may possess without being at all open to the softening, humbling principles of Christianity. He was in general just, generous, and self-denying, pure in his life, and devoted to what he considered the duties of his high station. But he seems to have had one great defect—a defect common to all heathens—he was proud, and pride made him a persecutor. Firm in his own religious belief, he saw no need of any other. He considered himself virtuous, and so undoubtedly he was in outward conduct—and therefore he had no interest in the faith which was founded upon the fact of man's sin and God's Redemption. From his childhood, Marcus Aurelius had been placed in a position which led him to think highly of himself. When he was only eight years old, the emperor Hadrian introduced him amongst some of the heathen priests, and caused him to be instructed in the services of the priesthood. At twelve, he wore the philosopher's cloak, and practised himself in the endurance of hardships, lying upon the bare ground, and being with difficulty persuaded by his mother to use a mattress and light coverlet.

15*

As he grew up, he attached himself to the sect of the Stoics, who were especially noted for their contempt of worldly advantages. All these things tended to foster the self-conceit which was probably part of the Emperor's natural disposition, and at length he became so prejudiced in favour of his own opinions, that he could not even see the facts which were before him. For instance, he thought it a noble thing to be above the fear of death, but when he beheld how the Christians could die, he supposed their fortitude to be merely the result of obstinacy. "Resignation to the prospect of death," he says in his writings, "ought to proceed from deliberate judgment, not from mere unintelligent obstinacy, as is the case with the Christians. It should be founded on grounds of solid reason, and be attended with calm composure, without any tragical raptures, and in such a way as may induce others to admire and imitate."

We, who know that millions of human beings, varying in age and sex, and in bodily and mental strength, have been enabled to meet death, in its most terrible forms, calmly, only through the support of the Christian faith, may smile at the ignorant sneer of the philosophic Emperor; but a man of such prejudices was likely to be a most severe judge of all who differed from him; and the Christians, and especially Justin, soon had occasion to feel the full force of his enmity.

To come forward in defence of Christianity was in those days to be a mark for general suspicion and dislike; but Justin was not a person to shrink from duty from this cause. During his residence in Rome, he publicly contended with and refuted a philosopher named Crescens, an ignorant man, of infamous character, and thus made him his enemy, and placed himself in danger; and this danger was afterwards much increased by a case of injustice which occurred at Rome, and which Justin hastened to bring before the notice of the Emperor in a second Apology.

A certain woman living at Rome, and who, with her husband, was notorious for an evil life, was converted to Christianity. On her conversion she renounced her former sins, and endeavoured also to reclaim her husband, but without success. Extremely indignant with her, especially when she sought to obtain a divorce from him on account of his wicked life, he publicly accused her of being a Christian. The woman, unprepared for an immediate defence, appealed to the Emperor, who granted her a respite,—and the husband, finding his malice thus checked, turned his anger against a Christian, named Ptolemy, who had been the instrument of his wife's conversion. He persuaded a centurion, his friend, to imprison Ptolemy,—and to inquire whether he was a Christian. Ptolemy boldly acknowledged the truth, and his imprisonment was prolonged for some time, and at length he was brought before Urbicius, the prefect of the city. But one question was put to him—whether he was a Christian? When he owned the fact, he was immediately led to execution. Lucilius, another Christian who was present, unable to endure such injustice, expostulated with Urbicius upon the iniquity of putting men to death merely for a name, and apart from any definite charge of guilt. " You too appear to me to be of the same sect," was all that the prefect deigned to reply, and Lucilius having also made his confession, followed his friend to death. A third person was condemned in a similar manner on this occasion. These facts

Justin brought before the notice of the Emperor, hoping probably to obtain some assistance from his sense of justice, and being aware also, as he himself openly stated—that with such tribunals his own life was in danger, especially from the malice of Crescens. The Emperor was, however, deaf to the appeal, and the event which Justin had foreseen soon after occurred. Crescens insinuated himself into the Emperor's favour, accused Justin of being a Christian, and caused him to be thrown into prison with six of his friends. He was brought to trial before Rusticus, prefect of the city, a wise statesman and philosopher, who had been the Emperor's tutor. Rusticus undertook to persuade Justin to obey the gods and comply with the Emperor's edicts; but Justin, unmindful of his arguments, replied, that " no man could be found fault with, or condemned, that obeyed the commands of our Saviour Jesus Christ." The prefect proceeded to inquire as to the learning and discipline in which he had been brought up. Justin answered that " he had endeavoured to understand all kinds of discipline, and had tried all methods of learning, but finding satisfaction in none, he had at last met with rest in the Christian religion, though it was little esteemed by those who were led by error and false opinions." " Wretch ! " replied the indignant magistrate, " art thou captivated by *that* religion ? " " I am," said Justin ; " I follow the Christians, and their doctrine is right." " What is this doctrine ? " inquired Rusticus. " It is this," replied Justin ; " we believe the one only God to be the Creator of all things visible and invisible ; and we confess our Lord Jesus Christ to be the Son of God, foretold by the prophets of old ; and that He is now the Saviour, Teacher,

and Master of all those who are duly submissive
to his instructions; and that he will hereafter be
the Judge of mankind. As for myself, I am too
mean to be able to say anything becoming His
infinite Deity. This was the business of the Prophets, who many ages ago foretold the coming of
the Son of God into the world." "Where do the
Christians usually assemble?" inquired the prefect. Justin replied, that "the God of the Christians was not confined to a particular place." The
prefect then inquired, in what place he instructed
his scholars. Justin mentioned the place where he
dwelt, and told him that there he explained Christianity to all who resorted to him.

The prefect then examined Justin's companions
separately, after which he again addressed Justin
himself. "Hear," he exclaimed, "thou that art
noted for thy eloquence, and thinkest thou art in
the truth. If I cause thee to be scourged from
head to foot, thinkest thou that thou shalt go to
Heaven?" "Although I suffer what you threaten,"
replied Justin, "yet I expect to enjoy the portion
of all true Christians; as I know that the Divine
Grace and Favour is laid up for all such, and shall
be so while the world endures." "Do you think,"
again asked the prefect, "that you shall go to
Heaven, and receive a reward?" "I not only
think so, but I know it," was the reply. "I have
a certainty of it which excludes all doubt."

The governor seeing that it was in vain to
argue, called out in a threatening tone, "Join
together, and offer a unanimous sacrifice to the
gods." "No man, whose understanding is sound,"
replied Justin, "will desert true religion for the
sake of error and impiety." "Unless you comply,"
exclaimed the prefect, still more angrily, "you

shall be tormented without mercy." Justin's courage rose higher at the threat. "We wish nothing more," he said, "than to suffer for our Lord Jesus Christ; for this will give us salvation and joy at His dread Tribunal, before which all the world must appear." The rest assented, saying: "Despatch your purpose quickly. We are Christians, and cannot sacrifice to idols."

The governor then pronounced sentence. "As to those, who refuse to sacrifice to the gods, and to obey the imperial edicts, let them be first scourged and then beheaded, according to the laws."

Justin and his companions were led back to prison, rejoicing and blessing God. The sufferings that remained for them to endure were quickly over. According to the sentence they were scourged and beheaded; and so entered upon their eternal rest, about the year 165.

The trial of Justin Martyr is a sufficient evidence of the spirit in which the examination of Christians was at this time carried on. The hostile feeling of the Emperor was well known to all the governors of the provinces, and when the heathen people clamoured for the destruction of those whom they hated, search was made, and accusations were instantly received; the victims of the persecution were cruelly tortured before condemnation, and when steadfast in their faith were doomed to the most barbarous and awful forms of death. They were crucified, burned, or thrown to wild beasts. But Christianity only spread the faster for these terrors. It increased indeed so rapidly as to threaten the religion of the state, and the Emperor and his heathen subjects looked on in wonder and fear, whilst they saw the educated and the ignorant, the wealthy and the poor, alike forsake the joys of the world, and give themselves over to agony and death for the love of the crucified Jesus of Nazareth.

Shortly before the death of Justin, Papias, Bishop of Hierapolis, is said to have been amongst the number of the martyrs. His name is worthy of mention from the fact that he wrote a work containing a collection of anecdotes and sayings, connected with our Lord and His Apostles, from which many early writers were accustomed to quote. He appears to have been a man of extensive reading, but not of sound judgment. He says of himself, "I have never, like many, delighted to hear those that tell many things; but those that teach the truth; neither those that record foreign precepts, but those that are given from the Lord to our faith, and that came from the truth itself. But if I met with any one who had been a follower of the elders anywhere, I made it a point to inquire what were the declarations of the elders; what was said by Andrew, Peter, or Philip; what by Thomas, James, John, Matthew, or any other of the disciples of our Lord."

Papias is mentioned as one of the first Christians who held the doctrine of the Millennium, or the belief that before the Great Day of Judgment there would be a resurrection of the just, who would reign with their Lord upon the earth for a thousand years. This idea was entertained also by Justin Martyr, who allows, however, that many excellent Christians differed from him. The Millennium was, in fact, never an article of faith, but every person was left to form his own opinion respecting it; and at length, in the following century, the belief in it ceased to be held, though it has arisen again at various times since.

Some notions respecting it are to be found in a very ancient work called the Epistle of St. Barnabas, which was believed by several of the fathers to have been the actual writing of that Apostle, though others speak of it as belonging to a later date. St. Barnabas, however, appears to have had a less material idea of the Millennium than Papias, who was a credulous person, and disposed to look upon the expected reign of Christ as upon the triumph of an earthly kingdom.

CHAPTER XIX.

MARTYRDOM OF ST. POLYCARP. A.D. 167.

THE loss which the visible Church had sustained by the death of Justin Martyr was quickly to be followed by another, perhaps even more deeply regretted. Polycarp, Bishop of Smyrna, was at that time a very aged man. He has been mentioned before as the disciple of St. John, by whom he was appointed Bishop of Smyrna; and also as the friend of the martyr Ignatius, who, it may be remembered, sought the comfort of his society on his journey from Ephesus to Rome, and commended to him the charge of his diocese. This personal acquaintance with the last of the Apostles was in itself a reason for reverence; but the saintly character of Polycarp added weight to the position, which, from other circumstances, he held. After the death of Ignatius, he appears to have occupied himself in the affairs of his diocese; but shortly after the period of Justin Martyr's sojourn at Ephesus, he visited Rome. The occasion of his visit, was a controversy, which more or less affected the whole Christian Church, and which no one was considered more capable of arranging than Polycarp. The Eastern Church had always considered the festival of Easter to be, like the Jewish Passover, a fixed feast, to be held at the time of the full moon. The Western Church looked upon it as a moveable festival, to be observed on the Lord's day following the new moon. Each practice was declared to be derived from the tradition of an Apostle. The Eastern Church appealed to St. John, the Western to St. Peter. Probably both were right. The Apostles, it is well known, complied in things indifferent with the customs of any place in which they might happen to be. Polycarp might know that St. John kept Easter at a certain time in Ephesus, and Anicetus, who was then Bishop of Rome, might have received a well-founded testimony that St. Peter kept it on another day at Rome. It was not an essential point; yet the feeling upon the subject was very strong, and Polycarp undertook a journey to Rome, in the hope that by a personal interview with Anicetus, some agreement might be arrived at. The Roman Bishop was not then looked upon as the person to whom all were to yield, or the difference would have been settled at once. The wish of Polycarp was to convince Anicetus that he was wrong. He did not feel himself called upon to defer to him. Anicetus, however, would not give up his opinion; but in order to show that there was no unkind feeling on either side, they joined in the holiest Christian rite, and Anicetus, to put the greater honour upon St. Polycarp, gave him leave to consecrate the Eucharist in his own church, after which they parted in friendship, thus pre-

16

serving the peace of the Church, though upholding their respective ancient customs.

The visit of St. Polycarp to Rome, though apparently without any marked results, as regarded the Easter festival, was, nevertheless, of considerable use in other respects. His influence was exerted whilst there to stop the progress of heresy, and many persons who had been led away by the false doctrines of Marcion were reclaimed by him. His indignation against the heretics was indeed as great as that of St. John. Upon hearing any thing said contrary to Christian truth, he was wont to stop his ears, and exclaim with reverent honour, " Good God, unto what times hast Thou reserved me, that I should hear such things ! " and immediately he avoided the place where the false doctrines had been set forth. This, and other particulars respecting Polycarp, are recorded by Irenæus, Bishop of Lyons, who was intimately acquainted with him, and tells us that whilst a youth, he was with St. Polycarp in Asia Minor, and noticed every thing respecting him so particularly, that he could perfectly remember the very place where Polycarp used to sit while he discoursed, the shape of his body, the manner of his life, his conversation, and the account he was wont to give of his familiar intercourse with St. John, and others who had seen our Lord; rehearsing their sayings, and repeating what they had told him respecting our Blessed Saviour, His miracles and doctrines; all of which agreed exactly with the narrative of the Sacred History.

Polycarp returned to Ephesus after his visit to Rome, and appears to have continued in his diocese, supporting and guiding his people during the terrible persecution which soon afterwards raged on

all sides, and was especially felt at Smyrna. The
bishop of a diocese was, from his position, at all
times, a mark for vengeance ; and the well-known
zeal of Polycarp rendered him especially con-
spicuous. His friends, anxious for his safety,
entreated him to leave the city, and much against
his own inclination, he was persuaded to retire to
a little village not far distant. There he remained,
occupying himself, according to his custom, in
incessant prayer for all men, and especially for the
Churches of Christ throughout the world. He
was one day in the act of prayer, when a singular
vision was vouchsafed to him. The pillow under
his head appeared to him to be on fire. The
meaning of this vision instantly suggested itself,
and turning to those who were with him, he exclaimed, "I must be burnt alive." Three days
afterwards he was taken, being betrayed through
fear by two of his own servants. The circumstances of his capture and of his subsequent trials,
are thus described in one of the most valuable of
ancient records, an epistle written in the name of
Polycarp's Church of Smyrna, " to the Church of
God which is at Philadelphia, and to all the other
assemblies of the Holy and Catholic Church in
every place."

"When those who sought for Polycarp drew
near, he departed into another village : and immediately his pursuers came thither. And when they
found him not, they seized upon two young men,
one of whom, being tormented, confessed. For it
was impossible he should be concealed, forasmuch
as they who betrayed him were his own domestics.
So the keeper of the peace, who was also magistrate elect, Herod by name, hastened to bring him
into the lists ; that so Polycarp might receive his

proper portion, being made partaker of Christ; and they that betrayed him might undergo the punishment of Judas.

"The officers, therefore, and horsemen, taking the young lads along with them, departed about supper time, it being Friday, with their usual arms, as if they were in pursuit of a robber. And being come to the place where he was, about the close of the day, they found him in a small house, lying in an upper chamber, whence he could easily have escaped into another place; but he would not, saying, "The will of the Lord be done." Wherefore, when he heard that they were come to the house, he went down and spake to them. And as they that were present wondered at his age and constancy, some of them began to say, ' Was there need of all this care to take such an old man as this ?' Immediately then he commanded to be set before them, the same hour, to eat and to drink, as much as they would; desiring them to give him one hour's liberty, that he might pray without disturbance. And when they had permitted him, he stood praying, being full of the grace of God, so that he ceased not for two whole hours, to the admiration of all that heard him; insomuch that many (of the soldiers) began to repent that they were come out against so godly an old man.

"As soon as he had finished his prayer, in which he made mention of all men who had ever been acquainted with him, whether small or great, honourable or obscure, and of the whole Catholic Church throughout the world; the time being come when he was to depart, they set him upon an ass, and led him into the city, it being the day of the great Sabbath. And Herod, the keeper of the peace, with his father, Nicetes, met him in a chariot. And having taken him up to them, and set him in the chariot, they began to persuade him saying, 'Why, what harm is there in saying, Lord Cæsar, and in offering sacrifice, and so being safe?' with other words which are usual on such occasions. But Polycarp at first answered them not; whereupon, as they continued to urge him, he said, 'I shall not do as you advise.' They, therefore, failing to persuade him, spake bitter words against him, and then thrust him violently off the chariot, so that he hurt his leg in the fall. But he, without turning back, went on with all diligence, as if he had received no harm at all; and so was brought to the lists, where there was so great a tumult, that no one could be heard.

"Now, as he was going into the lists, there was a voice from heaven, 'Be strong, Polycarp, and quit thyself like a man.' No one saw who it was that spake to him; but those of our brethren who were present heard the voice. And as he was brought in, there was a great disturbance, when they heard that Polycarp was taken. And when he came near, the Pro-consul asked him whether he were Polycarp. And, when he acknowledged (that he was), he persuaded him to deny (the faith), saying, 'Reverence thy old age;' with many other exhortations of a like nature, as their custom is, saying, 'Swear by the Fortune of Cæsar; repent, and say, away with the wicked.' Then Polycarp, looking with a severe countenance upon the whole company of ungodly Gentiles who were in the lists, stretched forth his hand to them, and said, groaning and looking up to heaven, 'Away with the wicked.' But the Pro-consul urging him, and saying, 'Swear, and I will release thee; reproach

16*

Christ;' Polycarp answered, 'Four-score and six years have I continued serving Him, and He hath never wronged me at all; how then can I blaspheme my King and my Saviour?'

"And when the Pro-consul, nevertheless, still insisted, and said, 'Swear by the Genius of Cæsar,' he answered, 'If thou art so vainly confident as to expect that I should swear by what thou callest the Genius of Cæsar, pretending to be ignorant of what I am, hear me freely professing unto thee, I am a Christian; and if thou further desirest to know what Christianity really is, appoint a day, and thou shalt hear it.' The Pro-consul replied, 'Persuade the people.' Then said Polycarp, 'To thee have I freely offered to give even a reason of my faith; for we are taught to pay to the powers and authorities, which are ordained of God, the honour which is due, provided it be not injurious to ourselves. But for the people, I esteem them not worthy that I should give any account of my faith to them.'

"The Pro-consul said unto him, 'I have wild beasts ready; to those will I cast thee, unless thou repent.' He answered, 'Call for them, then; for we Christians are fixed in our minds not to change from good to evil. But it will be good for me to be changed from my grievous (sufferings) to their just reward.' The Pro-consul added, 'Seeing thou despisest the wild beasts, I will cause thee to be devoured with fire, unless thou shalt repent.' Polycarp answered, 'Thou threatenest me with fire which burns for an hour, and in a little while is extinguished; for thou knowest not the fire of the future judgment, and of that eternal punishment, which is reserved for the ungodly. But why tarriest thou? Bring forth what thou wilt.'

" Having said this, and many other things (of
the like nature), he was filled with confidence and
joy, insomuch that his very countenance was full
of grace ; so that not only he was serene and undisturbed at what was spoken to him ; but on the
contrary, the Pro-consul was astonished, and sent
his own herald to proclaim thrice, in the midst of
the lists, ' Polycarp hath confessed himself to be a
Christian.'   When this was proclaimed by the
herald, the whole multitude, both of the Gentiles
and of the Jews, which dwelt at Smyrna, being full
of fury, cried out with a loud voice, ' This is the
teacher of Asia, the father of the Christians, who
hath overthrown our gods, and teaches so many
not to sacrifice, nor to pay any worship to the
gods.'   And so saying, they cried out and desired
Philip, the president of the spectacles, that he
would let loose a lion against Polycarp.   But
Philip replied, that it was not lawful for him to do
so, since that kind of spectacle was already over.
Then it pleased them to cry out with one consent,
that Polycarp should be burnt alive.   For so it
was necessary that the vision should be fulfilled
which was made manifest to him by his pillow,
when he saw it on fire, as he prayed, and said pro-
phetically to the faithful that were with him, ' I
must be burnt alive.'

" This then was done with greater speed than it
was spoken ; the whole multitude instantly gathering together wood and faggots out of the work-
shops and baths ; the Jews especially, according to
their custom, with all readiness assisting them in
doing it.   When the pile was ready, Polycarp,
laying aside all his upper garments, and loosing
his girdle, endeavoured also to loosen his sandals,
which aforetime he was not wont to do ; forasmuch

as always every one of the faithful, that was about him, contended who should soonest touch his flesh. For he was adorned by his good conversation with all kinds of piety, even before his martyrdom. Immediately then they put upon him the instruments which were prepared for the pile. But when they would also have nailed him to the stake, he said, 'Leave me thus; for He who hath given me strength to endure the fire, will also enable me, without your securing me by nails, to remain without moving in the pile.'

" Wherefore they did not nail him, but bound him (to the stake). But he, having put his hands behind him, and being bound as a ram, (chosen) out of a great flock for an offering, and prepared to be a burnt sacrifice, acceptable unto God, looked up to heaven, and said, ' O Lord God Almighty, the Father of thy well-beloved and blessed Son Jesus Christ, by whom we have received the knowledge of thee; the God of angels and powers, and of every creature, and (especially) of the whole race of just men who live in Thy presence ; I give Thee hearty thanks that thou hast vouchsafed to bring me to this day and to this hour, that I should have a part in the number of Thy martyrs, in the cup of Thy Christ, unto the resurrection of eternal life, both of soul and body, in the incorruption of the Holy Spirit; among which I may be accepted this day before Thee, as a fair and acceptable sacrifice, as Thou hast before ordained, and declared, and fulfilled, even Thou, the True God, with whom is no falsehood at all. For this, and for all things else, I praise Thee, I bless Thee, with the eternal and heavenly Jesus Christ, Thy beloved Son, with whom to Thee and the Holy Ghost be glory, both now and to all succeeding ages.   Amen.'

" As soon as he had uttered Amen, and finished his prayer, the men appointed for the purpose lighted the fire. And when the flame began to blaze to a very great height, a wonderful sight appeared to us who were permitted to witness it, and were also spared to relate to others what had happened. For the flame, making a kind of arch, like the sail of a ship filled with wind, encompassed the body of the martyr, which was in the midst, not as flesh which was burned, but as bread which is baked, or as gold or silver glowing in the furnace. Moreover, we perceived as fragrant an adour as if it came from frankincense, or some other precious spices.

" At length, when these wicked men saw that his body could not be consumed by the fire, they commanded the executioner to go near and pierce him with his sword. Which being accordingly done, there came forth so great a quantity of blood, as extinguished the fire, and raised an admiration among the people, to consider what a difference there is between the infidels and the elect; one of which this admirable martyr, Polycrap, was, being in our times a truly apostolical and prophetical teacher, and the bishop of the Catholic Church which is at Smyrna. For every word that proceeded out of his mouth either is (already) fulfilled, or will (in due time) be accomplished.

" But when the emulous, and envious, and wicked adversary of the race of the just saw the greatness of his martyrdom, and considered how blameless his conversation had been from the beginning, and that he was now crowned with the crown of immortality, having without all controversy received his reward, he took all care that not the least relic of his body should be taken away by us, although many desired to do it, and to have a share in his holy flesh. And to that end he suggested to Nicetes, the father of Herod, and brother of Alce, to go to the governor, and hinder him from giving his body to be buried; lest, said he, forsaking him that was crucified, they should begin to worship this Polycarp. And this he said at the suggestion and instance of the Jews, who also watched us that we should not take him out of the fire; not considering that it is impossible for us either ever to forsake Christ, who suffered for the salvation of all such as shall be saved throughout the whole world (the righteous for the ungodly), or to worship any other. For Him indeed, as being the Son of God, we adore; but for the martyrs, we worthily love them, as the disciples and imitators of our Lord, on account of their exceeding great love towards their Master and King; of whom may we also be made companions and fellow-disciples. The centurion, therefore, seeing the contention of the Jews, put his body into the midst of the fire and burnt it. After which, we, taking up his bones, more precious than the richest jewels, and tried above gold, deposited them where it was fitting. Where, being gathered together as we have opportunity, with joy and gladness, the Lord will grant unto us to celebrate the anniversary of his martyrdom, both in memory of those who have suffered, and for the exercise and preparation of those that may hereafter (suffer)."

The martyrdom of St. Polycarp took place A.D. 167.

His character stands out prominently in the records of those early days, yet the virtues for which he was distinguished were by no means peculiar to himself. The charity and fortitude of the Christians were amongst the most important influences which tended to the spread of the Gospel. Charity indeed was a virtue belonging only to Christianity. Heathenism had failed to produce it; but the unselfish love of the early Christians obtained the praise even of their enemies, and many marked instances of this love occurred about this period. The soldiers of the emperor Verus, the colleague of Marcus Aurelius, had brought back from the Parthian war a pestilential disorder, which continued for several years. It was an occasion when the hearts of heathens were sealed against natural affection. Each cared for himself alone, anxious only to spare himself suffering, and if possible, save his own life. But the Christians devoted themselves to the service of their sick friends, careless of infection, and having but one thought how they might best relieve the misery they saw around them. Many fell victims to this disinterestedness, but their deaths preached more powerfully than their lives. The heathens had never before beheld such conduct, and they could not but inquire into the motives which caused it. A celebrated Roman physician, named Galen, who lived at this time, speaks of the firmness, or the obstinacy, with which the Christians submitted to suffering rather than abandon their religion. This was the term he chose to apply to Christian fortitude, but it is certain that he could not but admire and marvel at it.

CHAPTER XX.

RISE OF MONTANISM.   A.D. 171.

WHEN looking back at such a distance of time upon the trials which the early Christians endured, they seem to stand out apart, as it were, from all ordinary events. We do not directly connect them with the triumphs or the misfortunes of the heathens; but there is no doubt that the prosperity or adversity of the empire had really a great effect upon the condition of the Church of Christ. Five years after the death of St. Polycarp, the emperor Marcus Aurelius, and his colleague Lucius Verus, left Rome to make war upon some German tribes, and the expedition being considered dangerous, the priests recommended that some extraordinary means should be used in order to obtain the favour of the gods. The same year also was marked by the inundation of the Nile, and was, therefore, a season of public distress. Both these circumstances were unfavourable to the Christians. For, according to the heathen superstition, what surer means could be used, to avert a general calamity, than the destruction of the enemies of the gods of Rome ? Persecution, therefore, was carried on with great rigour; but it failed to avert the fate of one of the emperors, and before the campaign against the Germans had begun, Lucius Verus was dead, and Marcus Aurelius returned to Rome, to bend all his energies to the restoration of the worship of the gods. It was not till the next year that his warlike preparations were carried out. He was then absent for several years, and during that time, he is said to have received a striking proof that the Providence which watches over the affairs of men is not indifferent to their prayers. The Romans had marched against the Quadi, a powerful German tribe, dwelling near the mountians of Sarmatia, and the banks of the Danube. The emperor's army was weary and faint from thirst, and there was no hope of relief. As they were about to attack their enemies, the Melitene legion, which consisted of Christians, fell upon their knees, and besought the Great God of heaven and earth to send them aid. Their prayers were immediately answered by a terrible tempest of thunder and lightning, which so alarmed the barbarians, that they took to flight, whilst a plentiful rain descended upon the Romans and thoroughly refreshed them. The facts of this story are undoubted; but heathen writers attribute the timely relief either to magic or to the prayers of the Emperor. It has been said that the legion was thenceforth called the thundering legion, and that the Emperor publicly acknowledged the service rendered him; but there is no sufficient evidence for these statements,* and the events which occurred only a few years afterwards, show that whatever might have been the impression of the moment, the feelings of Marcus Aurelius were in no way really changed with respect to the Christian religion.

It would have been happy for the Church if the persecution of open enemies had been her greatest danger; but whilst the Emperor was absent on his warlike expedition, and less able to oppose the spread of the Gospel, a noted error sprang up in the Church, which, in the end, carried away one of the most distinguished of the early Fathers.

* The title *Legio Fulminea*, or Thundering Legion, existed before the time of Marcus Aurelius.

17

Montanus, the author of this erroneous teaching, is supposed to have been a native of Ardaba, in Mysia, on the borders of Phrygia. About the year 171 he fell into a state of violent ecstasy, during which he predicted an approaching persecution, together with the judgments of heaven which should fall upon the persecutors. He exhorted the faithful to contend vigorously for the crown of martyrdom, and to prepare for the conflict by severe self-denial. The state of his mind was not the fervour of a saint; it was a wild enthusiasm, bordering upon fury; but its influence was strongly felt by many. Two noble ladies, Priscilla and Maximilla, who had forsaken their husbands, became followers of Montanus, and immediately imagined themselves to have been elevated to the rank of prophetesses. Probably at first there was some unintentional delusion on the part both of Montanus and his prophetesses. They were persons of a very excitable temperament, and Montanus may actually have believed, as he stated, that visions from heaven were vouchsafed him, and that he had the power of foretelling future events; the prophetesses, in like manner, may have supposed themselves inspired, but there can be little doubt that in the end Montanus voluntarily misled his followers. Numbers were soon found who gave entire faith to these new revelations, and although the bishop of the province examined the claims of the prophet, condemned his predictions, and excommunicated him, together with the two prophetesses, yet the delusion soon spread even beyond Asia Minor. The greatest attraction for people in general was the life of outward holiness and severe self-denial led by the Montanists. Ordinary persons find so much difficulty in giving up their accustomed luxuries, that they are apt to consider any one who lives a life of bodily self-denial, as for that reason alone, raised to the dignity of a saint; whilst it is difficult to suppose that falsehood in belief can exist with purity, uprightness, and zeal for God's service. But so it is, and has been from the beginning. Truth is a revelation from God. It remains always the same, and cannot be affected by the conduct of man. Balaam was a wicked man, but he spoke according to God's will. If we are to choose our religion by the virtues of the persons who proclaim it, we may have a new creed for every month in the year. There is perhaps no form of Christianity which has not produced men who have had a claim, from the excellence of their lives, to the title of saints. Yet God's Holy Truth has not therefore been altered. The testimony of the Bible and the witness of history, are the foundations of our faith, and though an angel from heaven should endeavour to make us believe things inconsistent with the Bible, and not held by the Apostles and the primitive Christians, we must, on the peril of our souls, reject his teaching. The peculiar tenets of Montanus referred, however, rather to matters of discipline than questions of doctrine. He owned that our Blessed Lord and His Apostles had declared all which it was necessary for mankind to believe in order to be saved; but he added, that the discipline of the Church, and the rules for a Christian's daily life in this world, had not been fully set forth, and that therefore a new revelation was required. This, he said, was given through him and his two prophetesses; who were therefore to be considered the persons chosen by God to teach men the extent of their duty. According to the revelations which Montanus pretended to have received, all those who after baptism had been guilty of very heinous sins, could never again be received into the communion of the Church. They might be exhorted to repent, and to show their repentance by submitting to open penance, and then they might hope that God would pardon them; but in this life,—amongst their fellow-Christians,—there was no prospect of regaining the privileges they had lost.

The Montanists forbade second marriages, and those who broke this law were expelled from the Church. They ordained new regulations as to fasting, and forbade Christians to flee or hide themselves in times of persecution, considering it as the greatest possible happiness to obtain the crown of martyrdom. But notwithstanding this professed sanctity, they have been accused of avarice and luxury. Montanus, it is said, appointed money receivers, and encouraged the people to offer gifts. Priscilla and Maximilla accepted presents, and the Montanist prophets are stated to have adorned their persons, practised usury, and been addicted to games of chance.

The teaching of Montanus naturally excited much disturbance and discussion. An account of the new errors reached the Churches of Gaul, and the two cities of Lyons and Vienne prepared to send a messenger with a letter to Rome, to inquire into the opinions which had arisen in the Church, and if possible to bring those who differed to agreement. This was the more necessary as Eleutherus, Bishop of Rome, showed some inclination to favour the Montanists; but it is a matter for wonder and admiration, that these distant Churches should have been able thus to interest themselves in questions of doctrine and discipline, since one of the fiercest persecutions which the Church had endured was at that very moment raging amongst them.

The immediate occasion of this persecution was a popular tumult caused by hatred of the Christians, the universal rage against them being increased by the cruel falsehoods of some slaves belonging to Christian masters, who, in order to escape torture, declared that the disciples of the Redeemer were guilty, in their assemblies, of the crimes commonly imputed to them. Many of the Christians fled. Against those who remained the terrors of the fire, the sword, and of wild beasts were employed. A few, about ten in number, lapsed, and this weakness seems to have caused greater anxiety and alarm amongst the Believers than the prospect of the most terrible sufferings. Examination was dreaded, not because it might be followed by death, but by apostacy. Very many, however, were left to bear witness by their fortitude to the steadfastness of their faith, and the superhuman power which upheld them. The most fearful torments could only extort from them the declaration " I am a Christian." This firmness in the case of a deacon named Sanctus, so exasperated the Roman governor, that having exhausted all ordinary methods of torture, he actually fixed hot brazen plates to the most tender parts of the martyr's body, though without producing the least effect upon his resolution. His frame, indeed, as we are told in an epistle written by the Churches of Lyons and Vienne, " bore witness to the ghastly tortures which he had sustained, being one continued wound and bruise, and altogether contracted, so as no longer to retain the form of a human creature," but his steadfastness was inflexible. His enemies hoped, after the respite of a few days, that

17*

by a renewal of the same methods of punishment, applied to his already mangled body, he might be brought to apostatise, and so lead others to a similar guilt; but, contrary to all expectations, during the second course of torture, the body of Sanctus was restored to its former shape, and thus instead of a punishment, the cruelty proved to be a cure. Many of the sufferers died before the day appointed for the infliction of the last sentence. Several young persons, unable to support the agony of torture, expired under it, and Pothinus, Bishop of Lyons, who was upwards of ninety years of age, died in prison, in consequence of the ill treatment he had received from the heathen mob. Many others, however, endured a public and violent death. Amongst those most remarkable for fortitude was Blandina, a Christian servant, who appears to have possessed so little bodily strength, that a general feeling of dread prevailed amongst her fellow-Christians, lest weakness should induce her to apostatise. Every variety and extremity of torture was inflicted upon her without success. The heathen tormentors themselves confessed that any one species of the torture was in itself sufficient to produce death. But Blandina needed only the support of faith, and when in the midst of her agony she could exclaim, " I am a Christian, and no evil is committed among us," it seemed as though all sense of suffering was for the time annihilated.

The persecutors at last suspended her to a stake in the form of a cross, and exposed her as a prey to the wild beasts. She was seen with her arms stretched out, engaged in earnest supplication; and the sight gave confidence to those who were preparing to suffer likewise, since it visibly recalled to them Him who for their sakes had suffered crucifixion.

Blandina remained untouched by the wild animals, and after some time was taken down, thrown into prison again, and reserved for the conclusion of the spectacles, though she was brought out, from time to time, to witness the agony and death of her fellow-Christians.

The hour of release, however, at length arrived. Blandina and Ponticus, a youth of fifteen, were produced on the last day of the public festival. Barbarities as before, were heaped upon them, and bravely endured by both, for Blandina exerted all her powers to support and confirm her young companion. She herself was kept to be the final victim, and after having suffered from scourging, the fury of wild animals, and the scorching of a heated iron chair, in which she was placed, she was inclosed in a net and thrown to a bull; and at length, unshaken in constancy, breathed her last, a conqueror even unto death through the strength of Christ, and the clear realisation of the Object of her faith.

The death of the martyrs was not sufficient to satisfy the rage of their enemies. Insults were heaped upon their lifeless bodies, and their friends were deprived the consolation of giving them Christian burial.

At the close of the Epistle before quoted, the writer says, "As for ourselves, our sorrow was greatly increased, because we were deprived of the melancholy satisfaction of interring our friends. Neither the darkness of the night could befriend us, nor could we prevail by prayer or by price. They watched the bodies with unremitting vigilance, as if to deprive them of sepulchre was to them an object of great importance. The bodies of the martyrs having been contumaciously treated and exposed for six days, were burnt and reduced to ashes, and scattered by the wicked into the Rhone, that not the least particle of them might appear on earth any more. And they did these things as if they could prevail against God and prevent their resurrection; and that they might deter others from the hope of a future life. As they said, ' Relying on this, the Christians introduce a strange and new religion, and despise the most excruciating tortures, and die with joy. Now let us see if they will rise again, and if their God can help them and deliver them out of our hands.' "

The same writer adds some remarks upon the character of the martyrs; their humility, meekness, and charity. " Though elevated to such a height of glory," he says, " and though they had borne witness for Christ not once or twice only, but often, in a variety of sufferings, yet they assumed not the venerable name of martyrs, nor permitted us to address them as such. But if any of us by letter or word gave them the title, they reproved us vehemently. For it was with much pleasure that they gave the appellation in a peculiar sense to Him who is the Faithful and True Witness, the First-begotten from the dead, and the Prince of divine life. And they remembered with respect the deceased martyrs, and said, ' *They* indeed were martyrs whom Christ hath deigned to receive to Himself in their confession, sealing their testimony by their exit, but *we* are low and mean confessors.' With tears they entreated the brethren to pray fervently for them that they might be perfected. They exhibited, however, in reality, the energy of the character of martyrs. Their magnanimity, undaunted, calm, and intrepid, was visible to all the world. In peace they went to God, leaving neither trouble to their mother the Church, nor faction and sedition to the brethren ; but joy, peace, unanimity, and charity."

This bitter persecution was the last which the Christians were called upon to endure under Marcus Aurelius, who died whilst still engaged in fighting against the barbarian tribes on the Danube. The fact is received by us as an ordinary matter of history ; but it is solemn and bewildering to think of the change which must then have come upon the mind of the stern heathen emperor ; the light which must have broken upon him in the world beyond the grave, showing the difference between the philosophy which he had worshipped, and the Christianity he had despised.

Athenagoras, an Athenian, and Hegesippus, a Jew by birth, are amongst the most noted Christian writers who flourished during the reign of Marcus Aurelius. The former wrote an apology for the Christian religion, and a treatise on the Resurrection. Hegesippus is the earliest ecclesiastical historian, but only fragments of his work have come down to us. He speaks with great satisfaction of the uniformity of faith which he found in all the Churches that he visited on his way to Rome, and gives a list of the Bishops of Rome from the earliest days of the Church.

CHAPTER XXI.

VICTOR, BISHOP OF ROME. A.D. 189.

It could have been little foreseen that the reign of
the savage Commodus, who succeeded Mar-
A.D. 180.   cus Aurelius, should bring a season of repose
to the Christian Church, but so it was. Commodus,
though cruel to all men, was too indifferent to every
form of religion to bestow particular notice upon
Christianity. He was also influenced by one of his
favourites, a woman named Marcia, who though a
person of infamous character, had once been a
Christian, and still retained a kindly feeling towards
her former associates. There was, in consequence,
no general persecution during the twelve years and
nine months of the reign of Commodus, but the
laws against the Christians still remained in force,
and even in Rome itself a member of the senate
was put to death on the charge of being a Christian.

This temporary lull must have been a very great
blessing to the Church after the hot persecution
which had so lately been endured. A period of
rest was a time for missionary efforts, and we have
several striking instances of the manner in which
the faith of Christ was now taking root, even in
the farthest regions of the known world. Lucius, a
king of Britain, is said to have written to Eleutherus,
Bishop of Rome, requesting that some person might
be sent to instruct his people in the truths of the
Gospel ; and though there are no sufficient grounds
for the whole of this statement, since we know that
Christianity had been planted in Britain before,

and that St. Paul held intercourse with British converts, yet it appears probable that up to this time the people only, and not their chiefs, had received the Gospel. Lucius may have been the first British chief who professed himself a Christian; and in that case it would have been only natural that he should apply for teachers and support to the Bishop of Rome. Britain was subject to the Romans, the Latin language was spoken in Britain, —all the instruction which the uncivilised Britons received came from their Roman conquerors, and if British Christians went to Rome, or Roman Christians came to Britain, they would equally find friends able to understand and sympathise with them. This established communication between the Christians of Rome and Britain, plainly marks the progress of the Church in the West. Bardesanes, of Mesopotamia, who was one of the most distinguished Christians of that day, although not entirely free from heretical opinions, bears witness to its powerful influence for good in Parthia and Persia; and Pantænus, of Alexandria, a man of great learning, and high reputation, was chosen about this time to be the instrument by which it should be more firmly planted in the remote regions of the East.

Pantænus was originally a follower of the Stoics, but was led to embrace Christianity by the teaching of persons who had themselves seen the Apostles of Christ. He settled in Alexandria, the favourite resort of learned men, both Christians and heathens. The Christians had established schools there for the purpose of training persons in divine knowledge, and the first principles of Christianity; and about the beginning of the reign of Commodus, Pantænus was elected to be the Catechist, or head of the school. The employment must have been well suited to his natural inclinations. His school was much frequented, and he gave a more free admission than had before been customary, to those who chose to receive his instructions. Alexandria being the centre of commerce as well as of learning, was visited by persons from all parts of the world. Ethiopians, Arabians, Bactrians, Syrians, Persians, were all to be found there. Amongst others came ambassadors from India ; not, as it is supposed, the country which we call Hindostan, but the southern part of Arabia, washed by the waters of the Persian Gulf. Many years before Christianity had been preached there by St. Bartholomew, but the knowledge of the true faith had died away, and now some one was needed to revive it.

Demetrius, the Bishop of Alexandria, was naturally the person to whom the ambassadors applied ; and he immediately turned to Pantænus, as most fitted for the mission. Great dangers and hardships were to be encountered, much opposition was to be expected, and Pantænus was called upon to leave a pleasant country and an employment for which his taste and intellect were peculiarly fitted ; but in those days of primitive zeal, such things were quickly set aside, when there was a prospect of spreading the knowledge of the Saviour in heathen lands. Pantænus placed one of his disciples named Clement, in the position which he had held as head of the Catechetical school, and leaving Alexandria, gave himself up to the duties of a missionary. The details of his work have not been handed down to us, but tradition says that the Christian faith had not been wholly lost by the people amongst whom he laboured ; and that a copy of St. Matthew's Gospel, written in Hebrew, and left with them by St. Bar-

tholomew, was found and brought back by Pantænus; when, after some years, he was again permitted to return and resume his duties at Alexandria, assisted by Clement, who was one of the most
remarkable persons in the Christian Church, famed
both for his writings and his zeal; and indeed the
most learned man who had hitherto employed his
pen in defending or explaining the Gospel. A
change had by this time come over the Roman
empire—Commodus was dead. He had been killed
by the wicked Marcia, and the people were no longer
in danger from his ferocious cruelty. But the
country was in a very disturbed state, and many
claimants for the throne appeared in different parts
of the world. Two emperors, Pertinax and
A.D. 192. Julianus, succeeded Commodus in the course
of a few months, and were followed by Severus, a
clever and prudent monarch, but noted for perfidy
and cruelty.

A.D. 195. The reign of this emperor brings us to
the close of the second century. Up to that
period, Severus showed no dislike to Christianity;
on the contrary, he allowed his son, Caracalla, to
have a Christian nurse, and retained in his own
household a Christian named Proculus, who had
performed a cure upon himself, and for whom he felt
sincere gratitude. Yet persecution had not, therefore, entirely ceased. Though the emperor did not
encourage it, yet whenever the heathen populace
were excited against the Christians, search was
made, and the suspected persons were put to some
test of a revolting or insulting kind; either they were
ordered to eat food mixed with blood, from which
it was known that their religion required them to
abstain, or they were told to cast incense into a

18

chafing-dish, when the incense was to be offered to an idol ; or, as we have seen when Trajan entered Antioch, they were called upon to take part in some procession, which was not only in honour of the emperor, but also of the gods. In all these cases to refuse was to bring upon themselves the sentence of death. Still, as no direct edict of the emperor was then in force, the period may be looked upon as one of comparative safety, and as usual at such a time, troubles are to be noticed amongst the Christians themselves.

One of the most prominent characters in the Church at this period, was Victor, Bishop of Rome, who succeeded Eleutherus, A.D. 189. To judge from the facts handed down to us, Victor must have been a man of violent opinions and determined will ; and soon after the accession of Severus, this disposition exhibited itself on an occasion which is particularly worthy of notice, as showing, amongst other things, the discipline of the early Christians, and the manner in which kindly communication was kept up between the different Churches.

Severus, finding himself opposed by the people of Byzantium (the present Constantinople,) who favoured his rival, Niger, laid siege to the city. The Christians dwelling there were unwilling to take part with the other inhabitants, and in consequence, many were tortured and killed. Theodotus, a person engaged in trade, but possessed of considerable learning, had the cowardice, though professing himself a Christian, to deny his faith when taken before the authorities. He escaped punishment; but he was bitterly taunted by his brethren, and at length he fled to Rome. In those days when a Christian had occasion to pass from one city to another, he generally carried with him a letter from his own bishop to the bishop of the Church which he was visiting; in which an assurance was given that the bearer was orthodox, or held the true faith. He was then admitted to partake of the Holy Communion. Without such letters, he was liable to be examined as to the soundness of his faith, and if his answers were not satisfactory, he was not admitted to communion.

This was the case with Theodotus. He brought no letters of commendation, and when the report of his conduct at Byzantium reached Rome, and an inquiry respecting it was set on foot, he attempted to justify himself by saying that he had not denied God, but man; evidently implying that he believed our Blessed Lord to have been only a human being. This is the first instance of the heresy which denies the Divinity of Christ. Up to this period, no Christian had as yet entertained such a doctrine. It had been said by some, that our Lord's Body was only a phantom, by others, that it was only after His Baptism that a Divine Being was united to Him; but no one had yet ventured to assert that He was a mere man, without any portion of Divinity. Such an impiety was reserved for Theodotus, at the end of the second century, and it immediately received its punishment.

Victor excommunicated Theodotus; but he could not prevent him from drawing others away from the truth. A party gathered around him, and as heretics even thought it necessary to keep to the government of bishops, the followers of Theodotus persuaded a person named Natalius, who had been a sufferer in some persecution, to adopt their doctrines, and to take the office of a bishop amongst them; and they provided him with a monthly salary of 120 denarii, or about three pounds five shillings and sixpence of our money. The party of Theodotus never appears to have had much influence in the Church. He himself was excommunicated by Victor. Natalius lived to renounce his errors, and was readmitted to communion. Soon after the condemnation of Theodotus, the zeal and decision of Victor were shown in a much more doubtful case, and in a way which excited universal attention and great controversy. The dispute respecting the time at which Easter should be kept had never been settled since the days when Polycarp and Anicetus discussed the question at Rome. But Victor, unlike his predecessor, could not be satisfied to allow it to remain undecided. His strong will, as it would seem, could not brook opposition, and he endeavoured to persuade all other Christian Churches to unite in excluding the Churches of Asia Minor from communion with them. But he found none to join entirely with him. Councils were held by various bishops in various places; Polycrates, Bishop of Ephesus, especially, supported the custom of the Churches of Asia; while Jerusalem, Antioch, and Alexandria, sided with Victor. But even those who agreed in opinion with the Bishop of Rome, did not consider the question of sufficient importance to demand a breach of Christian unity.

Victor, on that one point stood alone, yet he was not the less resolved upon putting his determination into practice. The Christians who came from Asia Minor to Rome, and wished to be partakers of the highest privilege of the Church, found themselves excluded. Several bishops remonstrated with Victor upon the violence of his conduct; and their earnest appeals appear at length to have been received in a right spirit; for although we are not informed by any contemporary writer whether Victor persisted in his excommunication, yet we know that many Churches in Asia afterwards adhered to the Jewish mode of reckoning Easter, and were not on that account deprived of Christian communion.

CHAPTER XXII.

MARTYRDOM OF ST. IRENÆUS. B.C. 208.

AMONGST the bishops who stood forth boldly to condemn the conduct of Victor in the Easter controversy, the most distinguished was Irenæus, Bishop of Lyons. He was not then for the first time brought into public notice. Many years before, when during a time of persecution, the Christians of Lyons interested themselves anxiously in the teaching of Montanus, Irenæus, then only a priest, was the person chosen to be the bearer of the letter written upon the subject to the Church of Rome. A Greek by descent, though born at Smyrna, he had been contemporary with St. Polycarp, and is said to have learnt from the lips of Papias many anecdotes of the Apostles and their first followers. He also states himself, that he was intimate with another contemporary of the Apostles, but the name of the individual alluded to has not been preserved. It is supposed that Irenæus accompanied St. Polycarp on his visit to Rome during the bishopric of Anicetus, and that he after-

18*

wards settled at Lyons; there his learning and piety must have recommended him to the favourable notice of his brethren, and caused him to be appointed to be the bearer of their letter. His errand probably saved his life, for he was not a person likely to be overlooked in a time of persecution, and it also gave him an opportunity of employing his talents in the way best suited to him. Irenæus was destined during his whole life to be a distinguished opposer of heresy, and on his arrival at Rome, his attention was drawn to the lax state of Christian doctrine prevailing in other instances besides that of the Montanist teaching. Marcion and Valentinus, the two noted heretics, had then for some time exercised a most evil influence in the city, and appear to have been but slightly condemned by Eleutherus the bishop. Marcion was probably dead at the time when Irenæus visited Rome, but his place was filled by Florinus, a priest, who had once been a companion of Irenæus under the instructions of St. Polycarp, and had at that time been particularly noted by him for his soft and delicate manners. It must have been a cause of great grief for a man so earnest as Irenæus, to find this departure from the true faith in one who had been blessed with such advantages. He at once published a book against the erroneous doctrines of Florinus, and he was afterwards induced to undertake a still further exposure of the absurd fancies of the heretics, and the abominable wickedness of their lives. The greater number of the false opinions of those days have long since died away, and the writings of Irenæus are chiefly interesting to the learned; but there are some facts mentioned by him which must attract the attention of all. He tells us that a great variety of extraordinary gifts and powers were exercised in the Church in his time, that the dead were raised by fasting and prayer, that devils were cast out, and those rescued from them converted to the faith; that the sick were recovered by imposition of hands, that several of the Christians had revelations imparted to them and prophesied, and that all kinds of miracles were wrought "in the name of Jesus Christ, who suffered under Pontius Pilate."

Several historical facts are also confirmed by the testimony of Irenæus. In his third book against heresy, he enumerates the bishops of Rome as they descended by succession down to Eleutherus, who was bishop at the time when Irenæus wrote. In the same book he also asserts the authority of the Four Gospels; and in his fifth book and elsewhere, he testifies to the authority of St. John's Revelation, and First Epistle, and of the First Epistle of St. Peter. He speaks of the "Epistles of Paul," generally, as among the Scriptures, and mentions them all separately, and he also quotes from the Epistle of St. James, and cites the First and Second Epistles of St. John.* These facts, and others of a similar kind, respecting the Scriptures, derived from the witness of early writers, are of the greatest consequence to us, as proving that the first Christians accepted as sacred the same books as ourselves. Without this historical testimony, or, as it is sometimes called, tradition, our faith in the Bible would rest upon an unsafe foundation. We might wonder at it and admire it, but we could not be sure that the doctrines it teaches are those which from the earliest days have been held to be the teaching of inspiration. When, however, we find

* See Blunt on the Early Fathers.

that the books now considered sacred, are the same which were admitted as such by the immediate followers of our Lord and His Apostles, our doubt is at an end, and our business is not to criticise the Scriptures, but to receive and obey them.

Irenæus returned to Lyons to find Pothinus, the aged bishop, dead, and the see vacant. He was immediately elected to fill it, and in this position he laboured for many years, guiding his people in a time of great danger, both from external persecution and internal dissension, until the hasty zeal of Victor, with regard to the Eastern controversy, induced him to take a more open part in the discipline of the Universal Church.

A synod of the Churches of France under the jurisdiction of Irenæus, was convened by him on this occasion. Thirteen bishops, besides himself, were present, and after careful consideration, a letter was written in the name of the council, assuring the Bishop of Rome, that they agreed with him in his view of the controversy, so far as it regarded the time at which the Easter festival should be celebrated; but earnestly advising him to take heed how he excommunicated whole Churches for observing the customs derived from their forefathers; and reminding him of the different conduct of Anicetus, who, although he was widely opposed to St. Polycarp, on this point, yet evinced the greatest desire for peace, and openly showed his willingness to remain in communion with him. The intervention of Irenæus is believed to have had great weight in inducing Victor to adopt milder measures with those who differed from him, and thus to restore tranquillity to the Church; an object the more to be desired, as the days of outward peace were now drawing to a close, and all the energy and fortitude of the Christians were required to face the storm of persecution which was about to burst upon them.

Nine years had passed since Severus ascended the throne. During the greater part of that period the emperor was engaged in war, his thoughts must have been engrossed by military affairs, and the only circumstance which would lead us to suppose that he took any interest in religious matters, is the fact that whilst visiting Alexandria, he made particular and curious inquiries into the mysteries of the religion of the Egyptians. Christianity seems to have been regarded with indifference, if not with favour; but the principles of the Christians were such as must sooner or later have given offence to a heathen monarch. Soldiers were required to take part in the religious ceremonies; on this account many Christians refused to enter the army; and grown bold by the respite from persecution, they probably professed openly their aversion to the duties required of them. Such a declaration could not be overlooked by a prince whose chief business was war, and who was painfully conscious of the increasing weakness of his dominions, exposed as they were to the ravages of the barbarians on the borders. Severus issued an edict forbidding all persons to embrace the religion either of the Jews or the Christians. The words of the edict have not been preserved, but from various facts it is evident that death, with the loss of property, was the punishment of the disobedient. From one end of the empire to the other the edict was hailed with satisfaction by the enemies of the Christians, and once more open persecution began.

One of the most important victims was the saintly Irenæus. - Severus had himself, in former days, governed the province of Lyons, and Irenæus and his fellow-Christians must then have been brought under his notice; perhaps for that reason the sufferings inflicted at Lyons were peculiarly severe. Irenæus is said to have been first tortured and then beheaded, A.D. 202; but the accounts handed down to us can only be considered authentic in so far as they relate the actual fact of his martyrdom. The labours of his life were thus sealed by his death, and his witness to the belief and practice of the early Church comes to us with all the authority of one who died for the truths which he maintained. He himself seems to have felt how important was to be his testimony to all future ages; for he thus concludes one of his books. "I adjure thee, whoever thou art that shalt transcribe this book, by our Lord Jesus Christ, and by His glorious coming, wherein He shall judge the quick and the dead, that thou compare what thou transcribest; and diligently correct it by the copy from whence thou transcribest it, and that thou likewise transcribe this adjuration, and annex it to thy copy."

So the testimony of Irenæus has been transmitted to us, and at this very day, we, in like manner, are answerable if we presume to alter it or choose to neglect it.

CHAPTER XXIII.

ORIGEN HEAD OF THE CATECHETICAL SCHOOL AT ALEXANDRIA. B.C. 203.

In the midst of the troubles which now befell the Church of Christ, one Christian was to be found bold enough openly to defend his principles by word as well as by deed.

Tertullian was a Carthaginian by birth. He was the son of a heathen soldier, a centurion, and had been educated in all the accomplishments which the learning either of the Greeks or Romans could impart. Poetry, history, philosophy, mathematics, were alike familiar to him; he was acquainted with the rules of science, and the facts of natural history, and was also admirably skilled in the knowledge of the Roman laws. His conversion to Christianity took place about the latter end of the reign of Severus. He had observed the power which the Christian faith exercised over the minds and lives of those who embraced it; he had studied the prophecies, and knew the testimony which had been given to the truth of Christianity even by heathens. All these things had, through the power of God's grace, made him a Christian. Now, in the time of persecution, when the cruelty of the heathens was so great, that the days of Antichrist and the end of the world were supposed to be at hand, Tertullian wrote to the martyrs in prison, exhorted and comforted them, rebuked the heretics, and in every way openly took the part of the Church. Yet in his own heart there was a seed of evil which was ultimately to injure seriously the very cause to which he had devoted himself. He was a man of a stern disposition, severe to others as to himself, and his temper seems to have led him into the sin of spiritual pride. The command given by the Redeemer to flee from persecution was set aside, and Christians were told by him that such conduct was cowardly and unworthy, and this opinion betrayed the first leaning to the Montanist errors which he afterwards more fully embraced. Notwithstanding his boldness, Tertullian escaped from persecution with his life, and is said to have lived to an advanced age; and although he was after a time excommunicated for his Montanist opinions, yet he appears to have always had great influence in the Church. From the writings of Tertullian much information may be gained as to the manners and ceremonies of the early Christians, for he was a most severe censor of every thing which, according to his opinion, showed worldliness or a tendency to self-indulgence. He found fault with the Catholics because their fasts were not sufficiently rigid, ridiculed the frivolities of the times, just as a very strict person in these days might laugh at any absurd fashion, called those who differed from him, *psychici*, or animal persons, and his own friends, *spiritales*, or spiritual people; and in short, resembled many in the present age who set up a particular rule of life for themselves, and condemn every one who does not follow it; forgetting that our Blessed Lord gives us no such precise laws, and warns us that without charity, or love to our brethren, neither faith nor zeal will profit us.

The same temper of mind which sems to have led Tertullian into error, also marked, though in a less degree, the character of another leader of the

Christian Church at this period. A man of singular piety and great ability, but who, from the speculative turn of his mind, and the want of caution with which he expressed himself, gave rise to many fanciful opinions. We first hear of Origen in connection with the persecution under Severus, in the beginning of the third century. He was the child of Christian parents, and his father, Leonides, of Alexandria, had instructed him from infancy in the knowledge of the Holy Scriptures. Even in those early days, Origen showed the quickness of intellect, and spirit of inquiry, which were to render his name famous throughout all ages. The questions which he put to his father often contained mysteries too deep to be solved. Leonides reproved him for his curiosity, yet in his heart he looked upon his child with admiration; and it is said that at night, when the boy was sleeping, Leonides would stand by his bedside, and uncovering his son's breast, kiss it with reverence, as being honoured with the dwelling of the Divine Spirit. As he grew older, Origen pursued his studies under Clement of Alexandria; and he also placed himself for some time under the teaching of a Christian philosopher, named Ammonius, who had devoted much time and thought to the doctrines of the heathen philosopher Plato. This kind of learning, no doubt, encouraged the acute, criticising nature of Origen's intellect; but it may probably have strengthened his dependence upon his own powers, and so, in the end, tended to lead him in a measure astray.

When the persecution of Severus began, Leonides, the father of Origen, was thrown into prison. Origen earnestly desired to share the same danger. His belief in the glory of martyrdom was such, that he could not endure the idea even of his father being saved from it. Knowing the effect which would probably be produced on the mind of Leonides by the condition in which his family would be left after his death, Origen addressed a letter to him, in which he earnestly exhorted him to be firm. "Take heed, father," he wrote, "that you do not change your mind for our sakes." Leonides remained steadfast, and was beheaded, and his widow and seven sons were left to struggle with the world. Origen still longed to share his father's glory. His mother entreated him to spare himself, if not for his own sake, at least for hers; but her prayers were of no avail, and at length in order to save him, she had recourse to artifice, hiding his clothes, that he might have no means of appearing in public. After being thus shielded from persecution by his mother's care, Origen was supported by a rich matron of Alexandria, who was aware that he and his mother and brothers had been left in poverty in consequence of the death of Leonides and the seizure of the family property. Origen's benefactress had adopted as her son, Paul of Antioch, a ringleader of heretics in Alexandria; but Origen, though he was quite dependent on the lady's bounty, would take no notice of her favourite; and at length, having perfected his studies, resolved to live no longer in dependence, but to open a school himself. He was then a mere youth; yet so great were his talents, that many of the learned philosophers of Alexandria did not disdain to be present at his lectures; and at the age of eighteen, A.D. 203; he was chosen by Demetrius, the bishop, to succeed Clement of Alexandria as master of the Catechetical School, in which instruction was given to persons seeking for the knowledge of Christanity. Clement himself left Alexandria, and took refuge at Jerusalem, with his intimate friend Alexander, bishop of that city, who had been formerly Bishop of Cappadocia, and whose removal from one see to another is the first instance of a practice which has since been common. Persecution still prevailed, and Origen in no way shunned it. He visited the martyrs in their dungeons, attended them to the place of execution, openly embraced and saluted them, and was once in imminent danger of being stoned to death on this account. He was, indeed, repeatedly in peril of his life. On one occasion, having shaved his head, after the manner of the Egyptian priests, the people set him upon the steps of the temple of Serapis, commanding him to follow the custom of the priests, and give branches of palm trees to those who went up to perform their idolatrous rites. Origen took the branches and cried aloud, " Come hither, and take the branch, not of an idol temple, but of Christ." His courage was not likely to lessen the enmity of the heathen. It was soon unsafe for him to pass through the streets of Alexandria ; multitudes beset his house, and because he had a vast number of scholars, they brought a guard of soldiers with them, who hunted him from house to house. Still crowds flocked to hear him, and day by day Christians were strengthened against the coming trials of martyrdom by the exhortations of the young and eloquent teacher. Origen's private habits at this time must have told strongly upon the minds of those who witnessed them. His life was one of the strictest self-denial. His nights were chiefly passed in watchfulness and study ; he was inured to cold, nakedness, and poverty. Following literally the words of his Lord, he would allow himself neither two coats, nor two pair of shoes, nor any provision for the future. He offended many by refusing to receive their presents. His abstinence was so great as to endanger his life. It can be no marvel that such an example was admired and imitated. They who felt the difficulty of renouncing the least luxury, might well think that such an entire sacrifice of comfort was an evidence of every Christian virtue, whilst others would deem it a wise preparation for the far greater trial which was likely at any moment to overtake the professed follower of Christ.

Many, strange and interesting, are the stories of the martyrs who suffered at that time. If we see reason to think that some of them may have been coloured by superstition, yet the evidence for them is so strong, that it would be presumption to reject them as entirely false. Several of Origen's scholars were to be found amongst the victims of the emperor's cruelty ; and women, as usual, distinguished themselves for their constancy. Potamiæna, a young woman remarkable for beauty, purity of mind, and firmness in the Christian faith, is especially mentioned as having suffered the most grievous torments. Aquila, the judge, caused her to be scourged very severely, and threatened to deliver her up to the insults of the mob ; but she remained unmoved, and was condemned to be burnt, together with her mother, Marcella. A soldier named Basilides, presided at her execution. Her gentleness and innocence touched his heart ; he pitied her, treated her courteously, and as much as possible protected her from the insolence of the people. Potamiæna acknowledged his kindness gratefully, and promised that after her departure she would entreat the Lord for him. Scalding pitch was poured on her whole body; she bore the agony with wonderful patience; and the fire afterwards relieved her from her torments. Some time after, Basilides, being required by his fellow-soldiers to take a profane oath, refused, confessing himself to be a Christian. He was at first disbelieved, but as he persisted in his assertions, he was carried before a magistrate, who sent him to prison. The Christians visited him there, and questioned him as to the cause of his sudden change. Basilides declared that Potamiæna had appeared to him three days after her martyrdom, and informed him that she had performed her promise, and that he would shortly die. After this confession, he suffered martyrdom. Similar instances of calm resolution were everywhere to be found. At Carthage, twelve persons accused of being Christians were brought before Saturninus, the proconsul. Amongst them may particularly be mentioned a man named Speratus, and three women, Donata, Secunda, and Vestina. As they came into the presence of the judge, Saturninus tempted them with the hope of pardon, "You may expect," he said, "the forgiveness of the emperor, our master, if you return to your senses, and observe the ceremonies of our gods. Swear all of you by the Genius of the emperors, our masters, that you may enjoy the pleasures of life." "I know not the Genius of the emperors," answered Speratus, "I serve God, who is in Heaven, whom no man hath seen nor can see. I have never been guilty of any crime punishable by the public laws. If I buy any thing, I pay the duties to the collectors. I acknowledge my God and Saviour to be the supreme Governor of all nations. I have made no complaints against any person, and, therefore, no one ought to make any

19*

against me." The proconsul turned from him, and addressed his companions. " Do not ye," he said, " imitate the folly of this mad wretch, but rather fear our prince, and obey his commands." " We fear none but the Lord our God, who is in Heaven," was the reply; and the sentence was immediately given that they should be fettered and carried to prison.

A second trial was made on the following day. The proconsul, seated on his throne, caused the prisoners to be brought before him, and said to the women, " Honour our prince, and do sacrifice to the gods." Donata replied, " We honour Cæsar as Cæsar; but to God we offer prayers and worship." Vestina and Secunda also professed the same constant faith. They were separated from the men; to whom Saturninus then spoke. " Dost thou persevere in being a Christian?" he said to Speratus. " I do. Let all give ear, I am a Christian," answered Speratus; and the confession was made equally by the rest, who declared that they should die joyfully for the sake of Jesus Christ.

The proconsul inquired still more minutely into their faith. He asked them what books were those which they read and revered. " The four Gospels of our Lord and Saviour Jesus Christ," answered Speratus, " the Epistles of the Apostle St. Paul, and all the Scripture that is inspired of God." Saturninus seemed unwilling to condemn them. He offered them three days for reflection, but Speratus replied : " I am a Christian, and such are all those who are with me. We will never quit the faith of our Lord Jesus. Do therefore what you think fit."

Then the proconsul, seeing their resolution, pronounced sentence upon them in these terms :

"Speratus and the rest having acknowledged themselves to be Christians, and having refused to pay
due honour to the emperor, I command their heads
to be cut off." The reply burst from the lips of
the Christians: "We give thanks to God, who
honoureth us this day with being received as martyrs in heaven for confessing His Name."

They were carried to the place of punishment;
where they fell on their knees, and having again
given thanks to Jesus Christ, were beheaded.

But a case of more grievous suffering occurred
at Carthage. Vivia Perpetua, a young married lady
of rank, about twenty-two years of age, who was a
catechumen, was there seized, together with four
other catechumens, Revocatus and Felicitas, Saturninus and Secundulus. A sixth, named Satur,
afterwards, by an excess of zeal, voluntarily joined
himself to them. Perpetua's father was a heathen,
but deeply attached to his daughter, and the most
earnest entreaties were used by him to persuade
her to fall from the faith. Her constancy appeared to him to be an absurd obstinacy, and when
he saw that his efforts were vain, he became indignant, and treated her with great severity. For
a few days the catechumens were put under a
guard, but not imprisoned, and during this time
they found means to be baptized. Perpetua boldly
looked forward to the consequences of the confession she had made, and her most earnest prayers
were offered that she might be patient under bodily
pain. As the catechumens continued steadfast,
they were thrown into a dark prison, and this
punishment must have been very formidable to
Perpetua, who had been accustomed to all the
comforts and elegancies of refined life. Her thoughts
also, for a while, dwelt anxiously upon her only

child, a little infant; but two deacons of the Church purchased permission for the prisoners to refresh themselves for some hours in a more commodious place, and she then saw her child, and committed it tenderly to the care of her mother, who appears to have been a Christian. Still her mind was deeply oppressed by the consciousness of the misery she had brought upon her family; and it required much faith, and the constant recollection that she was suffering for the truth, to enable her to bear her position with calmness; but peace was at length granted her, and her prison then became a palace.

Some time after, Perpetua's father visited her in prison. He was overwhelmed with grief, a feeling probably increased by the recollection of the angry violence into which he had been betrayed at their last interview. "My daughter," he said, "have pity on my grey hairs; have pity on your father. If I was ever worthy of that name, if I myself have brought you up to this age; if I have preferred you to all your brethren, make me not a reproach to mankind. Respect your father and your aunt; have compassion on your son, lay aside your obstinacy, lest you destroy us all; for if you perish, we must be silent in disgrace." He then threw himself at her feet in tears, kissed her hands, and called her no longer his daughter, but the mistress of his fate.

Perpetua had but one answer to give to this appeal. The only comfort she could offer was to desire him to acquiesce in the Will of God.

The next day the prisoners were brought into the court, and examined in the presence of vast crowds. The unhappy father of Perpetua appeared there with his little grandson, and taking his daughter aside, he conjured her to have pity on her child. The procurator, who was to try her, joined in the entreaty, but in vain. Perpetua's father endeavoured then to drag her away, but the procurator interfered, and ordered him to be beaten, and the sight of the blows which her father received from a staff, must have been one of the greatest afflictions that Perpetua was called upon to endure.

When the trial was ended, the prisoners were condemned to be exposed to the wild beasts. They heard their sentence cheerfully, and were sent back to their cells. Perpetua demanded permission to have her child with her, but her father refused to give it up. One of the catechumens, Secundulus, died in prison. Another, Felicitas, underwent great suffering and privation, for a child was born to her only three days before her execution. When, in her weakness and pain, she uttered moans of anguish, one of her keepers said to her, " Do you complain of this ? what will you do when you are exposed to the beasts ? " Felicitas answered, " It is I that suffer now, but then there will be Another with me, who will suffer for me, because I shall suffer for His sake." Her little daughter was given in charge to a Christian woman, who nursed it as her own.

A report seems to have been spread abroad that the prisoners would free themselves by magical arts, and in consequence they were roughly treated. Perpetua, however, made application for greater indulgence, urging as a reason, that it would be for the honour of their keeper if they appeared in health when brought forward at the public spectacles. Her representations had the desired effect, and greater comforts were allowed. On the day before the shows, they ate their last meal in public, converting their repast as much as possible into an Agape, or love feast. Their relations, and indeed many other persons, were allowed to visit them, and the keeper of the prison must have looked upon them with deep sympathy, for by this time he was himself converted to the Christian faith. Perpetua and her companions talked to the people, warning them to flee from the wrath to come. They spoke of the happiness of their lot, and only smiled at the curiosity shown by those who came to see them. " Observe well our faces," exclaimed Satur, " that ye may know them at the Day of Judgment."

On the day appointed for their execution, they appeared before the spectators with joy in their countenances. Perpetua sang a hymn of rejoicing ; while some of her companions endeavoured to affect the people by the terrors of God's vengeance upon sinners. " Thou judgest us," they said to the procurator, " but God shall judge thee."

In compliance with the demands of the enraged multitude, they were scourged before being exposed to the savage animals.

Perpetua and Felicitas were then stripped, put into nets, and given over to be torn by a wild cow. But the indignity thus offered them touched the hearts of the spectators, and the assisting executioner drew them back, covered them with loose garments, and again delivered them over to death. Perpetua was first attacked ; falling backwards, she put herself into a reclining posture, then drew herself aside to arrange her dress and gather up her hair, that she might appear less disordered, and lifting herself up, gave her hand to Felicitas, who had been bruised by the animal's attack, and assisting her to rise, went with her to the gate of the amphitheatre. She was there received by Rusticus, a catechumen who attended her. Her first remark showed how wonderfully the prayer that she might be supported to endure bodily pain had been granted. "I wonder," she said, "when they will expose us to the cow." She had been, it seems, insensible to what had occurred, nor would she believe her own sufferings, until she saw the marks on her body and her clothes. Perpetua's faith being thus strengthened by this wonderful instance of Divine Mercy, she was anxious to strengthen the hearts of others, and calling for her brother, who was present at the spectacle, and for Rusticus, she said to them, "Continue firm in the faith; love one another; and be neither frightened nor offended at our sufferings."

The people, anxious to see the martyrs die, now demanded that they should be brought into the midst of the amphitheatre, where they were to be executed by gladiators. Some of the sufferers rose up, and, after having given one another the kiss of charity, wen tforward of their own accord. Others, without speaking or stirring, suffered themselves to be killed. Perpetua fell into the hands of an unskilful gladiator. He pierced her between the ribs, so as to give her much unnecessary pain. She cried out, and then guiding his trembling hand to her throat, received the last thrust, and fell asleep in Christ.

The facts of this narrative have every mark of truth. There can, indeed, be no doubt that at this season the power of God was wonderfully displayed, especially by the sudden conversion of several persons who voluntarily suffered death for the doctrine which before they detested. Origen bears ample testimony to this circumstance, and he is allowed by all persons to have been a man of unquestionable veracity. So far, however, were the Christians from thrusting themselves forward as martyrs, that a practice arose about this period of purchasing safety by the payment of a sum of money. Whole Churches or communities of Christians appear to have submitted to a kind of yearly tribute, on the payment of which they were freed from persecution. Wealth was the great object of rapacious governors, and if they could obtain it by taxing the Christians, they were often willing to spare their lives. It does not follow that those who paid the tax were cowards, shrinking from martyrdom. They made an open profession of their faith, and if the government chose to inflict a milder punishment than usual, there was no command to lead them to seek for death, but rather a caution, which would induce them, if possible, to avoid it.

CHAPTER XXIV.

ORIGEN ORDAINED PRESBYTER AT CÆSAREA.
A.D. 230.

ORIGEN appears to have resided at Alexandria all the time that the persecution lasted. Whether the Emperor Severus took an active part in exciting his subjects to cruelty is unknown; but when he departed with his two sons, Caracalla and Geta, to conquer Britain, we hear less of the sufferings of the Christians; and after his death, which happened at York, about eight years after the persecution first broke out, a new state of things seemed A.D. 211. likely to arise. As has been stated before, Caracalla, the successor of Severus, had been brought up by a Christian nurse, and although he afterwards proved a monster of wickedness, yet there was something in the early association which seems to have touched his better feelings.   It is said, that when he was only seven years old, he felt so strongly the fact of one of his playfellows having been beaten because he was a Christian, that he could not, for some time after, endure the presence of his own father, or the father of the boy.   Enmity against Severus was, however, evinced by Caracalla on many other occasions; and the favour shown to the Christians when he ascended the throne may have been caused quite as much by a love of opposition to the line of conduct adopted by the late Emperor, as by any other motive.   Certain it is, that nothing like real Christian principle ever appears to have influenced the conduct of Caracalla.

But, in the mercy of God's Providence, the Church was benefited, notwithstanding the sins of the heathen Emperors.   Caracalla began his reign by allowing all exiles to return to their homes; and this edict, though not specially intended for the relief of the Christians, must have been of great service to them.   Other circumstances also show that at this time they were more free. Clement of Alexandria was able to visit his Christian brethren at Antioch; whilst Origen undertook a journey to Rome, being very desirous to see a place so venerable for its antiquity, and so much renowned.   Zephyrinus the successor of Victor, was then Bishop of Rome.   He had made great efforts for the suppression of heresy, and so increased the respect felt for the Roman Church; but Origen did not long remain with him; and having, as we may suppose, satisfied the curiosity which was his strong characteristic, he returned to

20

Alexandria, where he gave himself up to the close study of the Holy Scriptures, and set himself to learn the Hebrew language, with the assistance of the Jewish patriarch who resided in the city. He still continued his instructions in the Catechetical school; but finding his scholars increase so fast as to leave scarcely any leisure for private study, he chose Heraclas, who had once been his pupil, to assist him in teaching the younger catechumens. The others he instructed himself in geometry, arithmetic, and other necessary knowledge; after which he led them through a course of philosophy, explaining the writings of ancient authors, and sometimes writing comments upon them. Great numbers of heretics were amongst his hearers; amongst the rest, a man of rank and fortune, named Ambrosius, who had been led away by some of the errors of the Gnostics, but under the teaching of Origen returned to the true faith. He was a man of considerable talent, and, like his master, earnest in discovering the true meaning of the Scriptures. Much of his time seems to have been spent with Origen; and their conversation, when together, continually turned upon this subject; whilst walking, or at meals, or in hours of recreation, it was the one topic brought forward; and Origen himself tells us, that no supper-time was allowed to pass without discourses to the same purpose. A great part of the night was spent by Ambrosius and his master in study; and both by night and day, when prayer ended reading began, and when reading ended prayer began. Ambrosius, indeed, was a truly earnest-minded good man, and although he possessed riches and earthly rank, did not disdain to take upon himself the office of a deacon in the Church, and to undergo great hardships and sufferings for the sake of the faith. It has been objected against him that when he died he left no legacy to his old and valued friend Origen ; but probably Ambrosius knew the self-denying habits of Origen well enough to feel that his riches would be of no value to him.

The labours of Origen at this period were varied by a journey to Arabia, which he made at the request of an Arabian prince, who desired to be instructed in the Christian religion. This appears to have been the same country which had been visited by Pantænus about twenty years before. He returned to Alexandria, but did not long remain there in peace, for about this time Caracalla, being extremely. enraged with the people of Alexandria, in consequence of some reflections they had made upon his cruelty, arrived in person at the city, and presided at an extensive massacre of the citizens. Origen, and probably many of his Christian hearers, sought refuge in flight. Palestine was the most interesting country which could be visited, and Origen went thither. The Bishop of Cæsarea, with whom he became acquainted, struck with his learning and knowledge of the Scriptures, allowed him, although only a layman, to expound the sacred writings publicly in the Church ; but the ecclesiastical rules were strict in those early days, and when the tidings of this permission reached Demetrius, Bishop of Alexandria, he sent a remonstrance to the Bishop of Cæsarea, saying, that such a thing had never before been heard of in the Christian Church. This, however, was not strictly the case; instances of a similar kind had been known, and they were brought forward by the Bishop of Cæsarea, and also by Alexander of Jerusalem, the friend of Clemens

Alexandrinus. Demetrius, however, was not satisfied. He wrote to Origen, ordering him to return, and sent deacons to urge him to comply; and Origen, in obedience to the command of his bishop, went back to Alexandria. Great changes in the government of the empire were now approaching. The monster Caracalla was murdered, after a reign of six years; and Macrinus, who succeeded him, met the same fate about fourteen months afterwards. The empire was then given to Elagabalus, a young man who had been priest of the sun at Emessa, in Phœnicia.

A.D. 218.

The wickedness of this Emperor was as great as that of Caracalla, and his senseless folly could scarcely be surpassed. Yet the Christians were enabled to remain undisturbed. Elagabalus was bent upon establishing everywhere the worship of the sun, and with that view ordered all the symbols of superstition to be suppressed; but the Christians had long been accustomed to perform their acts of worship in secret, and one of the charges often brought against them was, that they had no temples nor altars. It was, therefore, easy for them to evade the Emperor's command; and whilst the heathen idols were destroyed, Christianity was enabled to make its way in secret. On one occasion, indeed, it was publicly noticed and honoured, for Mammæa, the aunt of Elagabalus, who had probably become acquainted with its doctrines during her long residence in Syria, sent for Origen, and requested him to meet her at Antioch, and discourse with her on matters of religion. Origen complied with the invitation, but there is no reason to believe that Mammæa became a Christian; yet both heathen and Christian writers, though they accuse her of avarice, agree in giving her credit for being really impressed with feelings of religion.

Elagabalus reigned only three years and nine months, and was then murdered. His cousin, Alexander Severus, the son of Mammæa, succeeded him. Like his mother, Alexander in a certain way favoured the Christians; but his religious principles must have been very vague. He had a domestic chapel, in which every morning he worshipped those deceased princes whose characters were most esteemed. Their statues were placed amongst those of the gods, and into this assembly he introduced also the statues of Abraham and of our Blessed Lord.

Many instances are recorded of the consideration shown to Christians by Alexander Severus. A certain piece of land was claimed by the keeper of a tavern: it had been without an owner for some time, and the Christians, who apparently at this time were so tolerated as to be allowed buildings set apart for public worship, had occupied it for that purpose. When the case was referred to the Emperor, he replied that it was fitter that God should be served there in any manner, than that it should be used as a tavern; and the building was given up to the Christians. The Christian sentence, " Do as you would be done by," was considered by Alexander so important, that whenever he was called upon to punish any person, he obliged a crier to repeat it; and he also caused it to be written on the walls of his palace, and on the public buildings. The names of governors of provinces, or other magistrates, were ordered by him to be proposed in public before their appointment, so that the people might be able, if necessary, to bring forward any accusation against them; and the reason given was, that it would be a shame not to do that with respect to governors, who were

20*

entrusted with men's properties and lives, which was done by Jews and Christians when they published the names of those whom they meant to ordain priests; a speech which shows how careful the Christians were in the choice of their pastors.

Origen spent this time of comparative peace in writing commentaries on the Holy Scriptures, at the entreaty of his friend Ambrosius, who not only urged him to the task, but furnished him with the means of carrying it on. Origen's daily maintenance was provided, and Ambrosius also allowed him seven notaries, sometimes even more. These notaries were very common, both amongst the Greeks and the Romans. They made use of what we now call shorthand, by which they were enabled to signify by signs, not only words, but entire sentences. In the primitive Church they were frequently employed to write the acts of the martyrs, for which purpose they frequented the prisons, were present at all trials and examinations, and followed the martyrs to the place of execution, there to mark and note down their sayings and sufferings. The origin of this institution is assigned to the time of Clement of Rome, or, as he is also called, Clemens Romanus; and it accounts for the long accounts of the answers and speeches of the martyrs which have been handed down to us. Besides these notaries, young women were employed to transcribe what the notaries had written in shorthand.

The diligence of Origen in these studies is described as almost incredible; but his work was interrupted by the claims of more public business; for he was summoned to Athens, to assist in putting a stop to some heresies which were gaining ground there. From thence he proceeded to Palestine, and at Cæsarea he was ordained priest by Theoctistus, Bishop of Cæsarea, assisted by Alexander, Bishop of Jerusalem, A.D. 230.

Origen was then forty-five years of age; his mind was in its highest vigour, and no doubt it was thought that, by being regularly ordained, his influence for good would be increased. But Demetrius, Bishop of Alexandria, who had long been jealous of his influence, expressed great indignation when he heard what had been done; considering it an affront to his jurisdiction, and a contempt of his authority, that Origen should thus have obtained his ordination from distant sources. He complained openly and violently, brought forward every reason that he could discover against the admission of Origen to his new office, and at length excited so strong a feeling of opposition, that a decree was obtained from two synods banishing Origen from Alexandria, and degrading him from the priesthood. Notwithstanding this condemnation, Origen still retained his holy office, publicly preached in the Church, and was received with honour by all wise and moderate persons. But Alexandria was no longer a place which he could make his residence, and having given up his Catechetical school to Heraclas, his colleague, he took up his abode at Cæsarea, in Palestine, where he opened a school, similar to that over which he had presided at Alexandria. Here he had many distinguished pupils, amongst others Gregory, surnamed Thaumaturgus, or the wonder worker, from the numerous miracles which he is said to have performed. Origen was also intimately acquainted with Fermilian, afterwards Bishop of Cæsarea, in Cappadocia, who was so much attached to him, and so greatly admired his talents, that he prevailed upon Origen to visit him from time to time in Cappadocia, in order that by his preaching he might edify the Churches in that province; whilst Fermilian himself would sometimes go to Palestine, and live for a time with Origen, in order to improve by his society and conversation. Firmilian was a person of great reputation, and held correspondence with most of the eminent men of those times, and few matters of importance were transacted without him.

There were, at this time, several Churches in Cappadocia, and their affairs were so well regulated, that the bishops held annual meetings among themselves to ensure uniformity in their proceedings. Lay councils, attended by deputies from different provinces, were also occasionally held in Cappadocia. One of them was convened about this period at Iconium. Firmilian was present, with fifty bishops from Phrygia, Galatia, Cilicia and Cappadocia. Its object was to debate whether baptism administered by Montanists was valid. The council of Iconium decided that it was not. We shall find this question as to the validity of baptism, when administered by persons not strictly members of the Catholic Church, arising again, and causing great divisions. On the present occasion, there seems to have been a very strong feeling against the Montanists, who were becoming more and more separated from the Church.

But persecution was near at hand, to withdraw the attention of the Christians from the consideration of questions of doctrine to those of personal safety. Alexander Severus, after reigning about thirteen years, was murdered by Maximin, A.D. 235. a gigantic Thracian. Maximin was a complete barbarian, but he was elected Emperor by the army ; and the Christians, who no doubt were attached to Alexander's government, from the security which they had enjoyed under it, were soon the objects of his wrath. A persecution was begun, which was felt all the more terribly after such a season of repose. Old superstitions also were brought forward to increase the hatred of the heathen. Some tremendous earthquakes, which swallowed up whole cities, took place in Cappadocia, and the calamity was viewed by the people as a special visitation from heaven on account of the progress of Christianity. Yet even Cappadocia was a safer residence than Palestine, and Origen left Cæsarea, and took the opportunity of visiting his friend Firmilian. He stayed in Cappadocia two years, being sheltered in the house of a lady named Juliana, who courteously entertained him ; and here he carried on the greatest literary task which he had ever undertaken, Juliana furnishing him with many valuable books necessary for his labours. This work was a new and corrected edition of that Greek translation of the Old Testament which is known by the name of the Septuagint. The translation had been made in obedience to the order of Ptolemy Philadelphus, king of Egypt, more than two centuries before the birth of Christ, by persons skilled both in Hebrew and Greek. It was used as a kind of authorised version by the Hellenistic or Greek Jews, but the copies were by this time corrupted, and full of variations. There were also three other celebrated Greek translations of the Scriptures ; one made in the reign of Hadrian, another in that of Commodus, and a third about the beginning of the third century. The original copy of this latter translation was the property of Juliana by inheritance, and she now gave it into the hands of Origen, who published the different versions in four separate columns, adding the text of the original Hebrew, both in Hebrew and Greek letters. This work was called the Hexapla. Two other versions of the Old Testament were afterwards added, and the whole was then termed the Octapla. This work must have been a great assistance to the proper understanding of difficult passages in Scripture. A particular mark was put against any passage which had been inserted in the Septuagint, but was not to be found in the Hebrew; and where anything was wanting in the Septuagint which yet was in the Hebrew, the words were inserted with an asterisk before them, to distinguish them from the rest of the translation. The difficult passages which had been rendered according to the same meaning by all the translators, were also signified by a special mark. Twenty-eight years, it is said, were spent by Origen in this great and valuable work, which, however, has unfortunately been lost. The art of printing being unknown, it would have been a task of enormous labour to make copies, and this probably prevented persons from engaging in such an undertaking, though some part of the Septuagint, thus corrected, was afterwards taken out and published.

The labours of Origen did not render him unmindful of the trials of his fellow-Christians, and especially of his own friends. He wrote, at this time, a book about martyrdom, which he jointly dedicated to a presbyter of Carthage and to his dear friend Ambrosius, who suffered greatly under the persecution of Maximin, and made a glorious confession of his Christian faith.

The persecution was, however, destined to be of comparatively short duration. Maximin was killed, after a reign of about three years. Four Emperors succeeded him in the course of six years. The first two, whose rule lasted but a few months, were so occupied in maintaining their own positions, that they could not interfere with questions of religion; whilst Gordian, and Philip the Arabian, who followed, were decidedly favourable to Christianity.

A.D. 243. Philip, indeed, is said by some to have been actually a Christian; but there seems no certain foundation for the assertion. He may have been acquainted with the doctrines of Christianity, and at some period of his life have been inclined to adopt it; and Origen is stated to have written a letter to him, and to his wife or mother Severa, but this is no proof of the Emperor's conversion, and all his public acts, after he ascended the throne, showed that he was attached to heathenism, though he did not choose to persecute Christianity. This period of repose must have been very favourable to the works undertaken by Origen. We hear, indeed, of a visit which he made to his friend Ambrosius, who, with his wife and children, was at that time living in Nicomedia; and he was also called into Arabia, to assist at a council summoned to denounce a heresy which had sprung up under the sanction of a bishop, named Beryllus, but his time seems to have been fully occupied in writing upon various subjects. Amongst other works, he undertook a most valuable defence of Christianity, and indeed of religion in general, against the attacks of Celsus, a heathen philosopher, and a man of much talent and wit; and he produced also a commentary on the twelve minor prophets, and upon the Gospel of St. Matthew.

He preached to his people every day, though it was not till he was sixty years of age that he permitted his discourses to be taken down by shorthand writers. Origen's exertions appear, indeed, to have been almost too great for human strength. It has been reported that he wrote six thousand volumes; the number being supposed to include epistles and single homilies. Amongst such a mass of writings it is perhaps not surprising to find some unsound opinions. There is, in fact, no doubt that Origen was a man of great eagerness and impulse; fond of speculating upon mysteries, and especially upon the condition of the soul after death, and who often expressed himself incautiously, and propounded ideas privately, which he had no intention of making public. He himself states this in a letter which he wrote to Fabian, Bishop of Rome, blaming Ambrosius for publishing things which he had never meant should go beyond the hands of his dearest friends. Many of his works have also been corrupted by heretics. This was the case even in his lifetime. A charge of blasphemy, he states, had been brought against him,— for something he was said to have written—but of which he was quite innocent, and he adds, that it was not to be wondered at if his doctrine was adulterated, since even the great St. Paul could not escape such misrepresentation. He was, as he himself tells us, careless of his manuscripts, and he narrates a story of an eminent heretic, who, having taken notes of a controversy which they had carried on, afterwards cut out and inserted whatever he pleased, changing the argument into something quite unlike the truth, and then carrying it about and glorying in it. Origen's friends, shocked at the publication, applied to him for an authentic copy of the discussion ; but it had been thrown aside, and was with great difficulty found, and sent to them without being revised. The same thing, it appears, had happened on other occasions, and if this was the case during Origen's lifetime, it is not to be wondered at that the practice should have continued after his death, when heretical sects had sprung up, bearing his name, and professing to obtain support for their false doctrines from certain doubtful passages in his works.

CHAPTER XXV.

GREGORY THAUMATURGUS BECOMES A PUPIL OF ORIGEN. A.D. 235.

DURING the season of peace, which lasted from the reign of Alexander Severus to that of Philip the Arabian, Origen's friend and pupil Gregory Thaumaturgus was fast rising into notice. Gregory, who was brought up from childhood as a heathen, had originally been intended for a lawyer. His father, a man of rank and fortune at Neocæsarea, the capital of Cappadocia, died when he was about fourteen ; but his mother placed him and his brother Athenodorus under very good masters, who taught Gregory the art of speaking and writing well, and encouraged him in the study of the Roman law. This course of instruction gave his mind a bent in the direction desired by his friends, and his family circumstances tended to the same end. His sister had married a famous lawyer, who was called to occupy a distinguished position in Palestine, that of assistant in the government of the province and it was in consequence of this connection that Gregory first visited Palestine.   His brother-in-law having first gone thither to settle himself in his new position, sent for his wife and her attendants, and begged Gregory to accompany them.   The journey could be made easily, for public carriages had been sent for the conveyance of the party, and Gregory felt that the visit might be advantageous, as there was a celebrated university for the profession of the Roman law at Berytus, in Phœnicia, and he was aware that he might greatly improve himself by studying there.   His friends, moreover, persuaded him, his sister greatly desired his company, and yielding to all these inducements, Gregory decided upon the step, which, through the Mercy of God, was to bring him within reach of Origen's instruction.   The result of that instruction has already been stated.   Gregory was converted, together with his brother Athenodorus, who like himself, had been blessed by the teaching of Origen. Much study was, however, required before Gregory could be prepared to instruct others, and when he left Origen and returned to Neocæsarea, Origen wrote him a letter commending his talents, which were likely to render him an eminent lawyer among the Romans, or a great philosopher among the Greeks ; but urging him, at the same time, to turn them to his own improvement in the knowledge of the Scriptures, and the practice of holiness.   He exhorted Gregory to read the Bible with the most profound attention ; not rashly to form his own opinions upon religious subjects, nor to speak of them without previous thought ; he warned him that he must not only *seek* but *knock*, he must pray not only with faith but fervency ; it being vain to think that the door would be opened when prayer was not sent beforehand to unlock it.   In compliance with this advice, Gregory withdrew from the applause and admiration of the friends who crowded around him, begging him at once to commence the task of instructing publicly, and retiring to a solitary place, gave himself up to the contemplation of the works of God, exhibited both in the human mind and the wonders of creation.

Neocæsarea was a large and populous city, but it was overrun with superstition and idolatry. Christianity seemed scarcely as yet to have found an entrance there.   But it had excited the attention and pity of Phædimus, the bishop of a neighbouring province, who earnestly desired to find some person equal to the task of converting the heathen inhabitants.   The fame of Gregory had reached him ; no one else seemed so fit for the work, but when Phædimus would have sent for the young philosopher, and ordained him, Gregory, aware of his wish, and afraid of the charge proposed to him, carefully hid himself.   Phædimus made many attempts to discover his place of concealment, but in vain ; and at length, being as much resolved that Gregory should be ordained as Gregory was to decline the important office, he one day set himself to very earnest prayer, and considering that Gregory, as well as himself, was then present before the Almighty, he addressed a discourse to him, in which he declared that he consecrated him to God's service, and made him Bishop of Neocæsarea.   We are not informed how it was that Gregory was made acquainted with what had been done, but when the information reached him, he considered this singular ordination as a Divine call, and felt himself obliged to acquiesce in it.   He was afterwards, with the usual ceremonies, consecrated to his sacred office.

Gregory had entered upon a very difficult work. The city and its neighbourhood was not only given up to idolatry, but heresies had spread over the adjoining countries; and he himself, though well skilled in the learning of this world, was not yet deeply acquainted with the mysteries of Christianity.   In order to remedy this deficiency, he is said to have prayed very earnestly for enlightenment from heaven, and his petitions were so mercifully answered, that he soon afterwards was enabled to write a clear exposition of those points of faith which before had perplexed him.   This Creed of St Gregory, as it is called, is very important, as showing how defined was the faith of orthodox Christians in those early days.   The words in which it is expressed resemble, in many respects, those of the Nicene Creed.

After this Gregory set himself diligently to his task of converting the heathen, an undertaking greatly assisted by the miraculous powers which appear to have been bestowed upon him, even before he was ordained to his bishopric.   The account of these miracles has doubtless been much exaggerated; but the evidence for them is too clear to allow of their being entirely set aside.   Some relate to the expulsion of demons, a power which no doubt existed commonly in the third century, and with regard to which the testimony of the early Fathers is unanimous.   Minutius Felix, a lawyer converted to the truth in this century, who wrote a Defence of Christianity in the form of a dialogue between a heathen and a Christian, thus speaks upon the subject.   " Being adjured by the living God, they (the demons) tremble and remain wretched and reluctant in the bodies of men.   They either leap out immediately, or vanish by degrees, as the faith of the patient or the grace of the person administering relief may be strong or weak."

Even before Gregory's arrival at Neocæsarea, the heathen populace had heard of his astounding powers, and hastened out to meet him. But he, we are told, was perfectly regardless of the applause of the multitude, and passed through the crowds without looking either to the one side or the other. His friends, who had accompanied him from the wilderness, were very anxious as to his entertainment, and the provision for his necessities; but Gregory reproved them, asking whether they thought themselves banished from the Divine protection, whether God's Providence was not the best and safest refuge and habitation, and warning them that whatever became of their bodies, it was infinitely more important to look after their souls, which were, by the virtues of a good life, to be trimmed and prepared, furnished and built up, for Heaven.

Persons, however, were not wanting who were ready to welcome so distinguished a guest. Amongst them Musonius, a man of the greatest rank and wealth in the city, was the first to entreat that the bishop would honour his house with his presence, and take up his abode there. This proposal being accepted, the other citizens who had made offers of hospitality were dismissed with courtesy and thanks. That very day, it is said, Gregory began to preach, and before night had converted many.

The following morning the doors of the house were crowded; persons of all ranks and ages flocking to the bishop, begging him to assist them in their distresses, and cure their maladies. Gregory granted their requests, being careful, whilst he healed them of their diseases, to instruct them in the truths which alone could show them the way for

21*

the healing of their souls. The converts were numerous, and having gathered a congregation, Gregory's next care was to erect a church. As contributions were cheerfully given, the building was soon begun and finished; and it is said to have stood unshaken, when almost the whole city was afterwards destroyed by an earthquake.

Amongst the numerous wonders related of Gregory Thaumaturgus, one instance of his powers has been transmitted to us, as having tended greatly to the conversion of the people. Soon after his acceptance of the office of Bishop of Neocæsarea, we are told that a public festival was held in honour of one of the gods of the country. The inhabitants of the surrounding districts poured into the city in vast numbers. The theatre, which was the great place of entertainment, was quickly filled, and the crowd was so great, and the noise so confusing, that the shows could not begin. A cry rose from the people, "Jupiter, we beseech thee, make us room." Gregory being told of this, sent them a message, that their prayer would quickly be granted, and that greater room than they desired would quickly be made. Immediately a terrible plague broke out. It spread like a flame; persons were taken ill and died in a few moments. The temples, whither many fled in hopes of cure, were filled with dead bodies; the fountains and ditches, to which the sufferers repaired to quench their burning thirst, were stopped up by the multitudes of those who fell into them; whilst some of their own accord fled to the tombs, and seated themselves amongst them, thus securing a sepulchre, which they were not likely to obtain from the good offices of the living. The cause of this great calamity was at length understood. It was the punishment of their sinful prayer to a false god; and when this was believed, the people applied to Gregory, whose power they believed to be divine, entreating that he would stop the pestilence. The prayers and faith of the bishop prevailed; the plague abated, and the people deserting their temples, oracles, and sacrifices, became Christians.

It is easy for us at this distance of time to pronounce such stories false; but we must remember that it is much more in accordance with reason to accept than to reject the well authenticated miracles of those early days; because, by accepting them, we have a simple explanation of a fact which is undeniable, namely, that Christianity, although preached at first by persons for the most part without worldly rank or wealth, and often without learning, overthrew the whole religious system of the vast Roman empire. If there were no miracles, and no Divine interposition, the progress of Christianity must be utterly unaccountable. Belief in the early miracles is also strictly in accordance with reason, because they stand upon the same evidence which we accept for other historical facts. This does not mean that all the stories which are related are necessarily true; but only that there are some for which the testimony is so great, that if we reject them, we must also reject the testimony to the existence of the individuals most famous in the history even of our own country. There may be exaggerations, mistakes, inconsistencies, but the fact that there were miracles is unquestionable; just as there can be no doubt as to the chief events in the reigns of our English monarchs, although the greatest difference of opinion may exist as to certain incidents connected with them. These observations have been made especially with reference to Gregory Thaumaturgus, because there has unquestionably been much exaggeration in the report of his miracles, and when persons are told they must accept them all, they are apt to say it is impossible, and so reject them entirely. But without entering into the evidence in detail, or pretending to decide how much or how little of these wonderful stories we are to believe, it may be sufficient for us to know that they are reported by persons of undoubted credit, and especially St. Basil and St. Gregory Nyssen, two of the early Fathers, who lived within less than a hundred years after Gregory Thaumaturgus, and derived much of their information from their grandmother, Macrina, herself a pupil and disciple of Gregory. St. Basil states that the Gentiles were accustomed to call Gregory a second Moses, because of his astonishing powers, and adds, that his memory was still as fresh among the people of that country, and was held in such universal admiration, that no time would be able to blot it out. The general belief of all ages in the miraculous powers of the Bishop of Neocæsarea, is indeed undoubted, and the title of Thaumaturgus, or wonder worker, is constantly ascribed to him in the writings of the Church. In his private character Gregory was worthy of as much reverence as in his more public capacity. St. Basil tells us that he was a man of an apostolic temper, living in the strictest obedience to the precepts of the Gospel. In all his devotions he showed the greatest reverence, his language was cautiously guarded, no word of anger or bitterness was allowed to proceed out of his mouth. Never would he approach the altar till first reconciled to his brother; slander and reproach cast upon others were an abomination to him, and envy and pride were unknown to him.

Such a man, so holy and so zealous, must have been well prepared for any trial, and it pleased God, in the ordering of His Providence, to bring the faith of Gregory, together with that of Origen, and many other faithful servants of Christ, who were living at the same time, to the test of one of the severest persecutions which had yet befallen the Christian Church.

CHAPTER XXVI.

THE DECIAN PERSECUTION.   A. D. 249.

PHILIP THE ARABIAN was put to death by the contrivance of Decius, one of his guards, who afterwards took possession of the throne. Early in the following year, A. D. 249, an edict was issued by which the Christians were ordered to sacrifice to the heathen gods. The motives of this decree have not been clearly ascertained, but it was given at a time when many of the believers in Christ were but ill prepared to meet persecution. Peace and prosperity had done their usual work in weakening strength of principle and power of endurance. The difference between heathens and Christians in the performance of moral and religious duties was no longer strongly marked. Curious speculations destroyed the simplicity and unity of the faith; the manners even of the clergy, as we are informed by a bishop and martyr who lived in those days, was becoming gradually corrupt; a worldly spirit was very apparent. Marriages were formed with heathens, and even bishops were seen to neglect their flocks, and employ themselves in the most ordinary occupations, from a desire to obtain money.

Origen bears witness to the same melancholy facts. He complains of the ambition of the clergy, and the wrong steps which they took to obtain preferments, and when speaking of the behaviour of the people during divine service, he says : " Several come to church only on solemn festivals, and then not so much for instruction as diversion. Some go out again as soon as they have heard the lecture without conferring or asking the pastors any questions. Others stay not till the lecture is ended, and others hear not so much as a single word, but entertain themselves in a corner of the church."

The persecution which now began was doubtless the means by which, through the Mercy of God, the Christians generally were roused from this state of apathy ; but at its commencement the fallen condition of the Church was painfully shown. Avarice and love of this world having taken deep root in the hearts of many, persons ran to the forum, even before they were accused, and sacrificed to the gods as they were ordered ; whilst the crowd of apostates was so great, that the magistrates would have delayed the retractation of some till the next day, but for the entreaty made by the wretched suppliants to be allowed to prove themselves heathens that very night. Yet there were many added to the noble army of confessors and martyrs, amongst them the aged and venerable Alexander, Bishop of Jerusalem, who had many years before been called to his diocese by a Divine revelation. He was Bishop of Cappadocia, when from feelings of religious interest, he resolved to visit Jerusalem. Narcissus, who then presided over that see, was a very old man, incapable of properly performing his duties. The Christians in Jerusalem were warned by a vision, and a Voice from Heaven, to go forth out of the city, and receive him whom God had designed to be their bishop. They obeyed, and meeting Alexander, welcomed him with the utmost respect, and constrained him to become the colleague of Narcissus in the government of their Church. Now, after having held his bishopric thirty-nine years, during which time he displayed singular prudence and earnestness, Alexander was called upon to endure various imprisonments and great sufferings, and at length died in prison, at Cæsarea, to the great grief of the whole Church, and to the especial sorrow of Origen, who had been ordained by him, and had ever found him a most steadfast friend. Origen himself, was in the end, summoned to bear his testimony to the value of the faith which he had so long and so heartily professed. He was cast into a loathsome dungeon, and was there loaded with irons. A chain was placed about his neck, and for many days together his feet were set in the stocks, with his legs most painfully stretched. He was also threatened with fire, and indeed actually tried with all the torments which his cruel enemies could suggest, short of those which would have put an end to his agony by death. It was their desire that he should live to suffer, and though he was an old man, and his bodily powers were weakened by a life of intense labour, he did survive the persecution, and being at length released from prison, lived some time afterwards, and wrote several letters for the consolation of those who were placed in the same circumstances. He died at Tyre, three years after the Decian persecution began.

Gregory Thaumaturgus, like his friend Origen, was too distinguished a person to escape suffering. The edict of Decius was carried out with great severity in Cappadocia, and the account given us of the condition of the province in consequence is very grievous. All other business, we are told, gave way to that of accusing and punishing the Christians, and the magistrates actually studied to invent methods of cruelty and instruments of torture. Swords, and axes, fire, wild beasts, devices for stretching and distending the limbs, iron chains made red hot, frames of timber set upright, in which the victims were placed and their bodies raked with nails that tore off the flesh,—these and many other modes of torture were daily used; every great man being anxious that another should not appear more fierce and cruel than himself. Some of the heathens took upon themselves the office of informers; others either became witnesses, or searched out the Christians who were endeavouring to conceal themselves, or else seized on those who fled; whilst many took advantage of the opportunity to gratify their avarice, and accused their neighbours only that they might get possession of their property A general consternation pervaded the country. Men were afraid of their nearest relatives. The father cared not for the safety of his child; the child took no heed of his duty to his parent. The Gentile son betrayed the Christian father; and the infidel father accused his Christian son. The woods were crowded, and the cities became empty; yet no sooner were many of the houses left by their owners, than they were seized upon for common gaols, the public prisons not being large enough to contain the multitude of Christians that were sent to them. It was impossible to go into the markets, or to any places of usual concourse, without seeing some persons apprehended, and others led to trial or execution, amidst the lamentations of their friends, and the mocking laughter of the heathens.   No regard was paid to age, sex, or virtue, but, as in a city stormed by an inhuman conqueror, everything was without mercy exposed to the mad rage of the merciless enemy.

Gregory Thaumaturgus knew well how few there were, especially among his recent converts, who would be likely to bear up under this terrible trial, and he therefore advised his people to flee, telling them that it was better in this way to save their souls, than to risk falling from the faith.   In order to show them that such a course might be adopted without sin, he himself set the example of retiring from danger, and retreated to a desert mountain, accompanied only by a Gentile priest, whom he had converted, and who ministered to him in the capacity of a deacon.   The greatest efforts were made to discover the place of his concealment, for, as the head of the Christians, it was considered very important to obtain possession of him.   Snares were laid for him on all sides, and when at length his hiding-place was known, vast numbers of persons collected together to hunt him out, and guard against his escape, by stationing themselves at the foot of the mountain.   A miracle is said to have been the proof that God was watching over His servant.   Gregory and his companion, we are told, finding themselves surrounded, knelt in earnest prayer, and committed themselves to their Heavenly Master's protection.   Their pursuers approached, searching every nook, examining every bush and tree, and at last, instructed by an informer, they drew near to the very spot were Gregory and his friend lay.

But they could see nothing.   God had blinded their eyes, and they returned to their companions,

22

affirming that they could discover nothing but a couple of trees, a little distance from each other. When the search was given over, the informer went to the place which he had pointed out, and found Gregory and the deacon still praying. He immediately concluded that their escape was the result of Divine interposition, and falling down at the Bishop's feet, gave himself up to be instructed in Christianity, and became from that time the companion of Gregory's solitude and perils.

Disappointment only increased the rage of the Cappadocian persecutors, and they hurried through all parts of the province, seizing upon men, women, and children, and torturing them for the Name of Christ. Gregory remained in his retirement as long as the time of trial lasted. When at length the severity of the storm was over, he returned to Neocæsarea, and visiting all parts of his diocese, established in every place anniversary festivals and solemnities in memory of the martyrs who had lately suffered.

Gregory Thaumaturgus is stated to have lived to a great age. His death was, like his life, marked by deep humility and zeal for the souls of others. When aware that his end was approaching, he made a strict inquiry through the city and the neighbourhood, whether any were still to be found strangers to the Christian faith. Being told that there were seventeen in all, he sighed; and lifting up his eyes to heaven, appealed to God to witness how much it troubled him that he should leave any whose salvation was incomplete; yet he added, that "it was a mercy demanding the deepest thankfulness, that whereas on entering upon his office, he found but seventeen Christians, he should leave but seventeen idolaters to his successor." When this inquiry had been made, Gregory's anxiety was at rest. After an earnest petition for the conversion of the heathen, and the increase in holiness of those who were already Christians, he resigned his soul to God. Gregory's simplicity of character was evinced even in the case of his interment. The last injunction he laid upon his friends was, that they should take no trouble for his funeral, nor procure him any peculiar place of burial. As in his life-time he had lived as a stranger and pilgrim in the world, so at his death he desired the portion of a stranger, and to be cast into the common lot.

CHAPTER XXVII.

ST. ANTHONY THE HERMIT BORN. A.D. 251.

THE Decian persecution seems to have raged universally, and,—as in Cappadocia, and in other places,—human ingenuity was excited to devise for the victims torments previously unknown. One martyr, after having endured the rack, and been covered with burning plates, was ordered by the judge to be rubbed all over with honey, and then exposed in the hot sun, lying on his back, with his hands tied behind him, that he might be stung by the flies.

The wrath of the emperor was especially excited against the heads of the Church. He was heard to say that he would rather endure a competitor in the empire, than a Bishop of Rome; and Fabian, who had filled that see for fourteen years, was now put to death; whilst the storm raged at Rome with such fury that a successor to the bishopric was not appointed for more than a year. Alexander, Bishop of Comana, suffered martyrdom by fire; but Eudemon, the Bishop of Smyrna, apostatised, and several other Bishops unhappily followed his example. Yet Smyrna was destined to produce one great example of Christian faith. Pionius, a presbyter of the Church, being daily in expectation of seizure, put a chain round his own neck, as a proof of his willingness to suffer; his sister, Sabina, and his friend, Asclepiades, did the same. Polemon, the keeper of the idol temple, came to them with the magistrates, and asked "if they knew that the emperor had ordered them to sacrifice." Pionius replied, that "they were not ignorant of the commandments; but they were those commandments which directed them to worship God." Polemon ordered them to accompany him to the market-place, and see the truth of what he had said.

They obeyed, and found crowds assembled. Polemon advised them to comply with the emperor's command, warning them that torture would be the consequence of a refusal. Pionius answered by addressing the multitudes. "Citizens of Smyrna," he said, "who delight in the beauty of your city, and value it as the birth-place of your poet Homer; and ye Jews, if any such there be among you, hear me whilst I speak in a few words. You deride both those who come of their own accord to sacrifice, and those who do not refuse when urged to it. Yet Homer himself would teach you never to rejoice at the death of any man. Jews! ought ye not to obey Moses, who says, 'Thou shalt not see thy brother's ass or his ox fall down by the way, and hide thyself from him; thou shalt surely help him to lift them up again.'   Does not Solomon warn you, ' Rejoice not when thine enemy falleth ?'   Whence then proceed those bursts of laughter, and the cruel scoffs of the Jews, pointed not only against those who have sacrificed, but against us ?   They insult us with a malicious pleasure, because our long peace is at length interrupted.   But though we were their enemies, still we are men.   What harm have we done them ?   What have we made them to suffer ?   Whom have we slandered ?   Whom have we persecuted ?   Whom have we compelled to worship idols ?   Have they no compassion for the unfortunate ? or, Are they themselves less guilty than the poor wretches who, through the fear of men or of tortures, have been induced to renounce their religion ? "

The speech of Pionius was long.   He reasoned with the Jews from their own Scriptures, and set before the Pagans the terrors of the day of judgment.   The hearts of the people were touched. ' Pionius," they said, " your uprightness and your wisdom make us deem you worthy to live, and life is pleasant."   " I own it," replied Pionius ; " life is pleasant, but it is that Eternal Life for which I long. Yet think not that I contemptuously reject the blessings of this world ; I do but prefer those which are infinitely better.   I thank you for your words of kindness, yet they sound to me as words of temptation."   He continued to discourse to them upon a future state, and his words, strengthened by his well-known sincerity, and his undoubted virtues, seemed to fill the people of Smyrna with veneration. His enemies dreaded an uproar in his favour.   He was carried to prison, together with Sabina and As-clepiades, who had both made their public confession of faith, declaring that " they worshipped God

22*

Almighty, and Jesus Christ, His Blessed Son." Many, both Jews and heathens, visited them in their captivity; and some even of those who had fallen away, sought them with tears of remorse. The Jews, bitterly hating Christianity, invited certain of the lapsed Christians to their synagogue, for they would fain have strengthened them in their rejection of Christ. When Pionius heard of their efforts, his spirit was deeply moved; the wilful blindness of the Jews excited him vehemently. "They pretend," he said, "that Jesus Christ died like other men, by constraint. Was that man, whose disciples have cast out devils for so many years, a common felon? Could He, for whose sake His disciples and so many others have voluntarily suffered the severest punishments, have been forced to die?" He urged these arguments earnestly, but finding them probably but ill received by the Jews who were with him, he requested them after a time to depart out of the prison.

A fresh attempt was soon made to shake the constancy of Pionius. He was ordered to go to the idol temple, and told that his Bishop, Eudemon, had already sacrificed. He refused, but was dragged thither with his companions. "We are Christians," they exclaimed as they stood at the entrance, "and they threw themselves upon the ground, that they might not be compelled to enter. Resistance, however, was vain. Pionius was forced in, and placed before the heathen altar. The unhappy Eudemon stood there also. He had sacrificed. The sight of the apostate must have inspired Pionius and his companions with courage, rather than fear; the questions of the judges were answered with boldness, their threats were listened to with indifference, and the prisoners were sent back to their captivity.

They remained in confinement until Quintilian, the proconsul, who had been absent from Smyrna, returned; then Pionius was examined before him. Tortures as well as persuasions were tried, but equally without success; and at last, enraged at such obstinacy, Quintilian ordered him to be burnt alive.

Cheerfully and willingly the martyr went to the place of execution, one feeling of gratitude being uppermost in his mind, from the thought that he had been preserved pure from idolatry. He was stretched, and nailed to the wood, and then a final effort was made to shake his fidelity. "Change but your mind," said the executioner, "and the nails shall be taken out." "I have felt them," was the answer of Pionius, and he remained thoughtful for a time. "O Lord," he said at length, "I hasten that I may be the sooner a partaker of thy resurrection." Another Christian, though one who held some heretical opinions, was nailed to a plank of wood in a similar manner. Whether Sabina and Asclepiades suffered in the same way, is not known. Pionius and his companions were placed upright, and a great quantity of fuel was heaped around them. Pionius with his eyes closed, remained motionless—he was absorbed in prayer whilst the fire was consuming him. Only at last he opened his eyes, looked cheerfully on the fire, and said, "Amen: Lord, receive my soul;" and with these words he entered upon his rest.

Instances of escape from danger at this period, as well as details of suffering, have been preserved to us. Dionysius, Bishop of Alexandria, who was deservedly honoured by all, thus relates, in a letter to a friend, the events which befell himself.

"Sabinus, the Roman governor, sent an officer to seek me during the persecution of Decius, and I remained four days at home expecting his coming. He made the most accurate search in the road, river, and fields, where he suspected I might be hid. A confusion seems to having seized him, so that he did not find my house. He had no idea that a man in my circumstances would stay at home. At length, after four days, God ordered me to remove, and—having opened me a way contrary to all expectation—I and my servants, and many of the brethren, went together. The event showed that the whole was the work of Divine Providence. About sunset I was seized, together with my whole company, by the soldiers, and was led to Taposiris. But my friend Timotheus, by the Providence of God, was not present, nor was he seized. He came afterwards to my house, found it forsaken and guarded, and learned that we were taken captive. How wonderful was the dispensation! But it shall be related precisely as it happened. A countryman met Timotheus, as he was flying in confusion, and asked the cause of his hurry : he told him the truth. The peasant heard the story, and went away to a marriage feast at which it was the custom to watch all night. He informed the guests of what he had heard. At once they all rose up as at a signal, hastened quickly to the place where we were, and shouted. Our soldiers, struck with a panic, fled. The people found us lying down on unfurnished beds. At first I thought they must be a company of robbers. They ordered me to rise and go out quickly. When at length I understood their real designs I cried out, and entreated them earnestly to depart and let us alone ; but if they really meant to be kind to us, I requested them to strike off my head, and so to deliver me from my persecutors. They compelled me to rise by downright violence, and I then threw myself on the ground. They seized my hands and feet, pulled me out by force, placed me on an ass, and conducted me from the place."

In so remarkable a manner was the life of Dionysius preserved, even, as it would seem, against his will, and without any direct intention of releasing him on the part of those who enabled him to escape, for the whole affair has the appearance of a drunken frolic. After his escape, Dionysius carefully concealed himself. This was not difficult in Egypt, where large tracts of mountains and desert furnished protection to the unfortunate Christians, whose forced retirement from the world was the commencement of a system of voluntary seclusion, which has continued down to the present day. Monks and hermits owed their beginning to the terrors of persecution. Paul, one of the Christian fugitives at this time, has acquired the celebrity of being the first hermit. He had received a learned education, and was left by his parents at an early age in possession of a considerable fortune. When the persecution broke out he was about twenty-two years old, and was living with a married sister, whose husband was base enough to give information against him, in order to obtain his estate. Paul, who was of a gentle temper and earnestly religious, having notice of this, retired into the desert mountains, where he concealed himself in a cave, and began a mode of existence in which he persisted for a long series of years. It is said, indeed, that finding a life of contemplation and devotion more agreeable than the struggle with the world, and believing that he was gaining the favour of God by shutting himself out from all the ordinary comforts which are the solace of human existence, he

dwelt in his cave till the beginning of the succeeding century, and died at the advanced age of 113.
The example set by him was followed by numerous others. The doctrines of Montanus had before
prepared the minds of Christians for a system of
outward self-discipline, and many who adopted
this course of life, were, no doubt, really humble
and sincere in their intentions; and believing a great
number of the usual enjoyments and occupations
of mankind—even of those who professed to belong to the Church of Christ—to be displeasing to
God, were for that reason resolved to give them
up. But there was a danger of an opposite kind
which they did not perceive. Customs begun from
real earnestness, may easily end in being followed
merely from a love of ostentation and singularity.
The best men are open to this temptation. When
we stand apart from others, and condemn what is
generally believed to be innocent, we are in great
peril of spiritual pride. Unquestionably there are
occasions when such a protest is required, and
when we are bound to make it, but this does not
appear to have been the case with regard to many
of the customs and habits of life which at this
period were matters of discussion among Christians.
The Church had never been required to give a
decision upon them, and they were wisely and
charitably left to the religious feeling and judgment of each individual. In a time of persecution
it was natural that the stricter line of conduct
should be adopted. Persons who had become easy
and self-indulgent during the repose of the preceding years, if they did not fall away entirely
from the faith, were roused to a more clear per-
ception of the nothingness of this life, and the
overwhelming importance of that which is to come.

Standing continually on the brink of the grave, the allurements of earth were despised. "What shall it profit a man, if he gain the whole world and lose his own soul?" must have been the question for ever sounding in their ears; and in order to save their souls they rushed away, not only from the enjoyments of the world, but also from its duties. The safer rule would probably have been to have accepted the enjoyments when they were found in the path of duty, and to have hallowed them by remembering gratefully that God was their Giver.

Personal safety, however, supplied a still stronger argument for retirement in a period of persecution. Many countries, thickly peopled with Christians, were but little calculated for concealment, and thus it was that the monastic system took its rise in the extensive deserts in Egypt.

But Paul the hermit, though acknowledged as the founder of this system of seclusion, is not so celebrated as Anthony, who afterwards adopted it. The life of this saint more properly belongs to after years, as he was only born in 251; but when referring to the origin of monastic institutions, his name can scarcely be omitted. Anthony was by birth an Egyptian; his parents were noble and rich, and being Christians, educated their son in the Christian faith. He was brought up in privacy, and received but little instruction in the fashionable literature of the day; indeed, it appears that he was never acquainted with the Greek language, though he interested himself in reading. When about eighteen or twenty years of age, Anthony's parents died, leaving him in possession of a large family property, and committing to his guardianship his little sister, then only six years of age.

This early sorrow may probably have deepened the strong religious feeling which was even then developed in his character. One day, whilst going as usual to church, he meditated upon the lives of the Apostles and their immediate converts, and the sacrifices made by them for the sake of Christ. As he entered the church the words which he first heard were, " If thou wilt be perfect, go and sell that thou hast, and give to the poor, and thou shalt have treasure in heaven, and come and follow Me." These words Anthony regarded as addressed to him; he believed that he had received a special call from Heaven; and, reserving only so much of his property as was necessary to make a provision for his sister, he gave up the remainder to the poor. The opportunity was afterwards offered of providing for his sister, by placing her under the care of a trustworthy female acquaintance; and Anthony, being struck by hearing at church the text, " Take no thought for the morrow," parted even with that which he had at first reserved.

From this period his ascetic life began. In the village next to his own lived an aged man, who had from his youth adopted a solitary life. Anthony determined to follow his example. He sought a retired spot in the neighbourhood, and, labouring with his own hands for the supply of his few daily necessities, gave himself up to prayer and the study of the Scriptures; whilst from time to time, he sought intercourse with persons famed for wisdom and holiness, with the view of imitating their example and increasing his own spiritual knowledge. Anthony's professional self-denial was extreme. He watched often through the whole night. His food was bread and salt; his drink water. He ate but once in the day, after sunset; and sometimes passed two and even four days without nourishment.

Finding the retirement which he had adopted insufficient for the entire subjugation of every earthly feeling, he, after a while, repaired to a more lonely asylum in a burial ground, and there made his abode in one of the sepulchres, arranging with a friend to supply him at long intervals with food. In this situation he imagined himself assaulted by demons, and almost beaten to death; whilst horrid forms of lions, bears, wolves, bulls, and serpents threatened to assail him, until the roof of the sepulchre opened, and a ray of light from Heaven descended upon him. Then the demons vanished, and a heavenly voice cheered him with the assurance of support.

We have no means of inquiring into the reality of these stories. That St. Anthony fully believed himself to be openly assaulted by Satan is undeniable; but he was a man of a very enthusiastic disposition, and his long fasts, by weakening his body, must more or less have had for a time an effect upon his mind. The personal conflict with evil spirits, which he supposed himself to have had, seems to have suggested a yet more distant flight from everything connected with his past life. He repaired to the desert, and made his habitation in a deserted fort, filled with reptiles. After laying up food for six months, he blocked up the entrance, probably with the idea of shutting out his enemies. But the same delusions followed him. The reptiles by which he was annoyed were considered to be demons in disguise, and the combat which he carried on with them was often heard from without.

Anthony spent about twenty years in this fort.

23

At the end of that time, when he was about fifty-five years of age, the eagernesss of his friends caused the doors of his retreat to be broken down, and he was compelled to come forth. Those assembled to see him were struck at the little change his person had undergone. He appeared in all ways the same as they had known him before his retreat: his mind seemed perfectly calm, and he evinced neither confusion at the sight of the multitude, nor elation at their respectful greeting.

Addressing them with kindness and courtesy, he urged them to despise the world, and to give themselves up to the service of Him who had died for them; urging them especially to choose the life of retirement, as that which would most surely set them forward on the road to Heaven. His words and his example operated powerfully upon those who heard him. Numbers forsook their homes, and devoted themselves to that which they believed to a belief of superior holiness. Monasteries were formed, in which persons of the same mind might live together in strict seclusion from the temptations of the world, and in habits of rigorous self-discipline. They gathered around Anthony as their leader, and he imparted to them his earnestness, discoursing with them frequently on the nothingness of earth, and the all-importance of Heaven; and when, in after years, the terror of persecution reached even to the desert, and some of the solitaries were led forth for martyrdom, Anthony accompanied them; attended them at the judgment seat, undeterred by the threatenings of the magistrate; encouraged them under their sufferings; at last followed them to the place of execution, grieving only that the same glorious death was not permitted to himself.

The last years of Anthony's life were passed in the wilderness. He settled at the foot of a lofty mountain, where a spring of cold water, and a small plot of earth, enabled him to provide support for himself and for those who, even in this remote place, resorted to him. Two inducements prevailed upon him on different occasions to quit his retreat. His sister, having remained unmarried, had formed a sisterhood, of which she was the head, and Anthony visited her and his former friends in the place at which he had first resided; and at a very advanced age he took part in the celebrated controversy with the heretic Arius, and repaired to Alexandria to preach against his errors. The effect he then produced was very wonderful. Even heathens flocked to hear him, and it is said that as many became Christians in one day as were commonly converted in a year.

St. Anthony lived to be a hundred and four years old. His last fear seems to have been lest his friends should show a superstitious reverence for his remains. Being aware that his end was approaching, he retired to a remote mountain, where he commonly dwelt, and calling to him two monks, who for fifteen years had shared his ascetic life, he gave various instructions for their conduct, and said to them, "I, as it is written, go the way of my fathers, for I perceive I am called by the Lord. Let them not carry my body into Egypt, lest they store in their houses. Bury it in the earth in obedience to my word, so that none but yourselves may know the place. In the resurrection of the dead it will be restored to me incorruptible by the Saviour. Distribute my garments as follows:— let Athanasius, the bishop, have the one sheep-skin, and the garment I sleep on, which he gave me new, and which has grown old with me; let Serapion, the bishop, have the other sheep-skin; as to the hair-shirt, keep it for yourselves. And now, my children, farewell; Anthony is going, and is no longer with you.'

After these words they kissed him. Then he stretched himself out, and seemed to see friends come to him, and to be very joyful at the sight (to judge from the cheerfulness of his countenance as he lay); and so he breathed his last, and was gathered to his fathers."

Such is the description of St. Anthony's death given by Athanasius, Bishop of Alexandria, and one of the most illustrious Fathers of the Church. He adds an enthusiastic testimony to the good effect produced in Egypt by Anthony's example; and although in the present day, when we have learnt to see the errors connected with the monastic system, we may probably look upon such testimony with suspicion, there seems no doubt that in the beginning the influence of monks and hermits was beneficial to the Christian Church, by keeping up a high standard of holiness, and acting as a continual protest against the follies and vices of the world.

CHAPTER XXVIII.

THE NOVATIAN SCHISM.   A. D. 251.

ABOUT the period of the Decian persecution, the attention of the Christian Church was directed to Africa, not only on account of the rise of monasticism in Egypt, but also from the respect and admiration felt for the bishop who then occupied the see of Carthage. Cyprian, Bishop of Carthage, was a man distinguished for learning, piety, zeal, and judgment. His guidance and example were eminently valuable to the Christians of his own day, and his writings still form a most valuable portion of the inheritance of truth, handed down to us by the early Church. Yet the whole of the Christian life of St. Cyprian may be included in twelve years. He was only converted about three years before the commencement of the Decian persecution. Up to that period he had been a heathen teacher of the art of eloquence in Carthage, living in the midst of luxury and distinction, surrounded by a stately retinue, dressed in splendid garments, and followed by admiring disciples. His conversion, which was very rapid, was brought about by Cæcilius, a presbyter of Carthage; and the state of his mind at the time when he was studying to escape from paganism, he thus describes in a letter to a friend.

"While I lay in darkness and the night of paganism, ignorant of my own life, and alienated from light and truth, it appeared to me a harsh and difficult thing to obtain what Divine Grace had promised; namely, that a man should be born again, and that, being animated to a new life by the salutary washing of regeneration, he should strip himself of what he was before, and, though the body remained the same, he should in his mind become altogether a new creature. How can so great a change be possible, I said, that a man should suddenly and at once put off what nature and habit have confirmed in him? How shall he learn parsimony, who has been accustomed to ex-

23*

pensive feasts? And how shall he who has been accustomed to purple, gold, and costly attire, condescend to the simplicity of a plebeian habit? Can he who was delighted with the honours of ambition live in obscurity? He must still be assailed by temptation; drunkenness, pride, anger, rapacity, cruelty, ambition, must still domineer over him. These reflections engaged my mind very often, for they were peculiarly applicable to my own case. I was myself entangled in many errors of my former life, from which I did not think it possible to be cleared. I favoured my vices, and, through despair of what was better, I clung to them as part of my very nature. But after the filth of my former sins was washed away in the laver of regeneration, and Divine Light from above had infused itself into my heart, now purified and cleansed; after the new birth had made me a new creature indeed, immediately and in an amazing manner, dubious things began to be cleared up, and what before seemed difficult now appeared easy and practicable. I saw that that which was born after the flesh, and had lived enslaved by wickedness, was of the ' earth, earthy; ' but that the new life now animated by the Holy Ghost began to be of God. . . . You know what these opposite states have done for me. I need not proclaim it. To boast of one's own merits is odious, though that which ascribes nothing to the virtue of man, but professes all to proceed from the gift of God, cannot be called an expression of boasting, but of gratitude. . . . Of God it is, of God, I say, even all that we can do; thence we live, thence we have strength . . . and even now, though placed here below, have some clear foretaste of our future felicity. Only, let fear be the guardian of innocence, that the Lord, who mercifully shone into our minds with His heavenly grace, may, by the steady obedience of the soul which delights in Him, be detained as our guest,—lest pardon received should beget careless presumption, and the old enemy break in afresh.

" But," he adds, " if you keep the road of innocence and of righteousness ; if you walk with footsteps that do not slide ; you will then find that, according to the proportion of faith, so will your attainments and enjoyments be. . . . As much of capacious faith as we bring, so much abounding grace do we draw from Him.   Hence an ability is given, with sober chastity, uprightness of mind, and purity of language, to heal the sick, to extinguish the force of a poison, and cleanse the filth of dismtepered minds, . . . to compel by menaces unclean and wandering spirits to quit their hold of men, to scourge and control the foe, and by torments to bring him to confess what he is."

The last sentence has been quoted to show how naturally miracles were at that time mentioned as facts commonly known and acknowledged. Much more Cyprian wrote in the same strain, owning with the deepest gratitude the blessings which God had bestowed on man through Jesus Christ, but urging a holy life as the necessary fruit of faith, and the only proof of sincerity ; and his own conduct fully exemplified the doctrines which he taught.   Whilst yet only a catechumen, his piety and self-denial were evident to all, for he not only practised the strictest temperance and sobriety, but, trampling over all the temptations of his worldly position, he at once sacrificed his wealth, selling the greater part of his estate, and causing the money to be distributed amongst the poor.   After his baptism, he was quickly called to the inferior ecclesiastical offices, and then admitted to be a priest.   The Bishop of Carthage died soon afterwards, and the reputation of Cyprian was by this time so great, that both the clergy and the people almost unanimously desired to have him as their head.   But Cyprian was very unwilling to accept the office.   His conversion was too recent, and he thought too humbly of himself, to suppose that he could rightly accept such a responsibility. The proposal was therefore declined, but the people were not to be disappointed.   They crowded his doors, and blocked up every passage by which he might have escaped.   Even when he endeavoured to make his exit by the window, it was in vain. They still waited for him impatiently, divided between hope and fear.   At length he came forth, conquered by their determination, and his decision was received with universal joy.   He was to be Bishop of Carthage ; and upon this high office he entered on the last year of the reign of Philip the Arabian.   The Church was then at peace, so that Cyprian was enabled to direct his attention to the restoration of discipline, which had latterly been much relaxed.   Of the details of his government we have only a few particulars, but we know that he earnestly endeavoured to raise the minds of his clergy, and detach them from worldly interests. His character must have exercised a great in- fluence, and he had besides the advantage not only of talent, but of an attractive personal appearance. His countenance and manner are thus described : " His look had the due mixture of gravity and cheer- fulness ; so that it was doubtful whether he were more worthy of love or of reverence.   His dress also corresponded with his looks.   He had renounced the worldly pomp to which his rank in life entitled him, yet he avoided affected penury." Zeal, united with what we generally call good sense, seemed indeed to have been characteristic of Cyprian, and such qualities were especially needed at this period.

The Church, as it has already been stated, had become corrupted by prosperity. Sincerity and humility were declining, and when at length in the reign of Decius the storm of persecution burst forth, the Christians at Carthage, as elsewhere, were but ill prepared to meet it. Cyprian himself was amongst the first to be attacked. The voices of the heathen populace were heard again and again in the circus and the amphitheatre, calling for the bishop, that he might be thrown to the lions ; and when thus warned of his danger, Cyprian felt himself at liberty to obey the command of his Divine Master,—and also, as he himself tells us, to follow special directions given him at the time,— and to flee from the city. On this occasion he was proscribed by name, and his property seized by the government. The place and the companions of Cyprian's first retreat are unknown, but we learn incidentally from the letters which at various times he addressed to his friends and to the clergy, that he had not retired from Carthage without leaving behind him for the poor of his diocese a provision, secured probably before the seizure of his property, which he committed to the care of the presbyter, Rogatian. In the mean-while, though absent in body, he was yet in spirit present with his people, sparing neither efforts nor prayers, neither encouragements nor reproofs, to preserve them in the true faith, and to keep them within the limits of apostolical order. His endeavours were not without fruit: a noble witness was borne by many; and Cyprian, in his place of retreat, gloried in their firmness, whilst he was incessantly anxious for all who were in any way exposed to a like trial. "Let the poor," he says, when writing to his clergy, "be attended to as much as possible—those I mean who have stood the test of persecution; suffer them not to want necessaries, lest indigence do that against them which persecution could not. I know that the charity of the brethren has provided for very many of them, yet—as I wrote to you before, even while they were in prison—if any persons do want meat or clothing, let their necessities be supplied." The portion of the Church revenues especially applied to the use of the bishop, seems to have been relinquished by Cyprian on this occasion, for the use of his poorer brethren.

Cyprian's joy on account of the faithfulness of the martyrs was, however, considerably damped by the disorderly conduct which began to take place in his absence. Several persons, who, in the weakness of their faith, had denied the truth, being anxious to be received again into communion with the Church, applied to certain presbyters of Carthage for re-admission, and were actually permitted to partake of the Lord's Supper without any just evidence of their repentance.

Cyprian did not conceal his displeasure on this occasion. He wrote to the presbyters, saying that it was quite unprecedented to transact these things without the consent of the bishop; and that, even in lesser offences, a regular time of penitence was insisted upon, and a certain course of discipline took place; open confession of sin being made, and those who had fallen away being re-admitted to

Communion by the imposition of hands of the bishop and his clergy. He begged that the irregular practice might be stopped, till, on his return, everything could be arranged with propriety. But the question as to the treatment of the lapsed was not settled by the letter from the bishop, it was continually recurring, and was rendered more difficult by the interference of those who had suffered tortures for Christ, or who were on the point of martyrdom. It had long been the custom for such persons to present petitions for any in whom they were specially interested; and now, acting upon what, no doubt, they considered to be Christian charity, they took upon themselves to give to lapsed persons letters of general recommendation, without mentioning the circumstances, which might render their cases worthy of peculiar pity. This was perplexing to Cyprian, for confessors and martyrs were at that time regarded with such exceeding reverence, that their wishes became almost commands. Yet to listen to them in every instance, was likely to endanger the whole discipline of the Church, and to set a most dangerous example for future ages. One especial instance of this interference may be mentioned. A confessor named Celerinus, who lived in some part of Africa, most probably in banishment, was much grieved on account of the apostacy of his two sisters, Numeria and Candida. He mourned for them night and day in sackcloth and ashes; and hearing that Lucian, a man distinguished for piety, was then in prison at Carthage, and reserved for martyrdom, he wrote to him, to entreat that either he himself, or any of his suffering brethren, particularly whosoever should first be called to martyrdom, would restore his sisters to the Church. He begged the same favour for Etcusa, who had not sacrificed, but had given money to be excused from the act. Persons who did this, were called Libellatici, from *libellus*, which meant a short written certificate, given by the magistrate as a testimony that the individual either was not a Christian, or had abjured Christianity. The petition of Celerinus was particularly inexcusable, because the case of his sisters had been brought before the clergy of their own Church, which it seems was at that time without a bishop, and its settlement had been deferred till a bishop was appointed. Celerinus, however, was too eager to allow of any delay, and therefore made his application to Lucian. He was the more likely to obtain his request, because Lucian had already decided, in the name of the whole body of confessors, to re-admit into communion all the lapsed who applied to them ; and had written a very short letter to Cyprian, desiring him to inform the rest of the bishops of what had been done, and expressing a wish that he might acquiesce in the views of the martyrs. In replying to the request of Celerinus, Lucian gave a vivid description of the sufferings which he and his brethren were then enduring, and which probably were in his own eyes a sufficient excuse for what might otherwise have been called an unlawful interference with the bishop's authority. They were shut up, he says, and pressed together excessively close in two small cells, where they suffered greatly from intolerable heat. Numbers had already died, and his own end seemed near. For five days they had received very little food, bread and water being measured out to them. He added, that he granted the petition of Celerinus, most especially, because Paul, a martyr who had lately suffered, had while yet in the body visited him, and thus spoken : "Lucian, I say to thee before Christ, that if any person after my decease beg of thee to be restored to the Church, thou must, in my name, grant his request." This command Lucian was now willing to obey. He referred Celerinus to the general letter which he had already written in behalf of the lapsed, though owning, at the same time, that they ought to explain their cause before the bishop and make their confession.

That some spiritual pride was mingled with this exercise of power can scarcely be doubted. Yet when we are inclined to condemn it, we must remember that Lucian was only acting in accordance with what was at that time a commonly received custom in the Church. Of his real piety there can be no doubt; but earnestness and sincerity, though they may be an excuse for the individual in the sight of God, cannot be accepted instead of good judgment by man; and this and similar instances of interference on the part of the martyrs, gave evidence that a spirit extremely dangerous to the cause of piety and humility was spreading fast in the African Church.

In this trying condition of affairs all persons of discernment looked to Cyprian, as the only individual able to restore discipline. The Roman clergy especially sympathised with his trials, and supported him by their approbation; for constant communication was kept up between the two Churches, even in the time of persecution. The Bishop of Rome had, as it has been said before, suffered martyrdom, and for more than a year no successor had been appointed, probably because of the difficulty that would have attended his election; for the neighbouring bishops could scarcely

24

have been present, and yet without them the election would not have been valid. But though thus deprived of their head, the Roman clergy acted with admirable discretion, each presbyter managing the affairs of his own congregation; whilst, when any communication was received from a foreign city, the whole body appear to have assembled in council to decide upon the answer that should be given. The superior discipline of the Roman Church gave great weight to the opinions expressed by the presbyters, and the support offered by them to Cyprian, must have been no slight consolation. " Our sorrow," they wrote to him, " is doubled, because you have no rest from these pressing difficulties of the persecution, and because the immoderate petulance of the lapsed has proceeded to the height of arrogance. We are astonished that they should proceed to such lengths in a time so mournful, so unseasonable as the present; that they should not so much as *ask* for re-communion with the Church, but claim it as a right, and even affirm that they are already forgiven in heaven. Never cease, brother, in your love for souls, to moderate and restrain these violent spirits, . . . the patients themselves will in process of time be thankful for that delay which was absolutely necessary for a wholesome cure; provided there be none to arm them with weapons against themselves, and demand for them the deadly poison of an overhasty restoration."

The unanimity of different churches upon this subject is remarkable; and as they were agreed with regard to the strict discipline which was to be observed, so they also joined in permitting a charitable leniency under peculiar circumstances. If any lapsed person was in danger of death, and had received a paper from a confessor, he might be admitted to the Communion without delay. Whether the dying penitent would have his pardon sealed in Heaven or not, it was impossible for man to decide; but it was charitably supposed that if he confessed his Saviour with his last and dying words, he could not be unfit, at the same moment, to partake of the Eucharist.

The persecution of Decius was now drawing to a close: to the last Cyprian continued his untiring care for the welfare of his people, supplying, with the bountiful liberality which was one of his peculiar characteristics, the necessities of the poor; rewarding persons who had endured with constancy, or who had shown kindness to the martyrs in their death, by placing them in honourable positions in the Church; urging his brethren to attend carefully to the burial of those who died in torture, or under the lengthened misery of imprisonment, and begging them also to mark the days on which the martyrs had departed this life, or, as he expresses it, were transmitted to immortality, in order that their commemoration might be observed. Instances of this custom have been mentioned before. The " Acts of the Martyr," or the circumstances attending his sufferings and death, were generally committed to writing, and on the anniversary of the martyrdom the account was usually read, either at the spot where his remains were deposited, or at some place of religious meeting. Many of these " Acts of the Martyrs" have come down to us, and some of them are unquestionably as old as the second century; and although, as the number increased, legends were introduced into these accounts, which make it very difficult to decide how much is true, and how much false, yet this ought not to make us reject the whole collection; any more than the superstitious reverence for saints and martyrs exhibited in later times, should make us condemn the affectionate piety shown by Cyprian and his clergy to those who had suffered for the Name of Christ.

But Cyprian was not to be permitted to return to his see in peace. Though the persecution of the heathen was nearly over, a far more dangerous enemy had risen up in his own fold, who was to cause him grief as great, if not greater, than any which it was in the power of his pagan enemies to inflict. There existed at this time in the Church of Carthage a person of bad character, named Felicissimus. He had long been opposed to the bishop, and in the troubled period through which the Church had lately passed, he had managed to draw away some of the Christians of Carthage, and induce them to celebrate, on a certain mountain, what he called the Communion. Whilst this practice was carried on, persons arrived who were authorised by Cyprian to discharge the debts of the poor, to furnish them with small sums of money to begin business again, and also to make a report of their ages, circumstances, and characters, in order that, if properly qualified, they might be appointed to some office in the Church. These designs were thwarted by Felicissimus. Several of the poor who first came to be relieved by Cyprian's deputies, were severely threatened by him because they refused to communicate on the mountain; and at length he proceeded as far as to collect a party, and set himself up as their leader. After a time he was joined by five other presbyters; one of whom, Fortunatus, was actually elected bishop in opposition to Cyprian. These shameful proceedings were strongly supported by

Novatus, a presbyter of Carthage, whose character was so notoriously bad, as not only to unfit him for his sacred office, but even render him unworthy to be admitted into lay-communion. The examination of his conduct was about to take place, when the persecution broke out and put a stop to it. Novatus now sided with Felicissimus, and yet he had not the courage to await at Carthage the return of Cyprian. Already had the bishop sent orders to his clergy to suspend from communion those who were the abettors of these disorders; and there was no doubt that on his arrival he would himself follow up this measure with zeal and promptitude. Under these circumstances, and perhaps wishing to extend the schism still further, Novatus crossed the sea and went to Rome. Here he joined himself with a man whose name, singularly enough, was so similar to his own, that the two have often been confounded. Novatian, before he became a Christian, had belonged to the philosophical sect of Stoics, famed for their severity and rigorous self-discipline. Novatian retained these stern principles after his reception into the Church, and he exhibited them in his judgment of the lapsed, who, he said, ought not to be received again into the Church, though they gave the sincerest marks of repentance. This apparent zeal for church discipline led away many; and Novatus, amongst others, upheld Novatian, though it was strangely inconsistent in him to do so, since one of the complaints which he had made against Cyprian, had been that of too great severity in his treatment of his lapsed. Novatus and his party cared, however, for nothing but schism; and at length, breaking out into open rebellion, they contrived to have Novatian elected bishop, in opposition to Cornelius, the Bishop of

24*

Rome, who, after a long delay, had been appointed in the place of the martyred Fabian.

This was the first instance of what we now call Dissent—a separation from the Church, not on some question of doctrine, but of discipline and government. The Novatianists are not said to have held opinions contrary to the faith of the Gospel; their offence was schism, or the breaking up of church order and unity. With regard to Novatian himself, he professed to lead an austere life, wrote several treatises in defence of the Christian faith, and in the end is said to have suffered martyrdom; but the evil which he brought upon the Church was great and unquestionable.

CHAPTER XXIX.

CONTROVERSY REGARDING BAPTISM, BETWEEN CY-
PRIAN, BISHOP OF CARTHAGE, AND STEPHEN,
BISHOP OF ROME. A.D. 256.

The death of the Emperor Decius, which took place after he had reigned about thirty months, put an end to the persecution of the Christians. Under his successor, Gallus, the Church was, for a little time, allowed to be at peace.

A.D. 251.

Cyprian was now restored to his diocese, and many and great were the difficulties and labours which awaited him there. Almost the first question that came before him was the schism of Novatian. Only once before, in the case of Alexander and Narcissus of Jerusalem, had two bishops ever professed to occupy the same see. But in that instance an urgent reason for the arrangement existed. Alexander only took upon himself the duties which Narcissus was unable to perform. But no such plea was to be found for the present condition of the Church at Rome. If Cornelius was the rightly appointed bishop, Novatian could have no claim to the office; and the first wish therefore of the Roman clergy was, that the case should be examined and determined by Cyprian, whose judgment and virtues were acknowledged by the whole Church. A synod was accordingly held at Carthage. Novatian, who had fled to Africa, did not appear himself, but sent deputies to it. So also did Cornelius. A very little examination was sufficient to show where the right lay. The consecration of Novatian was proved to have been quite irregular. He had called three bishops from distant parts of Italy, under pretence that their presence was necessary in Rome to preserve the unity of the Church; and showing them letters which he had received from several confessors who approved of his consecration, he induced them, by wicked artifices, and even, it was said, after making them intoxicated, hastily to ordain him. Besides this, he had not hesitated to profane the most sacred of Christian rites in order to secure followers to himself. At the service of the Holy Communion he would seize the hands of the person to whom he had given the Eucharist, and thus address him, " Swear to me by the Body and Blood of our Lord, which you now hold in your hands, that you will not desert me, and that you will never pass to the party of Cornelius." Christians, therefore, could not receive the Eucharist until they had taken the oath.

Novatian urged, as his excuse, that he was elected against his will; to which Dionysius,

Bishop of Alexandria, who was present at the synod, replied in a letter addressed to him, " If what you say be true, that you were elected against your will, prove now the sincerity of your repugnance by a voluntary resignation.   You will endure this sacrifice rather than suffer the Church of God to be torn by schism ; for not less meritorious than martyrdom for the faith is death for the unity of the Church."

Cornelius was fully recognised as Bishop of Rome, and Novatian cast out of communion with the Church ; but his party still continued to have influence, and several bishops joined it.   Of Novatus, who first created the disturbance in Carthage, we hear only that, after supporting Novatian in Rome, he followed him to Africa.   The party of Felicissimus and Fortunatus were condemned by Cyprian, and soon sank into insignificance.

The case of the lapsed was now to be regularly considered, and strict decisions were to be made respecting them.

Severity seems to have been in all ages a distinguishing mark of those who separated from the Church.   The unforgiving principles of the Montanists were adopted rigorously by the Novatians. No penitence on the part of the offender, no course of discipline imposed by the Church, could entitle him to readmission to communion.   It was considered right only to exhort him to repentance, and leave him to the judgment of God.   But the decision of the Church at large was very different. The question was discussed at the Synod of Carthage according to the rule of Scripture, and it was there resolved that as the cases of the lapsed must necessarily vary, the treatment should be determined according to the nature of the offence.

None were to be denied the hope of restoration, lest despair should lead them into a total apostacy from the faith. The *Libellatici*, who had only purchased libels, or certificates from the magistrates in times of persecution, to excuse them from offering sacrifice, were to have a shorter time of penance assigned them ; the *Sacrificati*, who had actually sacrificed to idols, were not to be re-admitted until after a very long penance. This determination of the Synod at Carthage was sent to Rome, and approved by Cornelius, and a council of sixty bishops, and as many presbyters and deacons ; and it was also confirmed by other heads of the Church in various countries. Perhaps the prospect of a renewal of persecution made Cyprian the more earnest in not driving to despair persons of a weak faith and timid disposition. Charity seemed especially required in times of difficulty, and such were again near at hand ; and in a second council, held in the same year, it was agreed that those who had shown from the first a sincere contrition should immediately be admitted to communion. The cause of the renewed outcry against the Christian faith appears to have been a terrible plague, which broke out in several parts of the empire, and was, as usual, attributed to the vengeance of the gods upon Christian impiety. Carthage had its full share in the calamity. Vast multitudes died every day ; the streets were filled with dead bodies ; and, in the universal suffering, feelings of kindness and sympathy seemed to be almost entirely lost. Each thought of himself, and sought his own safety, careless of the claims of father, mother, sister, or friend. Only Cyprian stood forth to urge a different line of conduct. Earnestly he exhorted the Christians to be Christians indeed—to extend their charity not only to their brethren, but to the heathen; to overcome evil with good; and, according to their Lord's advice, to pray for those that persecuted them. "God," he reminded them, "makes His sun to rise and His rain to fall, not only for the advantage of His own children, but of all men. Surely, therefore, they ought to act as became the nobility of their new birth, and imitate the example of their Father." By this and many more arguments of the same kind, he persuaded the Christians, and after a while many of the heathens also, to give help to the sufferers. Those who were poor and unable to afford money, came forward with the offer of time and labour; all were eager to engage in the work over which Cyprian presided, and the benefits of an abundant charity were quickly felt, not only by the Chrstians, but by all without distinction.

The threatened persecution soon broke out. Gallus renewed the edict of Decius, by which Christians were ordered to sacrifice; and in consequence Cornelius, bishop of Rome, was put to death, and Lucius, who succeeded him, was obliged to flee from the city, and at length also suffered martyrdom. Cyprian had the grief of seeing many of his clergy dragged to prison or to death, but he contrived to preserve his own life without leaving Carthage. His active benevolence was still exerted in all cases of suffering, and when a great number of prisoners were carried off from some part of Numidia by an invasion of barbarians, he raised a subscription for their ransom, which amounted to 850*l.* The pestilence still continued to rage; it even survived the persecution, for

A.D. 253. Gallus was killed after a short reign, and Valerian, who succeeded him, had shown himself favourable to Christianity so that his accession was hailed as a signal for peace ; but the sufferings from the plague lasted some time longer. In the meantime, certain events occurred, which, though in themselves not remarkable, are yet very interesting, as marking the exact limits of the episcopal power in those days, and especially what was then understood by the sentence of excommunication. The schism of Novatian, and the severe treatment of the lapsed, had been adopted by Marcianus, Bishop of Arles, in Gaul ; and several of the neighbouring bishops wrote to Stephen, the newly elected Bishop of Rome, and to Cyprian of Carthage, to consult them as to what their conduct should be towards him. Cyprian urged Stephen to join with the Gallican bishops in excluding Marcianus from communion ; but Stephen, it must be remembered, could only join with them, he could not command them. His authority did not extend beyond his own diocese. All he could insist upon was that his own clergy should not communicate with the offending person. In another diocese, another bishop would be called upon to give his own decision for his own people. This was the constant practice of the early Church. The opinion of the bishops was happily almost always unanimous, and, after consulting together, they ordinarily agreed to adopt the same line of conduct. In another case, however, which happened about the same time, Cyprian and Stephen differed. Two Spanish bishops having been deposed for lapsing, and for other offences, afterwards went to Rome, and by making a false statement, persuaded Stephen to receive them favourably. The bishops elected in their stead proceeded to Carthage, and laid their case before Cyprian, who immediately summoned a council of thirty-seven bishops to inquire into it. These facts then appeared so plain, that a letter was written to the Spanish bishops, in the name of the African Council, advising them to adhere to what they had done, and apologising for the imprudence of the Bishop of Rome, by observing that he lived at a great distance, and had been deceived by a false account. There was no idea of submitting to Stephen's decision, as to that of the Supreme Head of the Church, for Cyprian added, very plainly, that if any person held communion with the lapsed and degraded bishops, he became a partner in their guilt.

But a more important question, as concerning the Church generally, was now to be discussed. It had been the custom in the eastern and African churches to baptize those persons who came over from heresy to the orthodox faith, although they had already gone through some form of baptism. In the Church of Rome the practice was different; the individuals who came over from heresy being admitted to communion without a second baptism. This difference probably arose from the fact, that the Roman Church, and indeed all the churches of Italy, had been less infected than others by heresy. It had therefore been unnecessary to make any rule upon this point. Almost every religious party, whatever their opinions might be, administered baptism with the same form of words which had been prescribed by our Saviour, and which was used in the Catholic Church. The bishop and clergy of Rome were satisfied with this. But in Asia, where Montanism had made such successful progress, it was thought necessary to check the evil, by pronouncing all baptisms invalid except when administered within the Catholic Church.

For some cause which has not been explained, the Bishop of Rome had a controversy upon this subject of baptism with certain African bishops. Probably some member of the Roman Church, when travelling in the East, had been forbidden to communicate, on account of the invalidity of his baptism. If the circumstance became known to Stephen, he was likely to remonstrate strongly against such an insult to a member of his own Church, for he entertained high ideas of the dignity of his see, and was besides a man of hasty temper, and expressed himself violently when his feelings were roused. In this respect he was no doubt inferior to Cyprian, who, though equally firm and fully conscious of the independence of his see, kept a better guard over his temper.

When the question of baptism was brought forward at Rome, several important members of the Eastern Churches went thither in person; but Stephen would not even give them an audience, and threatened to hold no communion with the Churches of Asia Minor. Eighteen African bishops at the same time appealed to Cyprian for his opinion. Cyprian never acted without consulting some members of his Church. Two councils—the latter of which was assembled at Carthage, in the spring of the year 256—decided that heretical baptism was invalid. The decision was communicated to Stephen by a letter from Cyprian, mild and courteous in its language, though in it the bishop of Carthage asserted strongly that every Church had a right to make rules for itself.

Stephen's reply was in a very different tone. He declared that his opponents were perverters of the truth, and traitors to the unity of the Church, and again threatened to exclude them from communion with the Church of Rome. The discussion was carried on for a long time; the bishop of Carthage adhered firmly to his own opinion, and was supported by a large number of other bishops, one of whom was less cautious in his language than Cyprian, and openly denounced the bishop of Rome as a schismatic and worse than all heretics. He even went so far as to say that his just indignation was excited by the folly of Stephen, who boasted of his rank and of being the successor of St. Peter, and yet allowed many things to be done at Rome which were contrary to apostolical order. In after years, as the power of the bishops of Rome increased, their authority in all disputed points was more generally submitted to, and thus the question as to heretical baptism was, in the end, decided according to the opinion expressed by Stephen and the Roman Church. The same opinion is held by the English Church. Baptism, administered by dissenters, is not considered invalid, if the form prescribed by our Blessed Lord has been used. When any doubt exists upon this point, the Rubric in the Prayer-book is observed, and the words said are: "If thou art not already baptized, I baptize thee in the name of the Father and of the Son and of the Holy Ghost." Dionysius, bishop of Alexandria, whose singular escape in the Decian persecution has been previously mentioned, agreed with the bishop of Rome concerning the re-baptizing of heretics; but he mentions a remarkable case which for a time shook his opinion, and which certainly proves how much more seriously persons thought of baptism then than they do now. "When the brethren were gathered together," he says, "and when there was present one who had been before my time an ancient minister of the clergy, a certain person allowed to be sound in the faith, upon seeing our form and manner of baptism, and hearing the questions and responses, came to me weeping and wailing, falling prostrate at my feet, and protesting that the baptism which he had received was heretical, and could not be the true baptism; that it had no agreement with that which was in use among us, but on the contrary was full of impiety and blasphemy. He owned that the distress of his conscience was extreme, that he durst not presume to lift up his eyes to God, because he had been baptized with profane words and rites. He begged therefore to be re-baptized; with which request I durst not comply; but I told him that frequent Communion, many times administered, would suffice. This man had heard thanksgiving sounded in the Church, and had sung to it 'Amen.' He had been present at the Lord's Table; had stretched forth his hands to receive the Holy Food, had actually communicated; and indeed, for a long time, had been partaker of the Body and Blood of our Lord Jesus Christ. Therefore I durst not re-baptize him, but bade him be of good cheer, and of a sure faith, and boldly approach to the Communion of saints. Notwithstanding all this, the man mourns continually, and his horror keeps him from the Lord's Table; and he scarce with much entreaty can join in the prayers of the Church."

CHAPTER XXX.

MARTYRDOM OF ST. CYPRIAN. A.D. 253.

DURING the first four years of the reign of Valerian,
who had associated his son Gallienus in
A.D. 253. the government, all seemed to promise
peace for the Christian Church. The emperor's
household was filled with Christians, and the
favour shown them by Valerian surpassed that of
even the most lenient of his predecessors. But
these tranquil days were not long to last. Valerian
was under the influence of a favourite, named
Macrianus, a man who took delight in superstitious
and magical rites. The Christians discovered and
exposed the delusions practised by the persons
whom Macrianus encouraged, and the rage of the
favourite was excited against them. He poisoned
the mind of the emperor, and the old edicts were
renewed, and persecution once more began. All
persons, especially bishops and presbyters, were
called upon to join in the heathen ceremonies, and
exile was to be the punishment of disobedience.
Private meetings also were forbidden ; and it was
especially decreed that no person should enter the
cemeteries, these being the excavations or catacombs
which had now for so many years been the refuge
of the living Christians who fled from danger, and
the resting-place of the dead, who had no longer
cause to fear it. The punishment of death was not
expressly mentioned in Valerian's decree, but it
was easy so to interpret it, and one of the first to
suffer martyrdom was the hasty but earnest-minded
Stephen, bishop of Rome.

Very shortly afterwards, a copy of the edict was

delivered to Paternus, proconsul of Africa, who immediately prepared to execute it. Cyprian, like his opponent Stephen, had then but slight chance of escape, and all thoughts of enmity and controversy in the mind of the warm-hearted bishop of Carthage, must have been lost in sorrow and admiration for him who had already so nobly borne his witness to the truth; and in the absorbing preparation for the trial which was awaiting himself. A message from Paternus summoned him to the council-chamber. Paternus was probably not his enemy. Cyprian and he had lived in the same provinces, and the proconsul must have learnt to acknowledge the unwearied charity and the holy self-denial of the Christian bishop. He wished but to work upon Cyprian's fears, to lead him to an acknowledgment which might be a ground for his acquittal. When Cyprian was brought into his presence, he thus addressed him :— "The sacred emperors, Valerian and Gallienus, have honoured me by directing to me letters in which they have decreed that all men ought to worship the gods whom the Romans adore, on pain of being slain with the sword if they refuse. I have heard that *you* despise the worship of the gods; wherefore I advise you to consult for yourself, and to honour them." "I am a Christian and a bishop," replied Cyprian. "I know no god but the one true God, who created heaven and earth, the sea, and all things in them. This God we Christians serve. To Him we pray night and day for all men, and even for the emperor." "To persevere in this disposition, will be to die the death of a malefactor," observed Paternus. "That is a good disposition which fears God," answered the bishop, "and therefore it must not be changed." "Then,"

25*

exclaimed Paternus, "it is the will of the princes that, for the present you should be exiled." "He," replied Cyprian, "who has God in his heart is no exile, for the earth is the Lord's and the fulness thereof."

It was in vain to endeavour to shake a constancy based on such a firm foundation; yet Paternus, wishing to carry out his instructions, strove to extract from Cyprian some information respecting the presbyters then in the city. He even threatened him with torture if he refused to state what he knew concerning them. But Cyprian turned upon him with an answer from the very laws which the proconsul thought he was upholding. The best of the Roman princes had issued edicts against informers. It was wrong, therefore, he said, to require him to break the law. "Our princes," persisted Paternus," "have ordered that Christians should hold no meetings, and that whoever breaks this rule shall be put to death." "Do what you are ordered," was Cyprian's calm reply ; and the proconsul, wearied by his steadfastness, passed the sentence of exile.

It was not, however, a severe one. Cyprian was only sent to Curubis, a little town by the seaside, about fifty miles from Carthage, and opposite to Sicily. The place was agreeable, the air healthy, and he was allowed to have the comfort of a private lodging. The inhabitants also treated him with great kindness, and he was repeatedly visited by the Christians. Here he remained for eleven months, occupied in holy meditations, and acts of charity and usefulness. But the news which reached him must have effectually interfered with any thoughts of rest. Nine bishops had been seized, together with several priests and deacons, and a great number of Christian believers, including maidens and children. They had been beaten with sticks, and then sent to work in the copper mines among the mountains. The sense of his own comparative security must have been actually bitter to Cyprian under such circumstances; he could but comfort himself by endeavouring to support those who were suffering, and earnestly he poured forth his sympathy in the letters which he wrote to them. The sympathy, however, was not such as human feeling might have dictated. It was rather a triumphant exultation in the honour conferred on those who suffered for Christ. "O happy feet!" he writes, "shackled indeed, at present, with fetters, ye will quickly finish a glorious journey to Christ! Let malice and cruelty bind you as they please, ye will soon pass from earth and its sorrows to the Kingdom of Heaven. In the mines ye have not a bed on which the body may be refreshed; nevertheless, Christ is your rest and consolation. Your limbs are fatigued with labour, and lie on the ground; but so to lie down when you have Christ with you is no punishment. Your allowance of bread is but scanty; be it so—'man doth not live by bread alone, but by the word of God.' Ye have no proper clothes to defend you from the cold, but he who has put on Christ is clothed abundantly."

The power of the comfort thus offered to others was soon to be proved by Cyprian himself, and it is said that God was pleased to reveal the trial that awaited him. Many months before it took place, a vision was vouchsafed to him one night as he was going to rest. A young man of a prodigious stature appeared, and seemed to lead him to the Prætorium, the house of the Roman governor.

He was presented to the magistrate, who gazed upon him, and then wrote something in a book. Cyprian's guide looked over the shoulder of the proconsul, extended one of his hands, and made a cross stroke over it with the other. The action was received by Cyprian as an intimation of the manner of his death. He earnestly begged but one day's respite to order his earthly affairs; and the countenance of the proconsul, and the signs made by his guide, seemed to show that his request was granted. He awoke from his vision with the certainty that he had one year, and one year only to live.

That year was not to be passed in exile. Cyprian was permitted to return to Carthage, yet not to his former home, his friends, and his position in the eyes of the world. A garden near the city, which he had sold on his conversion, was now Providentially restored to him, and there he lived, regulating the affairs of the Church and distributing all that was left of his income to the poor; grudging himself, for their sake, even his last home, which he would have parted with, but for the fear of exciting the envy and cruelty of the heathen persecutors. For still the fierceness of Gentile rage was burning against the Christians, and from Rome especially accounts were received which excited the deepest anxiety. "Valerian,"—so said the messenger whom Cyprian despatched to inquire into the condition of his brethren,—" had given orders that bishops, presbyters, and deacons should be put to death without delay; that senators, noblemen, and knights should be degraded, and deprived of their property, and lose their lives, if still they persisted in calling themselves Christians. Women of rank were to be banished; Cæsar's freedmen were to be stripped of their goods, and sent to labour in chains on the imperial property." These were Valerian's directions to the Senate, and fearfully had they been obeyed. Persecution was carried on at Rome in all its horrors, and Xystus, the bishop, the successor of Stephen, had already borne the penalty of his high position, and suffered martyrdom in the cemetery, where the solemn assemblies of the Christians were held. Letters from the emperor, enforcing the edict, were daily expected to arrive in Africa; and this alarming intelligence Cyprian now strove to circulate throughout the province, in order, as he himself expressed it, "that all might think of death,—but not more of death than of immortality, and that, in the fulness of faith, they might rather with joy than with fear expect the approaching events." For himself, he had still the means of escape within his reach. Heathen senators, reverencing his virtues, and fearing for his life, came to him and offered to conceal him. But ·the offer was declined. Cyprian was probably too generous-minded to endanger the lives of his friends by accepting it. He complied, indeed, .with their advice, and hid himself, when told that the proconsul, who was then at Utica, had sent soldiers to seek and carry him thither; but he desired to escape at that time, only that he might die amongst his own people at Carthage. Yet there was no change in his principles whilst he thus steadily faced his coming martyrdom. Although ready, even thirsting for it, he did not court it by any open act, and the instructions which he had previously given on this subject were renewed. "Let none of you," he says, in his last letter to his clergy, "excite any tumult on account of the brethren, nor offer himself voluntarily to the Gentiles. He who is seized and delivered up ought to speak. The Lord who dwells in us will speak at that hour. Confession, rather than profession, is our duty."

Paternus, the governor, had died during the exile of Cyprian, and Galerius Maximus was now proconsul of Africa. Being out of health, he left Utica and retired to Sextus, a place by the sea-side, six miles from Carthage. Cyprian then ventured forth from his place of concealment, and returned to his garden. But the proconsul had not forgotten him. Two officers, with a party of soldiers were again sent to seize him, and this time he was unable, or unwilling, to conceal himself. The officers placed him in a chariot, making him sit between them, and drove to Sextus. Galerius Maximus was too ill to see them, the trial was deferred till the next day, and Cyprian was carried back and given in charge to the chief of his two captors, whose house was very near the Prætorium. Here he was guarded courteously, and his friends were permitted to visit him.

In the mean time the news of his apprehension had spread through Carthage, and both Heathens and Christians were in a tumult of excitement, for Cyprian was revered by all. Many Christians gathered round the house in which their bishop was a prisoner, and passed the night in the street. Cyprian's kindness of heart showed itself still in his thought for the young women who were amongst the crowd, and to whom he begged that particular attention might be shown. The following morning he walked to the Prætorium, followed by a vast concourse of people. When he arrived the proconsul was not ready to see him. He sat down to rest on a seat covered with a white cloth, which was remarked as being a sign of the episcopal honour due to him even in his humiliation. Here a soldier, who had once been a Christian, seeing him overcome by heat and fatigue, and wishing perhaps to carry away something which had actually belonged to him, offered him the refreshment of another suit of linen; but Cyprian only replied,—" Shall we seek a remedy for that which may last no longer than to-day ?" and he remained patiently waiting till the judge should be ready for him. At length the moment arrived, and Cyprian was taken into the judgment hall. Galerius Maximus looked at him and said : " Art thou Thascius Cyprian, who hast been bishop and father to men of an impious mind ? The sacred emperors command thee to do sacrifice ; —be well advised, and do not throw away thy life." " I am Cyprian," was the reply ; " I am a Christian and I cannot sacrifice to the gods. Do as thou hast been commanded. As for me, in so just a cause there needs no consultation." " You would judge better to consult your safety," persisted the proconsul. " My safety and my strength is Christ, the Lord," answered the bishop. " I have no desire that things should be otherwise with me than that I may adore my God, and hasten to Him ; for ' the afflictions of this present time are not worthy to be compared with the glory which shall be revealed in us.' " The proconsul, growing crimson with indignation at this bold avowal, then enumerated the offences of the prisoner, and pronounced the sentence of death. " You have lived sacrilegiously a long time ; you have formed a society of impious conspirators ; you have shown yourself an enemy to the gods and their religion, and have not hearkened to the equitable counsels of our princes. You have ever been a father and a ringleader of the impious sect ; you shall, therefore, be an example to the rest, that, by the shedding of your blood, they may learn their duty. Let Thascius Cyprian, who refuses to sacrifice to the gods, be put to death by the sword."

"God be praised ! " was the answer of the martyr, and he was led forth to die.

A strong guard of soldiers surrounded him, and a vast concourse of people followed, and from amongst them arose the cry of the Christians, " Let us also be beheaded with him ! " They reached the place of execution—a field surrounded by trees, into which numbers climbed, eager to behold the spectacle.

The bishop took off his cloak, folded it, and laid it at his feet ; then, kneeling down, he commended his soul to God. After this he put aside his under coat, which he delivered to the deacons who attended him ; and, dressed in only a linen vestment, awaited the arrival of the executioner, who, when he came, received, by Cyprian's orders, twenty-five golden pieces, equal in value to about six pounds.

At the last moment the brethren gathered around their bishop, and spread linen cloths around him, that so his blood might not be spilt upon the ground. Cyprian bound a napkin over his own eyes, a presbyter and a deacon tied his hands, and his head was severed from his body by the sword.

Pontius, his biographer, says that " the longing of his heart was to have died with him." There must have been many among the Christians who gazed on the lifeless form of the kind, noble-hearted Cyprian of Carthage, that shared the wish.

CHAPTER XXXI.

THE COUNCIL OF ANTIOCH CONFUTES AND DEPOSES PAUL OF SAMOSATA. A.D. 270.

It has been said that Cyprian, shortly before his death, heard of the martyrdom of Xystus, bishop of Rome. In pursuance of the edict of Valerian, Xystus had been seized with some of his clergy. As they bore him to execution, Laurentius, his chief deacon, accompanied him, weeping, and said, " Whither goest thou, father, without thy son ? " " Thou shalt follow me in three days," replied Xystus.

The bishop was killed, and the prefect of Rome, hearing a report of the immense riches of the Roman Church, sent for Laurentius, and ordered him to deliver them up. The deacon demanded a little time, that he might set everything in order, and take an account of each particular. Three days were granted him. In that time Laurentius collected together all the poor who were supported by the Roman Church, and then sent this message to the prefect :—" Come, behold the riches of our God. Thou shalt see a spacious court filled with golden vessels." The prefect obeyed the summons, but when he arrived at the place where Laurentius was waiting for him, and saw only the poor who were assembled, he turned to the deacon with a countenance full of wrath. " What are you displeased at ? " asked Laurentius. " The gold you so eagerly desire is but a vile metal taken out of the earth. The true gold is that Light whose disciples these poor men are. These are the treasures which I promised you ; to which I will add pre-

26

cious stones. Behold these virgins and widows; they are the Church's crown; make use of these riches for the advantage of Rome, of the emperor, and of yourself."

The mind of the prefect of Rome was unable to comprehend the lesson thus taught him. Charity to the poor was not one of the heathen virtues. Filled with indignation, he exclaimed, " Dost thou mock me ? I know that you Christians value yourselves for despising death ; therefore shalt thou die at once." He then ordered Laurentius to be stripped, extended, and fastened to a gridiron, and in that manner to be broiled to death by a slow fire. His command was executed, and the martyr was placed before the fire. After being left there for a considerable time, he said to the prefect, " Let me be turned, that is sufficient for one side." They turned him ; he looked up to heaven, prayed for the conversion of Rome, and died.

Another instance of amazing fortitude was exhibited at Cæsarea, in Cappadocia, by a child named Cyril. His father was a pagan, but Cyril, having been taught the faith of Christianity, made an open profession of his belief. Several children of his own age persecuted him, and his father at length drove him from his home. The magistrate of the city, hearing of him, gave orders that he should be brought before him. " My child," he said, when Cyril was presented to him, " I will pardon your faults, and your father shall receive you again. It is in your power to enjoy your father's estate provided you are wise, and take care of your own interests." " I rejoice to bear your reproaches," replied the boy. " God will receive me ; I do not grieve that I am expelled from my home, I shall have a better mansion. I fear not death, because it will introduce me into a better life." On hearing this confession the judge commanded Cyril to be bound, and led as it were to execution; yet at the same time he gave secret orders that he should be brought back again, trusting that the sight of the fire might overcome the boy's resolution. Cyril, however, remained unmoved. The judge continued his remonstrances, but the only answer he could obtain was, "I go to a better house. I go to more excellent riches. Despatch me presently that I may enjoy them." Some persons who were present looked at the little fellow with weeping eyes, but Cyril comforted them. "Ye should rather rejoice in conducting me to punishment," he said; "ye know not what is my hope, nor what a city I am going to inhabit;" and uttering these words, he went to his death.

The strength vouchsafed to true Christian charity, and the weakness of a proud temper, were exemplified in the case of another martyrdom, which is recorded as having occurred at Antioch during the persecution of Valerian. There were living in that city, a presbyter, named Sapricius, and a deacon, Nicephorus. These men, through some misunderstanding, became so estranged that when they met in the streets they would not even salute each other. Nicephorus, however, after a while relented, and going to the house of Sapricius, threw himself at his feet and entreated his forgiveness. But the proud spirit of Sapricius could not overlook an affront, and he refused to relent. About this time the Valerian persecution broke out. Sapricius, being carried before the magistrate, made a bold confession, and was sentenced to be tortured, and then beheaded. Nicephorus followed him to the place of execution, still entreating for pardon, and reminding him of the words of his Divine Master, " Ask, and it shall be given you." But the unforgiving heart of Sapricius was not touched even in that moment of extreme danger. He thought he could die for Christ, but he could not die to his own will; and God proved to him the blindness of his self-confidence. Forsaken by the Holy Spirit, he suddenly recanted, and promised to sacrifice. Nicephorus entreated him to be steadfast; but his words had no effect. Then Nicephorus turned to the executioner and said, " I believe in the name of the Lord Jesus Christ, whom he hath renounced." The confession received its allotted punishment. Nicephorus was beheaded, and went to his rest in Paradise, and Sapricius lived to linger out a miserable, though, it is to be hoped, a repentant existence on earth.

Dionysius, bishop of Alexandria, was banished during this persecution; but his punishment was the means of the further spread of the Gospel in Egypt, as he and his companions took occasion to instruct the people amongst whom they dwelt, and converted many. Dionysius himself has left a description of his feelings at this time, which is interesting from the simplicity with which he speaks of his own weakness and natural shrinking from suffering. " As soon," he says, " as I heard that Æmilian (the prefect of Alexandria) had ordered us to depart from Cephro (the village to which he was first exiled), I undertook my journey cheerfully, though I did not know whither we were to go; but upon being informed that Colluthion was the place, I felt much distress; because it was reported to be a situation destitute of all the comforts of society, exposed to the tumults of travellers, and infested by thieves. My companions well remember the effect this had on my mind. I proclaim my own shame. At first I grieved immoderately. It was a consolation, however, that it was nigh to a city. I was in hopes, from the nearness of the city, that we might enjoy the company of dear brethren, and that particular assemblies for Divine Worship might be established in the suburbs, which indeed came to pass." The sufferings of Dionysius, though no doubt severe, appear light when compared with those which others were undergoing at the same period; but, after a persecution of three years, peace was restored to the Church by the death of the Emperor, which took place under the most painful circumstances. Valerian, being engaged in a war with Sapor, king of Persia, was made prisoner, and after enduring the most insulting and cruel treatment, —Sapor using his neck as a footstool when mounting his horse,—he was flayed alive. Gal- A.D. 259. lienus, his son and successor, showed no willingness to follow the footsteps of his father in his severity to the Christians, whose teaching he allowed to spread undisturbed. But repose was, as usual, the signal for heresy to spring up. Sabellianism, a false doctrine respecting the Holy Trinity, was propounded by Sabellius, an African presbyter, and ably refuted by Dionysius of Alexandria. The belief in a Millennium, or the personal reign of our Lord on earth for a thousand years, was also opposed by the same bishop; Dionysius was indeed, at that time, the most distinguished upholder of the Catholic faith, and even at the last moment of his life was engaged in setting forth the truth handed down from the Apostles. He died whilst a council was sitting which had been called to consider the errors that had for some time been set forth by Paul of Samosata, bishop of Antioch. Dionysius was unable to attend because of his advanced age, yet he delivered, in writing, his strong condemnation of the teaching of Paul, whose false doctrine related chiefly to the Divinity of our Lord. Paul himself was a rapacious, arrogant, and profligate man, and it is singular that the Church should so long have endured him. He is said to have owed his position chiefly to the support of Zenobia, Queen of Palmyra, who estimated him highly for his abilities; and especially valued his political talents. When an inquiry into his errors was first made, Paul protested that he repented of them; but his after conduct showed that this declaration was only a pretence, and, by the decree of a council held at Antioch, A.D. 270, he was finally deposed. Gregory Thaumaturgus and his brother Athenodore both attended the council of Antioch, which was the most important event of that period.

Claudius, Aurelian, Tacitus, Probus, Carus, and his two sons, Carinus and Numerian, who reigned jointly with him, succeeded each other in the space of sixteen years. They seem to pass before us, for the most part, as actors on a stage, who are playing their part in the pageant exhibited, but with whom we ourselves have no concern. Aurelian is the only exception. A.D. 270. The Christians at Antioch appealed to him, on one occasion, to put them in possession of the building used for divine service, which had been retained by the wicked Paul of Samosata after his deposition, instead of having been delivered up to Domnus, the bishop appointed to succeed him. Aurelian could not have known anything of the rights and pretensions of Paul, but he made an important decision. Instead of consulting the clergy of the place, who were likely to be prejudiced, he declared that the individual with whom the Italian bishops, and especially the bishop of Rome, held communion, should be the lawful bishop. The decision was accepted, and Domnus was put in possession of his rights. Thus the singular spectacle was exhibited of the Church unable to enforce its own decree, and calling in the aid of the government, which was in the hands of a heathen. At the time of his death Aurelian was meditating a persecution of the Christians, but though it may perhaps have begun in Rome, and in the places where the Emperor was personally present, it ceased when he died, and certainly did not at any time reach the provinces.

Porphyry, a Platonic philosopher, and one of the bitterest enemies that the Gospel ever encountered, about this time wrote a work against Christianity, which was answered by Methodius, bishop of Tyre. Neither the attack nor the defence have come down to us.

<hr>

CHAPTER XXXII.

THE DIOCLETIAN PERSECUTION. A.D. 293.

DIOCLETIAN, who succeeded Carinus, and will always be remembered as one of the A.D. 284. fiercest persecutors of the Christian Church, showed no signs of enmity to Christianity, when he first ascended the throne. His wife and daughter are said to have been Christians, and his household was filled by persons professing the true faith, several of the imperial officers who had the care of the

Emperor's ornaments, robes, furniture, and private money, being Christians.   Heathenism was indeed by slow, yet sure degrees, dying away.   The religion of Christ was now professed openly by the rich and noble ; believers in the Saviour held honourable offices in the state ; crowds attended the Christian worship ; and when the old buildings could no longer receive them, larger edifices were erected without remark or interruption.   Yet even at this period, as a proof that persecution was always more or less carried on in different parts of the empire, we find the first instance of martyrdom in Britain.   Alban, of Verulam, a Roman officer of noble birth, and a heathen, received into his house a Christian priest, who had fled to him for refuge ; and, whilst thus exercising charity, he was so struck with his guest's piety and earnestness in prayer, that his own heart was touched ; he listened to the new teaching, and became a Christian.   In the mean time soldiers were sent to apprehend the priest, who was known to be harboured in Alban's house.   They were received by Alban, who had dressed himself in the cassock usually worn by his friend.   The soldiers, though deceived for the moment, soon discovered their mistake, and Alban was seized and dragged before the Roman governor, who ordered him to confess where the Christian priest had taken refuge, and bade him also offer sacrifice himself to the gods of Rome.   Alban refused to obey either of these commands, and was immediately beaten with rods, and sentenced to death.   On his way to the place of execution he was obliged to cross a bridge over the river Ver. It was thronged with people eager to behold him. Alban, anxious that no delay might take place, without waiting for the bridge to be cleared, made his way through the river, an act of intrepidity and zeal, which had such an effect on the person appointed to be his executioner that, throwing away his sword, he asked to die with the prisoner. The request was granted, and the two Christians received the crown of martyrdom together, and were beheaded. A church was afterwards erected at Verulam in honour of Alban, and the town has since been called by his name.

The Roman empire was now fast hastening to its decay. Hordes of barbarians poured in upon the outlying provinces; rivals for the throne sprang up; the task of government became too great for Diocletian; and, in order to strengthen himself, he admitted a partner in the empire, Maximian, one of his generals. Even this was not enough. Two other joint rulers, or Cæsars, as they were called, were, after a few years, thought necessary for the safety of the state; and thus the will of Diocletian was no longer the one law of government. The change was soon felt by the Church. Christians were favoured or the contrary, according to the will of the Cæsar under whom their lot was placed; and soon it became evident that Diocletian himself was inclined to share the feelings of those who regarded them with suspicion.

The first symptom of a persecuting spirit appeared in the steps taken to prevent the spread of a set of novel doctrines, known by the name of Manichean, and more hateful to those who held the Catholic faith, than they could have been to the heathen Emperor, but which appear to have been at times confounded with Christianity. Manes, the founder of this sect, was born in Persia, and was originally a slave, and afterwards a painter and engraver. He became a convert to Christianity, but having been brought up in the Persian or Magian religion, he endeavoured to blend it with Christianity, and formed a system, which, though full of monstrous absurdities, spread rapidly, especially in the East. The chief heretical falsehood had hitherto concerned the Divine Nature of our Blessed Lord. But Manes introduced a new creed, and taught that the universe was subject to the control of two eternal and independent beings, one good, the other evil, and that from the conflict of these powers arose all the confusion which we behold on earth. The good soul of man, he declared, proceeded from the good spirit, and the evil soul, together with the body, and all corporeal creatures, from the evil spirit. To these errors he added a system of wild speculation as to the spiritual world and the Divine Being, which, though bearing some resemblance to Christianity, was really utterly destructive of it. Manes denied the resurrection, used a form of baptism different from that of the Church, forbade alms to be given to any who were not of his own sect, prohibited his followers from the use of eggs, cheese, milk, and wine, which he said proceeded from a bad principle, condemned marriage, and would not allow that magistrates should be obeyed. Amongst other absurdities, he held that the sun and the moon were ships, and that the soul of a man and of a tree were of the same substance, and both of them a part of God. His followers professed to lead strict lives, but they were, notwithstanding, allowed by the doctrines of their religion, to commit the grossest sins. Why Diocletian should have so strongly opposed this sect is uncertain; but the edicts passed for their punishment were very severe, and showed that the Emperor was zealous for the old heathen religion, and did not shrink from persecution. Galerius, his son-in-law, who had also been chosen to be Cæsar, encouraged his prejudices. He hated the Christians himself, and did not conceal the fact from Diocletian. But it was some time before he could excite the Emperor to any act of violence. At length he urged that the encouragement given to the Christians excited the anger of the gods, so that they would not accept the sacrifices offered them. This argument influenced the mind of Diocletian. He had been attempting to pry into futurity, by practising superstitious rites, and whilst so engaged a Christian servant had made in his presence the sign of the cross on his forehead. The Emperor's divination was unsuccessful, and he attributed it to this cause. In great anger he issued an order that all persons holding office about the court or in the army should be obliged to be present at sacrifices. This was in the year 298. The edict was proclaimed, amongst other places, at Tangiers, in Mauritania, at a time when every one was engaged in feasting and sacrificing. Marcellus, a centurion, took off his belt, threw down his arms, and exclaimed: "I will not fight any longer under the banner of the Emperor, or serve gods of wood and stone. If the condition of a soldier be such that he is obliged to sacrifice to gods and emperors, I quit the service." He was ordered to be beheaded. Cassianus, the registrar, whose business it was to write down the sentence, protested against its injustice, and a month afterwards he was also martyred.

From that time the persecution spread rapidly. Only in Gaul and Britain, which were under the government of the Cæsar Constantius, was there any safety. Diocletian was roused to tyranny, and the first objects of his anger were his wife Prisca and her daughter Valeria, the wife of Galerius, both of whom were compelled to join in a sacrifice. The details of the sufferings endured by the Christians have been thus given by Eusebius, the celebrated Church historian, who was actually living at the time.

"In the nineteenth year of Diocletian, in the month of March, upon the vigil of Easter, came abroad the imperial edicts for a general persecution of the Christians, commanding the Churches to be demolished, the Bibles burnt, all Christians in public offices disgraced, and those of a more private condition disenfranchised; and soon after more edicts were issued out, which ordered that the bishops should be laid in chains, and all other Christians obliged to do sacrifice at their utmost peril. A great number of our bishops persevered with all bravery and courage to the very last moment, under the sharpest anguish of the tortures, whilst others came presently to terms. There was no method, no instrument of death or barbarity, as scourges, pincers, dray-hooks, and the like, but what was employed against the disciples of the Blessed Jesus. They were half killed, and then thrown to expire upon the ground, many of them among the dead bodies of those who, it was asserted, had been induced to sacrifice; for the policy of the heathen had a double edge, either to force the Christians to do sacrifice, or, if they could not get the better of them, at least, to set them forth as sacrificers. At Nicomedia, the Imperial edict was no sooner stuck up but a zealous Christian of that place, and a person of the best condition and quality, came and tore it down in the face of the city (where Diocletian and Galerius then resided), and to the last moment underwent, without the least discomposure, the first sallies of their fury, which, consequently, were the fiercest. Even the Emperor's court yielded a plenteous harvest of martyrs, particularly the noble Dorotheus and several others, all gentlemen of the bedchamber. Peter, one of the number (for the present opportunity will not suffice to give the history of them all), being required, in the presence of the emperor now mentioned, to do sacrifice, and, absolutely resisting, was flayed with scourges to the very bone. Salt and vinegar were then poured into the wounds, and he was laid out upon a gridiron and broiled over a slow fire. After some time he yielded up the ghost, asserting resolutely his faith in his Saviour to the last moment of his life.

"The number of those who suffered to death in Africa, Mauritania, Thebais, Egypt, and all the provinces were so great that it required some skill in arithmetic to compute them. In Palestine, and in the city of Tyre, myself was a spectator of the tortures which my blessed brethren endured; of their impregnable constancy and patience, and of the mighty supports which they received from the Divine mercy; while an extraordinary presence of the Holy Spirit was manifested in them, and even the living instruments of execution, the lions, the leopards, the wild boars, the bulls were so restrained and overruled at the pleasure of their Creator, that, although they were goaded with red-hot irons, and the infidels forced the holy confessors to provoke and urge them, either they would not so much as make approaches to their bodies, or else they retreated as soon as they came on, sweating, trembling, and bellowing, while several of the heathens coming in their way were gored and tossed by the

27

bulls, and carried off for dead.   In the conclusion, when the persecutors had often tried in vain, and many of them, to their great disappointment, to set the wild beasts upon the martyrs, they put them to the sword, and flung their bodies into the sea.

" Apphianus, born in Lycia, descended of a very rich family, and trained up to philosophical studies at Berytus (where he led a life of severe and strict sobriety), secretly left his father and relations, before he had attained the twentieth year of his age, because their dissolute and irregular way of life gave great disturbance to his pious disposition, and, being conducted by the direction of the Holy Spirit, he came directly to Cæsarea.   There, it so fell out, that I had the commission of instructing him in the elements of the Christian religion, and of expounding the Holy Scripture to him ;   and there, after he had passed some time in the exercise of ascetical duties, inflamed with a Divine ardour, and quite unmoved by the terrors which the pro-ceedings of the persecutors had occasioned in that place, he went up calmly and unconcernedly to the prefect, who was then upon the point of performing a libation, and, interrupting the ceremony, took him by the hand, and soberly reasoned the case with him, dissuading him from the practice and showing him the grossness of the absurdity.   Upon this he was violently seized by the soldiers, abused and beaten, and thrown into a dungeon, where for four and twenty hours he was kept upon the torture ; and afterwards, when he protested over and over against the proposal of doing sacrifice, they slashed and scarified his body to the bone, and battered his face and neck with mallets of lead.   Then his feet were wrapt with flax, soaked in oil, which was set on fire.   But the martyr defied the force of all

these or any other torments they could expose him
to ; so he was again laid in chains, and, three days
after, having just life enough left to declare his
faith, he was thrown into the sea, when presently
both sea and sky were convulsed with an earthquake and tempest that rocked all the buildings in
Cæsarea ; and the dead body of the martyr, emerging
back on a sudden to the surface of the waves, was
floated ashore to the place where he had suffered.
Of this all the people of Cæsarea were witnesses.

" The persecution had now lasted seven years,
when a short respite of connivance intervened, till
the prefect, a very cruel man, sent malicious complaints of us to the tyrant the year following, and
then came down the procurator of the mines, who,
ranging the confessors into separate companies,
ordered away some to Cyprus and others to
Libanus ; the rest were dispersed in Palestine and
made slaves. Those confessors who were not in a
condition to work by reason of their age or in-
firmities of body, had a peculiar place of residence
assigned them. The chief of them was Silvanus,
a most worthy bishop, upon whom the persecutors
had taken all opportunities of indulging their
malice from the very beginning of the persecution.
He had a great many Christians of Egypt to bear
him company ; and among the rest, one John,
whose eyes had been thrust out before. This excellent person had a prodigious memory, and was
able to repeat without book all parts of the Holy
Scriptures, as I myself can attest, for I have often
been present when he has pronounced the lessons
at Divine Service, as exactly and easily as if he
had read them. Besides these two, there were of
the same company thirty-seven more, who by constantly performing the public duties of worship

and discipline, in a little time so provoked the prefect, that he beheaded all the thirty-nine at one execution. In Egypt, men, women, and children innumerable, steadfastly professing their faith and trust in their Saviour, endured the scourge, the rack, the pincers, and every other torture, were burnt, drowned, beheaded, famished, crucified, some in the usual manner, others with their heads downwards, and left to hang in a miserable destitute condition upon the cross. Scarce a day passed for several years, but a number of Christians were tortured and destroyed; and as soon as one company had received their sentence, another crowded up to the tribunal to declare themselves, and afterwards ran exulting and rejoicing to their execution, and, under the very keenest extremities of torture and the last agonies of death, sang psalms and songs of praise to their Blessed Creator; insomuch that there returned a frequent necessity for a fresh supply both of executioners and their weapons, to which I myself was eye-witness."

Such is the account of this terrible persecution given by Eusebius, and confirmed by the fact of the spread of Christianity in the midst of such apparently overwhelming trials.

CHAPTER XXXIII.

CONVERSION OF CONSTANTINE. A.D. 312.

DIOCLETIAN and Maximian resigned the empire, after the former had reigned twenty years, A.D. 304. but the persecution still continued under Galerius, and Maximin, who was associated with him. Constantius, however, who became Emperor of the West, and chose Severus to be his Cæsar, continued to show mercy to the Christians. He would not suffer them to be injured, and though at length persuaded to displace the Christian officers of his household who would not change their religion, he sent away in disgrace the few that consented to apostatise, saying, that those who were not true to their God would never be faithful to their prince.

Britain was the country in which Constantius spent the last years of his life. He took up his residence at York, and there finding himself seized with a serious illness, he began to make arrangements for the succession to his share of the empire. His son, Constantine, had been left with Galerius as a kind of hostage, but Constantius, being desirous to give him his last instructions, sent orders that he should join him with all speed. Constantine arrived only just in time to see his father alive. Constantius received him with the greatest affection, expressed it as his will that he should succeed him, enjoined him to protect the Christians, and then expired. Constantine, however, was not to be permitted thus easily to inherit his father's dominion. Galerius was indignant at his advancement, and raised up rivals to oppose him. The first years of Constantine's reign were spent in perpetual warfare, and although he gave perfect toleration to the Christians in the West, so far as his authority extended, he was unable to protect them in the East, where their sufferings were still very terrible. Palestine and Egypt, which were subject to Maximin, were especially the scenes of wanton and inhuman barbarity. Amongst other martyrdoms which attracted particular attention, may be mentioned that of Pamphilus, a man of great learning, who had written out nearly all the

27*

works of Origen with his own hand. Eusebius, the Church historian, was his pupil, and admired him so much, that he is often called Eusebius Pamphilus. Pamphilus was kept in prison for two years before his death, and during that time employed himself in writing a defence of Origen, whose opinions were now beginning to be called in question. He was beheaded with twelve other Christians, and the bodies of the martyrs were, by order of the governor, exposed for four days that the birds and beasts might eat them.

But punishment was soon to fall on one of the persecutors who countenanced these inhuman actions. Galerius was preparing to march into Italy in order to oppose Severus, the partner of Constantine, when he was seized with a horrible and loathsome disease. He lingered for more than a year in intense suffering; an object of terror and disgust to all who approached him. Worn out with agony, his conscience at length began to reproach him for his cruelty, and a few days before he breathed his last, he issued an edict by which the Christians were allowed to rebuild their places of worship, and were entreated to pray for the health of the dying Emperor. This was, in fact, an order for the cessation of the persecution, and hundreds of victims, who had been imprisoned or sent to the mines, soon afterwards returned to their homes.

After the death of Galerius, the Roman empire still continued under the government of four rulers. Licinius, who was one of the Emperors appointed by Galerius in opposition to Constantine, seized upon Asia Minor; Constantine was lord over the western countries; Maxentius, the son-in-law of Galerius, governed Italy; and Maximin was acknowledged

as Emperor in Syria, Egypt, and the countries
dependent on them. It was a season when no open
proclamation of enmity against the Christians was
made by the government, yet the Church was not,
therefore, really secure. Maximin hated the Christians as much as Galerius had done; but his
colleagues in the empire were not disposed to persecute them, and he could not at once venture to
set up his own will in opposition to theirs. All,
however, which lay in his power, he did. An
excuse was needed for their destruction, and in
order to furnish this the grossest calumnies were
invented. A work was forged under the name of
the Acts of Pilate, which gave a false and disgraceful account of the life of our Blessed Lord.
Copies were circulated throughout Maximin's dominions, and schoolmasters were directed to deliver them to their pupils, and to insist upon
lessons being learnt from them. Some unhappy
persons, professing Christianity, were hired to
confess dreadful crimes, which it was said were
committed at the Christian assemblies; and reports
of this kind being sent to the Emperor, were, by
his order, distributed throughout the land. Punishment followed necessarily. Loss of sight, am-
putation of limbs, and other tortures, were devised
for the Christians; yet Maximin deemed himself
merciful, because he spared their lives. Conscience,
however, was awake in others, though it might be
dead in him. The officer, who invented and pro-
mulgated the false confession, perished afterwards
by his own hand.

The condition of the Church was at this time
almost worse than at any previous period, for no
arts were left unemployed to root out the Christian
doctrines from the minds of the people, and edu-

cate the next generation in a confirmed aversion to it. Force had been proved to be useless, but corruption, it was trusted, might prove effective.

Truth, however, was not thus to be uprooted by the wickedness of evil men. If the heathen could teach and argue, so also could the Christians. For two centuries successive attacks had compelled them to explain and defend their religion, and few writers of eminence had ventured to appear against them. The facts upon which their faith rested were acknowledged even by their enemies. That Jesus Christ lived, taught, and was crucified, and that the belief in his resurrection was so strong as to lead his friends to face death, rather than deny it, were truths so undeniable that the fiercest enemies of Christianity had been unable to deny them. Doctrines might be perverted, miracles might be supposed accounted for by natural causes, heretics might talk of the Body of our Lord as an appearance and his sufferings as imaginary ; but still the Christian believer asserted without contradiction his unalterable creed : " I believe in Jesus Christ, who suffered under Pontius Pilate, was crucified, dead, and buried, and rose again the third day from the dead ; " and, as infidel after infidel started up in opposition, he was silenced by that strength of an undoubted fact against which no powers of reason or philosophy can prevail. And as it had been before, so it was now. Men of learning and genius stood up in defence of the faith. Lactantius and Arnobius, Africans by birth, and laymen, were amongst the most remarkable. They were men mixing in the world, who had no interested motives in the maintenance of Christian worship ; but they did not hesitate to give the full support of their talents and influence to the faith so grievously assailed; and their powerful exposure of the follies and impieties of paganism has never been surpassed.

Seasons of great suffering are almost universally acknowledged to be seasons also of great deliverance; and the time was now rapidly approaching when the Church was to be raised from what, in human eyes, was its position of degradation. The ambition and cruel government of Maxentius, the ruler of Italy, induced Constantine to undertake an expedition against him, in the hope of uprooting the tyrant's powers; and with this object in view he set out on his march from Gaul into Italy. The attempt was hazardous, for if it failed it would be ruin. Constantine must no doubt have been greatly oppressed by the thought of the dangerous and uncertain future; and at such a time the human mind is peculiarly alive to everything approaching to supernatural influence. How far the Emperor understood the claims of Christianity is uncertain; but that his wishes and prejudices were in its favour there can be no question. Toleration of the Christians had been the dying injunction of his father; and although Constantine himself had never yet openly professed his faith in Christ, it is known that, at the time of his Italian expedition, he condemned the worship of the many gods of heathenism, allowed multitudes of Christians to form part of his court, and amongst them some of the clergy, who openly offered up prayers for him.

The circumstance said to have given a final direction to his belief is by some supposed to rest on insufficient authority. But the facts that followed are an evidence which must be allowed to weigh greatly in favour of its truth. In the month of October, in the year 312, Maxentius was called upon to fight for his empire and his life under the walls of Rome. Constantine was advancing towards the city, and making ready for the battle. In the prospect of possible defeat and perhaps death, the Emperor was led to meditate upon the necessity of Divine protection. Such thoughts naturally lead to prayer, but Constantine knew not to whom to pray. The gods of the heathens he despised. The God of the Christians he had never yet acknowledged. In the disturbance of his mind he offered up some of those general petitions, which through the result of ignorance, are accepted in mercy. What he needed was, certainty as to his faith, and it was this for which he prayed. That very afternoon the answer was vouchsafed to him. As he looked upwards, whilst marching with his troops, the form of a bright Cross appeared in the heavens, and with it the words, " In this overcome." The soldiers also saw the sign. Constantine pondered on the event till night. When he fell asleep, the figure of our Blessed Lord appeared to him with the same token of the Cross, and he was directed to make use of the symbol as his military ensign. Eusebius, the Church Historian, tells us that he heard the story of the miraculous appearance in the heavens from the Emperor himself, who confirmed it with an oath ; and it is certain that under the banner of the Cross the army of Constantine gained a signal victory. Maxentius was drowned in the Tiber, and Constantine took possession of the city, and in memory of his success, ordered that the triumphal statue, which the citizens erected to his honour, should hold a Cross in the right hand. From that time Constantine's career was one of continued prosperity. Uniting with Licinius, he openly proclaimed freedom and toleration for the Christians. Maximin opposed the edict, but his power was soon at an end. Licinius, anxious to gain more authority in the empire, attacked him, and Maximin, after being defeated in battle, was obliged to flee for his life to Tarsus. He died there; some say from poison, others, of a fearful disease. In his last agonies, conscience accused him of his cruelty to the Christians. "It was not I, but others who did it," was the frantic cry which burst from his lips, and earnestly he implored that Christ would have compassion on his misery. He expired, confessing himself vanquished by the power of Christianity.

CHAPTER XXXIV.

CONSTANTINE BECOMES SOLE MONARCH. A. D. 323.

CONSTANTINE and Licinius now remained undisputed possessors and partners of the empire, but they were both too ambitious to remain long at peace. The quarrel which broke out between them is by heathen writers ascribed to Constantine, by Christian writers to Licinius. There can be no doubt that on one most important subject, the treatment of the Christians, the principles of the two Emperors differed widely. Licinius was a persecutor at heart, however he might, for a time, consent, from political motives, to join in supporting Christianity. Some of his cruelties incensed Constantine, who openly declared war against him.

The two armies came to an engagement in Pannonia. Previous to the battle, Constantine, in the midst of his Christian bishops, entreated the aid of the True God. Licinius through his priests, addressed himself to his pagan deities. Licinius was defeated, and though he made after attempts to recover his power, they were unsuccessful. He at length surrendered, on condition that his life should be spared; but, being discovered in the formation of new conspiracies, he was killed by the command of Constantine, who was then the sole and undisputed monarch of the Roman Empire.

Christianity was now the avowed religion of the state. Experience has shown that such a position, however greatly to be desired for many and most important reasons, is one which can never be free from danger to the cause of truth and earnestness. The interests of the world are mixed up with those of religion, motives become corrupted, and the dread of giving offence keeps back many from the open profession of the simple faith which their superiors in authority despise or condemn. Persecution strengthens truth—prosperity weakens it. But the fact is one which only experience can prove; and the Christians, who rejoiced in the undisputed sovereignty of Constantine, had no period of universal peace on which to look back for warning. The Church had been nurtured in suffering. To be suffered to pass unnoticed was the best that her children had hitherto been permitted to expect. It was no marvel that their hearts should beat high with exultation, and their voices be loud in thankfulness and praise when, for the first time, they found themselves not only admitted to the common privileges of their heathen fellow-subjects, but placed above them in the favour of the Emperor.

And, if the external support of Christian doctrines, and an attention to Christian forms, could be accepted as sufficient signs of genuine religion, there would be no doubt as to the claim of Constantine the Great to be placed amongst the most earnest disciples of the Saviour of the world.   It is only upon a deeper inquiry into his history, and a consideration of the facts of his reign, the support which, in several instances, he still gave to heathenism, and the crimes with which his life was stained,—that we are forced to suspend our judgment, and to question whether the religion he professed was anything more than an adoption of the creed which he believed would be most likely to further his political objects.   The life of Constantine is an inconsistent mystery; it has given rise to cavils, and arguments and assertions; but the opinions formed of his character must be as various as the facts, and as uncertain as the motives, of his conduct; and when all has been said, we can but confess our ignorance of the intricacies of every human heart, and leave the question of the emperor's sincerity to be revealed in the Great Day of Account by Him " to whom all hearts are open, and from whom no secrets are hid."

Yet, to human eyes, the sincerity of Constantine's profession of faith, at least at the commencement of his reign, was scarcely open to any serious doubt. He issued edicts requiring his subjects in the East to embrace the Christian religion; he forbade the use of sacrifices and other idolatrous rites of the heathen; and put an end to the inhuman entertainments of the Gladiators at Rome. He took care that all his prefects and inferior magistrates should be Christians; he was extremely liberal to the clergy; commanded the sign of the Cross to be marked upon the weapons and armour of his soldiers; abolished the punishment of crucifixion; and ordered the solemn observation of Friday as a fast, and of Sunday as a festival. He also exempted all ecclesiastical persons from taxes, allowed an appeal to be made to the bishops when persons were dissatisfied with the decision of any of the inferior civil magistrates ; and ordained that the determinations of councils and synods should be looked upon as sacred, and received as part of the imperial laws. Besides giving these marks of reverence for Christianity, Constantine built numerous churches, and epecially lent his assistance to his mother, Helena,—a British lady, who was remarkable for her devotion,—in the search made at Jerusalem for the place of our Lord's Sepulchre. The result of his search is said to have been the dicovery not only of the sacred tomb, but of the Cross, which according to Roman custom, had been buried near the place of crucifixion. The situation of the sepulchre was marked by a magnificent church built by Constantine's order. Such support was, however, an easy task ; it was far more difficult to act rightly with regard to the schisms which, during Constantine's reign, disturbed the place of the Church. The distinction between schism and heresy has already been shown in the case of the Montanists. Two other schismatical bodies, the Meletians and the Donatists, were formed at the beginning of the fourth century. The Meletians were the disciples of Meletius, bishop of Lycopolis, in Egypt, who objected to the mercy shown by one of the Alexandrian bishops to persons who had fallen away during the period of persecution. Pretending to hold stricter views of duty than their brethren, they were in the end led into grievous error, and induced to separate from the Church, and set up bishops of their own. Such was also the case with the Donatists, who took their name from Donatus, of Casa Nigra, in Numidia. This man was discontented with the condition of the Church of Carthage, and formed a party against the bishop Mensurius, whom he accused of having delivered up the sacred volumes to the heathen, and of having denied succours to the Christians in prison; Cecilianus, the bishop's deacon, was involved in the charge. The disputes were still going on when Mensurius died, and Cecilianus was chosen to succeed him. The quarrel then came to an open rupture. The party of Donatus became very strong, and was especially supported by a lady named Lucilla, whose riches gave her influence. On account of some slight informality in the consecration of Cecilianus, his election was declared by the Donatists to be invalid, and a bishop was chosen by them in opposition to him. The Church was now in open schism, and an appeal was made to the emperor, who convoked a council, at Arles, in Gaul, to decide the question. Three British bishops were present at this council. Cecilianus, after inquiry, was declared to be the rightful bishop, but the Donatists, instead of submitting to the decision, became furious. They asserted their pretensions more violently than before, and openly declared against the Catholics, whom they rebaptized; at the same time overthrowing their altars, burning their churches, consecrating new bishops, and thus for many years fatally injuring the tranquillity of the Christian world.

In this and all cases of appeal, Constantine seems to have been heartily anxious to restore unanimity to the Church; and to have shown a respect for the opinions and decisions of its rulers, and a sincere regard for the outward interests of the faith which he professed. According to what is said by an old writer, " the Church received all the proofs and pledges of his love imaginable, and thus favoured and fortified, might have long enjoyed, not only peace and security, but very profitable and magnificent privileges, had not such a flame been bred in her internally, that in comparison of it the worst persecutions had been a very great blessing."

CHAPTER XXXV.

COUNCIL OF NICE. A. D. 325.

It was in the same year in which Constantine openly professed his belief in Christianity, that Alexander, a man of great piety, just, charitable, and courteous, but deficient in strength of mind and intellectual gifts, was elected to the bishopric of Alexandria. The appointment was satisfactory to the people in general, but it excited a feeling of envy in the heart of Arius, an Alexandrian presbyter, who had himself aspired to the dignity. His ill-will, however, was not at once shown ; he continued to work under the bishop ; but as he could not attack Alexander's character, he determined to find some error in his doctrine. It happened, one day, that the bishop and several of his presbyters were occupying themselves in discussing the deep and difficult doctrine of the Trinity. Arius was very clever in controversy, and when the bishop expressed his opinions freely, he took occasion to differ from him, accusing him of the heresy called Sabellianism, which had arisen in the Church not very long before.

The bishop had probably spoken incautiously,

but there was not any real cause for the accusation. . Arius, however, insisted upon it eagerly, though, in the course of the discussion which ensued, he betrayed his own errors of doctrine, and showed that he had no real belief in the doctrine of the Trinity. He asserted that Christ did not spring from the nature of God the Father, but was created from nothing; that He had indeed an existence before the world, but not from eternity; and that He was capable of sin, although, from His perseverance in good, God had imparted to Him a dignity above that of all other creatures. This belief struck at the root of the great truth of the atonement, upon which the hopes of every Christian must rest. If Christ was not really God, the sacrifice offered upon the Cross must lose its priceless value. Alexander was much startled by the opinions propounded by Arius; but being unwilling at once to condemn him, he allowed several meetings to be called, in which Arius, and the friends who sided with him, might freely discuss the points in dispute. He himself listened to all that could be said on either side, and ended by positively determining against the doctrine which Arius maintained. A synod was assembled at Alexandria, and Arius, with nine of his followers, was expelled from the Church. Athanasius, a deacon, and afterwards a very distinguished father of the Church, is said to have had great influence with Alexander, and to have urged him to the strong measures against Arius which he at this time adopted. But the sentence of condemnation had but little effect upon the mind of Arius. He was a man of quick intellect, cunning, and restless, and particularly well qualified to be the leader of a party. Now that he was no longer permitted to

28*

exercise a public ministry in the Church, he set up conventicles for his followers, and thrusting himself into society, forced his discourse upon persons, whether they were willing or not to listen to him, thus filling the city with clamours against Alexander and the censures of the synod. A large number of weak men were drawn over to his side, and they increased the disturbance by taking upon themselves to plead the cause of Arius even in the streets and highways, repeating for this purpose the most idle tales; whilst some of them even ventured to solicit the interference of the courts of justice, and to entreat that they would take upon themselves to rescind the sentence of the bishop.

In consequence of their efforts, the party of Arius increased in strength at Alexandria, whilst the reputation of the heretic was skilfully advanced in distant places by letters and despatches, written by him to several of the most eminent bishops of the East. In these communications he represented his case so plausibly that many were induced to appeal to Alexander, hoping to effect a reconciliation between him and Arius. Eusebius, bishop of Nicomedia, was the chief supporter of the heretic. He was a clever but daring man, and his mind had for some time been deeply infected with the principles that Arius had openly proclaimed; he now placed himself at the head of the Arian party, which was spreading in all directions. Alexander did everything in his power to repel the growing evil; he wrote no less than seventy letters to various bishops, explaining the true principles of Arius; he convened a second synod at Alexandria, at which nearly a hundred bishops out of Egypt and Lybia were assembled; and, at length, in a general, or, as it is called an encyclical epistle, he called upon all the bishops and governors of the universal Church to sympathize with and support him in his condemnation of the new errors.

The Christian world was now unhappily a scene of almost universal contention. The orthodox and the heretical alike did their utmost to support their several doctrines, and it is to be feared that, in the eagerness of disputation, the principles of Christian charity were too much forgotten by both parties.

The spectacle must have been very perplexing to Constantine, who could have had but a slight acquaintance with the abstruse doctrines of Christianity. A considerable time elapsed before he took any part in the controversy. At length, finding himself securely established as the sole possessor of the throne, and being therefore at liberty to attend to ecclesiastical affairs, he wrote both to Alexander and to Arius, expressing an earnest desire for their reconciliation, but giving no opinion upon the disputed question ; rather, as he stated, considering it to be one which was beyond the reach of the human mind, and which it would therefore be wiser to leave unsettled. This letter was sent to Alexandria by Hosius, a Spanish bishop, whose faith and piety had been remarkable in the last persecution.

The advice of the emperor would have been easily followed if the question under discussion had referred only to the belief of the human imagination ; but the doctrine of the Saviour's Divinity was to the orthodox Christians no matter of speculation, but a truth which had been taught from the very beginning of the Christian Church. They were not at liberty to put it aside as a point of no practical importance. Apostles, they believed, had proclaimed it, martyrs had died confessing it. Man could not venture to pronounce that what God had been pleased to reveal was not necessary for salvation; and the only question really in the power of the Church to argue and decide, was whether the evidence for the doctrine was complete; whether it really formed part of the original faith delivered to the apostles, or was only a subtlety of human invention. The letter, of which Hosius was the bearer, was ineffectual to produce peace, and he returned to the emperor to give an account of his unsuccessful mission. Only one means then remained by which unity might be restored to the Church, and Constantine resolved to adopt it.

A summons was issued to the bishops and clergy in all parts of the Christian world, commanding them to meet together in council, and decide as to the truth or falsehood of the Arian doctrine. The place appointed for the assembly was Nice, the metropolis of Bithynia, and in the same province with Nicomedia, where Constantine then kept his court. Nice was a large city, remarkable for its handsome and regular buildings; it was situated on the bank of the Ascanian Lake, and surrounded by an open, pleasant, and fertile country. Hither came three hundred and eighteen bishops, besides a great number of presbyters, deacons, and persons holding inferior offices in the Church; the bishops, their attendants, and followers, being brought to the place of meeting in public conveyances, and the emperor undertaking to maintain them at his own cost whilst the council was sitting.

It was on the 20th of May, or, as some have asserted with greater probability, on the 19th of June, A. D. 325, that this great synod met.

Before the business of the meeting was regularly entered upon, the bishops spent some days in preliminary discussions, in which Arius himself was frequently called before them, and his propositions were carefully debated; and they also entered into controversy with some heathen philosophers, who had either been drawn to the meeting from curiosity, or had been brought thither by Arius to retard and entangle the proceedings of the synod. One of these men, who prided himself upon the talent displayed in his discourses, spoke scornfully of the fathers of the council. The insolence was so intolerable, that an aged Christian, who had suffered much in the late persecution, but was quite unacquainted with the rules of argument, rose up and offered to contend with the philosopher. Some laughed at the proposal, others took it seriously, and expressed themselves afraid of the result. But the Christian confessor was not to be daunted, and turning to his adversary, he bluntly, but earnestly, exclaimed, " In the Name of Jesus Christ, philosopher, give ear. There is One God, the Maker of Heaven and Earth, and of all things visible and invisible, who made all these things by the power of His Word, and confirmed them by the holiness of His Spirit. This Word, whom we call the Son of God, pitying the sons of men involved in error and sin, chose to be born of a woman, to converse with men, and to die for them ; and He will come again to sit as the Judge of all things which men have done in the body. These things we plainly believe. Labour not then in vain, seeking to confute what ought to be received by faith, or to discover how these things may or may not be ; but if thou dost believe answer me now that I ask thee." The philosopher, awe-struck by the old man's zeal and simplicity, replied, "I do believe;" and addressing his companions, he solemnly declared that by the power of a divine influence which he could not withstand, he was converted to the Christian faith; and now returned thanks to God for IIis enlightenment, whilst he earnestly exhorted his brother philosophers to reconsider the truths which they had been accustomed to deride.

But this discussion was of slight moment compared with the great controversy which was to follow. It must have been a magnificent spectacle when, on the day appointed for the examination of the doctrines of Arius, the procession of bishops reached the emperor's palace, and entered the magnificent hall prepared for the meeting of the council. Amongst them were men still bearing the marks of the dire persecution through which the Church had but lately passed. Paul, bishop of Neocæsarea, was amongst those who had most grievously suffered; two other bishops had each lost one of their eyes; scars and mutilations were visible on the persons of many besides; and, as they had borne witness to the faith amidst the scoffs of the heathen, so now they came from the most remote Churches of the known world to proclaim, before a Christian assembly, the truth which each Church had received, that the Lord Jesus Christ is Perfect God as well as Perfect Man. The bishops ranged themselves in the hall, standing. In the centre of the apartment was a copy of the Sacred Scriptures, by which the controversy was to be regulated, and at the upper end, was a golden chair, prepared for the emperor.

Constantine, dressed in his purple robes, and adorned with jewels, but without guards, followed the prelates. Advancing to the throne, he stood by it, declining to seat himself until requested by the bishops. He then placed himself upon the golden chair, and the whole council seated themselves at the same instant.

Silence was commanded, and the Bishop of Antioch opened the council by an address to the emperor, in which he magnified the goodness of God in securing Constantine on the imperial throne. Eusebius, of Cæsarea, the historian, added a speech to the same effect; and when he ceased, the emperor himself addressed the assembly in the Latin language, his words being translated into Greek by an interpreter.

"There was nothing," he said, "which he had more earnestly desired than to behold the venerable assembly then met. For the gratification of this wish he returned hearty thanks to God, praying that none might be able to interrupt the prosperity of the Church; and that, having been delivered from the power of tyrants, Satan might not be permitted to injure it by internal commotions." Then, producing a number of written accusations against various bishops which had been presented to him on the preceding day, he gravely reproved those who had at such a time brought forward their private complaints, reminding them that "these things were reserved for the decision of the Great Day of Judgment, and that it was the duty of all to lay aside their quarrels, and attend only to the things that concerned the faith, for which end they were there met together." Casting the papers into the fire, he protested that he had not read one word of them, and added that "it was not fit that the faults of priests should be published to the scandal of the people, who might from thence derive a warrant to themselves to sin more boldly." When the emperor had finished speaking the discussion began.

The case at first was argued with warmth on both sides; extracts from the writings of Arius were read, and their meaning canvassed. Athanasius of Alexandria exhibited wonderful powers of mind in the arguments which he brought forward in proof of the Catholic faith. Seventeen of the bishops openly defended the heretical doctrine, a few others appear to have supported it less publicly. The emperor acted as moderator, and endeavoured to bring them to agreement; but the task was one of immense difficulty, and it soon appeared that, without some explanations pointing out decidedly what the Scriptures had revealed, it would be impossible to guard against the subtleties of the Arians. The same words were used by both parties, but the Arians offered to them a meaning of their own. They allowed, for instance, that Christ was God, but it was only in the sense in which holy men and angels are styled gods in Scripture. They admitted, with the Catholics, that the Son was the Power, Wisdom, and Image of the Father; but they immediately falsified the truth by adding that men also are said to be the Image and Glory of God. In this difficulty it was resolved to collect together the passages of Scripture which speak of the Divinity of the Son of God, and from them to draw up a definite confession of faith.

This was done by Hosius, the Spanish bishop, and the creed, when completed, was brought forward for the confirmation of the synod. In essentials it was the same as that which we now call the Nicene Creed, and which the English Church requires should be repeated in the office for the administration of the Holy Communion. It ended, however, with the words, "I believe in the Holy Ghost," the remaining portion being added on a subsequent occasion, when it was thought fit to explain more definitely the Catholic doctrine as to the nature and offices of the Blessed Spirit. Only two bishops objected to subscribe this declaration of faith; the rest were unanimous in affirming the scriptural truth of the Nicene Creed, and its accordance with the doctrines handed down from the beginning of Christianity. Yet it is to be feared, from after circumstances, that about twenty still endeavoured to affix an Arian interpretation to the words used, though they would not openly declare their opinion. It only remained to pronounce sentence of condemnation upon Arius and his followers. They were solemnly anathematized by the council, and by the command of the emperor exiled to Illyricum. The writings of Arius were ordered to be burnt.

Two other questions were decided by the Nicene council; one concerned the schism occasioned by Meletius, who was ordered to be divested of all authority in the Church, and the other referred to the time of keeping Easter,—a controversy which had been renewed with great eagerness. By order of the Nicene council the festival was to be solemnised in all places on one and the same day, namely, the Lord's Day following the Jewish Feast of the Passover.

The last act of the council was to draw up some rules for ecclesiastic discipline, and the government of the Church, embodied in twenty canons or laws, which have been transmitted to our own day.

The business being concluded, the emperor, we are told, invited the bishops to a public dinner,

29

ordering guards and officers to be ready to receive them. The most distinguished were entertained at Constantine's own table, and the rest in apartments prepared for them. The greatest respect was shown to such as bore the marks of suffering from persecution; the emperor showing them all outward signs of reverence, and entreating their blessing. When dinner was ended, the bishops were loaded with gifts suitable to their dignity, and Constantine then took his leave of them, again pressing them to maintain unity of faith, and to live in peace amongst themselves; and, as a last request, begging that they would offer up prayers for himself, his children, and the prosperity of his empire.

Thus ended this great council after it had been sitting rather more than two months. The creed which it framed has ever been held as the standard of Church doctrine, while its laws, and the rules by which it was conducted, are regarded as setting forth the true principles of Church authority.

The history of the first centuries of Christianity might well close at this point, yet it may be interesting to trace shortly the after conduct and the fate of some amongst those who took a prominent part in the Nicene council. Of Constantine himself, little that is satisfactory can be told. Political motives appear to have greatly influenced him in his support of Christianity; and his acknowledgment of the Catholic faith seems to have been made in ignorance, and with greater desire for peace than for truth. By the entreaty of his sister, who was an Arian, he was induced to recall Arius from banishment, and to accept his declaration of belief in the creed of the council of Nice. And not content with this, he showed much harshness and injustice to Athanasius, who, after the death of Alexander, had been elected to the bishopric of Alexandria. The character of Athanasius appears to have been a remarkable compound of zeal, humility, and piety. Though engaged in controversy during the greater portion of his life, he seems never to have lost the spirit of true piety and charity. The idea of accepting the high office of bishop was so oppressive to him that he fled to the desert, in order to avoid it, and it was with the greatest difficulty that he was afterwards prevailed upon to accept it. But in the cause of the true faith, Athanasius was as firm as in other respects he was gentle. The emperor, having given permission to Arius to return to Alexandria, issued his commands that Athanasius should receive him into the Communion of the Church. The bishop refused to comply, and was threatened with banishment. He was still inflexible, and Constantine for the moment yielded. Eusebius of Nicomedia, and other supporters of the Arian party, then brought forward the most atrocious accusations against Athanasius. A synod was held at Tyre to examine into the truth of the complaints. Eusebius and his friends declared that Athanasius had mutilated and murdered Arsenius, an Egyptian bishop; and they boasted that when the day of trial should arrive they would give ocular proof of the bishop's guilt. With this view, at the appointed time, they produced before the court a withered arm, which they asserted had belonged to Arsenius. A shout of triumph rang through the assembly. Silence was commanded, and Athanasius, who stood unmoved in the midst of his enemies, enquired of the judge if any of them knew Arsenius. Several members of the council replied in the affirmative. Athanasius retired for a few moments. When he re-entered the hall, he was accompanied by a man, wrapped in a large cloak, who walked with his head bent down. At the request of Athanasius he looked up, and the assembly recognised Arsenius. He had heard of the plot against Athanasius, and, travelling night and day, had arrived in Tyre just in time to crush the conspiracy by his presence. Athanasius presented him to the council, saying: "Behold Arsenius with his two hands. God has given him no more. It is for my accusers to say where a third could be placed, or where that has come from which they have just exhibited to you."

The fury of the Arians at this exposure was so great that they would have torn Athanasius to pieces, if he had not been conveyed out of their reach by the soldiers of the emperor, who carried him on board a ship. Yet the bishop, although apparently triumphant, was not so in reality. He had excited the deadly hatred of a faction, and his enemies contrived during his absence to have sentence of condemnation passed upon him.

Athanasius then repaired to Constantinople, the city before termed Byzantium, which had been greatly beautified and enlarged by Constantine, and called after his name.

The emperor was entering the metropolis on horseback when Athanasius met and addressed him. At the first moment Constantine did not recognize the bishop; when he did, he refused to concern himself with his affairs; but Athanasius was importunate, and succeeded at length in obtaining a hearing. He explained that all which he desired was to be permitted to confront his accusers in the emperor's presence; the request was so reasonable that Constantine felt constrained to comply with it. Eusebius, of Nicomedia, and some other enemies of Athanasius were summoned to Constantinople. But when they came, it was with a new charge. Athanasius, they said, had threatened to stop the fleet which brought corn from Alexandria to Constantinople. This accusation, as they probably knew, was one likely to touch the emperor keenly. He had lately beheaded a man on a similar suspicion. Athanasius, taken by surprise, asked for time to enable him to prove his innocence, and Constantine, in a fit of indignation, ordered him to be banished to Treves.

Arius now returned to Alexandria, but disturbances followed, and he was soon afterwards summoned to Constantinople, that the emperor might be more fully satisfied as to the opinions which he held. On the day fixed for the interview, Constantine required him to declare, without evasion, whether he did or did not hold the Nicene faith. Arius produced the same confession which, when recalled from exile, he had before delivered to the emperor. It expressed his faith in Scripture words to which he was known to attach a peculiar meaning. Constantine was not satisfied. "You must," he said, "forthwith sign in my presence the decrees, and the creed of the council without alteration." With a smiling countenance, Arius complied. Constantine was surprised, and insisted still further that he should swear that he had subscribed sincerely without evasion. This oath was also taken, and the emperor allowed Arius to depart, saying: "Arius hath well spoken, if his words have no double meaning; if otherwise, God will avenge." It is

29*

said that when Arius went to the palace, he carried, concealed in his bosom, a form of faith which he had signed, and that to this he referred when he swore that he believed the creed which he had signed. By this miserable deceit he hoped to gain his end, and yet save himself from the suspicion of heresy. But God could not be deceived, though man was.

Constantine, confident in the sincerity of Arius, ordered Alexander, the bishop of Constantinople, to admit him to Communion. Alexander was an old man, earnest and zealous. The command he had received greatly distressed him, for he was fully aware that Constantine had been deceived. The feeling of distrust was indeed prevalent throughout the city. For seven days the bishop and his people gave themselves up to fasting and prayer, whilst vainly seeking to persuade Constantine to recall his order. It was on a Saturday night that Eusebius and several of the friends of Arius came to Alexander, as he was in the church called Irene, and insisted that the heretic should at once be admitted to Communion. The bishop replied that it was impossible, and the Arian party, knowing the next day to be a festival, went away, saying, " To-morrow, in this very church, he shall join with us whether you will or not."

The bold words made a deep impression on the mind of Alexander. Closing the church, he prostrated himself before the altar, and offered this fervent prayer : " Lord, if it be certain that Arius shall to-morrow be admitted to the Communion of the Church, take now Thy servant out of the world, and confound not with the wicked, him who serveth Thee with the principles of true piety. But if Thou wilt vouchsafe to spare Thy Church, as I know Thou wilt, hear what Eusebius hath dared to utter against Thee, and suffer not Thine heritage to be put to confusion and brought to ruin. Root out Arius from the earth, lest, being received into the Church, his heresy be received with him, and impiety henceforth be regarded among Christians as true piety itself." The following day Eusebius and his followers waited upon Arius, who was residing in the palace, and formed a procession to conduct him with triumph to the cathedral. As they reached the forum of Constantine, Arius was seized with a sudden and horrible illness, and being unable to proceed was left for a short time alone to recover himself. His friends waited, but he did not rejoin them. At length becoming uneasy, they sought for and found him dead.

There is perhaps no fact more striking than this in the whole history of the Christian Church. The Arians, unable to deny it, attributed it to magic, a sure testimony to the truth of the circumstances and the impression caused by them. Happy indeed would it have been for the Christian Church, if the awful death of the heretic had awakened men's minds to the danger of tampering with the truths which God has been pleased to reveal. But the Arian doctrine has, under different forms, appeared again and again in all ages of the Church. Choosing to be wise above that which is written, men still continue to reason upon subjects which are beyond reason, and refuse to believe because they cannot understand : not considering that the mind which can comprehend the Nature of God, must be itself divine.

CHAPTER XXXVI.

GENERAL REMARKS UPON THE SERVICES, RITES, MANNERS, AND CUSTOMS OF THE EARLY CHRISTIANS.

THE reign of Constantine the Great is, according to human estimation, perhaps the most important period in the history of the Christian Church. Christianity was then "established," for it was supported by the civil government, and its influence acknowledged even by those who were in no way converted to its belief. Many causes had tended to this result. The purity of Christian doctrine; the hopes held out by the new faith; the holiness and constancy of the first disciples, together with their power of working miracles, healing the sick, raising the dead, and casting out devils, were all, in the Providence of God, instrumental to it. That the last-named power was really exercised is undeniable, though it is difficult to ascertain in what manner the miserable condition of the persons styled Energumens, or Possessed by devils, exhibited itself.

Justin Martyr, Irenæus, Origen, Cyprian, Lactantius, Eusebius,—all, indeed, who in any way attempted to defend Christianity,—refer, however, to the fact itself as one known and acknowledged by all men; and appeal to the power exercised over Satan as one of the most striking testimonies of the truth of the claims made by the Church of Christ. Individuals so afflicted were permitted to be present at some of the Church services, and particular persons were appointed to take care of them, and provide them with easy and innocent employments.

The effects of the supernatural powers conferred

upon the Church were early seen. The Christians were by them enabled to confront their enemies with an evidence and an authority against which nothing could stand ; and, as time went on, and in the face of persecution and death, the Church spread far and wide, its members gathered boldness in the profession of their faith, and no longer hesitated to avow it in public assemblies, as well as in the secrecy of private intercourse. Upper rooms, or places of secret meeting for divine service, were common from the beginning, and services were also held in the catacombs, or excavations, from which it is probable the materials for building the city of Rome had originally been taken. These quarries extended to a distance of from fifteen to twenty miles. The sand-diggers who worked in them were slaves, a large class of whom were converts to Christianity, and these men, from their knowledge of the intricacies of these subterranean labyrinths, proved a great assistance to their brethren in guarding them from detection when engaged in devotion, or endeavouring to conceal themselves in times of persecution. But, by the close of the second century, buildings dedicated to Christian worship were openly recognised. They are mentioned by Clemens Alexandrinus, and more especially referred to by Tertullian, who calls a church " Domus columbæ," the house of a dove, and describes it as " simple,—built on high,—and delighting in light, as the figure of the Holy Spirit, and the east as the representation of Christ." Pictures and images were not at that time introduced, and the altar was of wood, and movable. For many years, indeed, churches must have been small buildings, without ornament. The Christians, when poor and persecuted, could have had no means of adorning them ; but Eusebius tells us that, during the time of peace which, for fifty years, the Christians enjoyed, "from the persecution of Valerian to that of Diocletian, the number of Christians so grew and multiplied that their ancient churches were not large enough to receive them, and therefore they erected from the foundation more ample and spacious ones in every city." When Constantine came to the throne, he spared no expense to build beautiful churches in all parts of the East, but especially in Constantinople, where the walls of the " Ecclesia Constantiniana," a church dedicated to the memory of the Twelve Apostles, were covered with marble, while the roof was overlaid with gold in the inside and with gilded brass on the exterior. Constantine also laid the foundation of the famous church now converted into a mosque, but still called by the name of St. Sophia.

From the earliest times churches appear to have been built with the entrance towards the west and the altar to the east ; but this rule was not so strict but that it might be altered if necessity required. Their construction differed in several respects from those of the present day. There were more parts or divisions in them, arising probably at first from the distinction made between those persons who were only preparing themselves for baptism, and were called Catechumens, and those who were actually baptized, and were admitted to the Holy Communion. In front of the building, which may more strictly be considered the church, was a court, open to the air in the centre, but surrounded with porticoes or cloisters, and having a porch for the entrance. These cloisters were intended for such persons as were not allowed to enter farther into the building, but who stood there to ask the prayers of their brethren who were entering the church. Notorious criminals were even obliged to wait in the open air, and, as part of their penance, to stand there exposed to the weather. In the middle of the court, or Atrium, there was commonly a fountain, or a cistern of water, at which the people were accustomed to wash their hands and faces before they went into the church. The atrium and porticoes were also used as places of burial. At Milan there is a church still standing called the church of St. Ambrose, which was originally built in the fourth century, and is formed upon the plan described.

The entrance from the atrium into the church itself was generally by three inner porches, leading from the cloisters into the lower portions of the sacred building,—a long but narrow part, crossing the front of the church, and which is often called the narthex, from a Greek word, signifying any oblong figure. Here the catechumens were assembled, with any Jews or heathens who might be interested in hearing the Psalms and lessons from Scripture and the sermon.

Some of the persons who had been excommunicated, but were showing true signs of repentance, were also admitted to the narthex. All these were termed Audientes, or hearers, and were dismissed without any prayers or blessing.

The nave, or body of the church, was separated from the narthex by rails of wood. It was usually of a square form, and in the lowest part of it the penitents, who were more nearly admitted to forgiveness, were stationed. As soon as the sermon was ended, they were accustomed to prostrate themselves before the bishop or priest, to receive his benediction and partake of the prayers offered for them by the congregation, after which they were obliged immediately to depart, before the Communion service began.

The Ambo, or reading-desk, joined the nave. This was a raised place made for the persons who read the Gospels and Epistles, indeed for all the clergy who ministered in the first service for the catechumens and penitents. The singers also were stationed in the ambo, and the books, in which the acts of the martyrs were noted, were read from the same place. The sermon was usually preached from the steps of the altar, but the ambo was occasionally used for the purpose. Beyond the ambo was the position for the communicants, and for an order of penitents called Consistentes, who were allowed to remain and hear the prayers of the Church after the catechumens and other penitents were dismissed, but who were yet not admitted to partake of the Eucharist. Men and women sat apart; the women, in the Greek churches, being often placed in galleries.

The third and innermost part of the ancient churches was that which we now call the chancel. The name is derived from the Latin word " cancelli," the term applied by the Western churches to the carved rails of wood by which this most sacred part of the building was shut out from the nave, and rendered inaccessible to the multitude. Curtains were also often used to conceal the view of the altar from those who were not fully Christians, or who had undergone the sentence of excommunication. The chancel was generally semicircular, and the highest part was for this reason called the Apse, a word signifying any circled or spherical building. The bishop's throne, with the thrones of his presbyters on each side of it, were also fixed in this part of the church,—in a semicircle above the altar, or Holy Table, which was not close to the wall at the upper end, but at some little distance, so that space was left to pass behind it. Within the church there was also a kind of vestry, in which the deacons placed the vestments and utensils belonging to the altar, that they might be in readiness for divine service. At other times they were kept in an outer vestry, or Diaconicum as it was termed. The words altar and table are used indiscriminately by some writers, although some epithet, such as holy, mystical, &c., is usually applied to the latter term, to imply its sacred signification in the Christian Church. Stone altars appear to have been first brought into use in the time of Constantine. It is important to remark that in the first ages of Christianity only one altar was ever placed in a church. It was always ornamented with some covering of fine linen or silk; and sometimes, as in the case of the altar in Constantine's Church at Jerusalem, with tapestry. The sacred vessels were originally of common materials, the poverty of the first Christians not allowing of any more costly substance; but it is evident that vessels of gold and silver were soon used, from the accusation brought against Laurentius, the deacon, that he would not deliver up the golden plate, the riches of the Church. Candlesticks or lamps were of the same rich material, but they were only used for the services held at night, not as being necessary for the ceremonies of the Church. Crosses, censers, incense, and images, appear to have been introduced in later ages.

In many churches, there was, besides the Communion Table, a place where the offerings of bread and wine, made by the people, were received, and from these offerings the elements consecrated at the altar were taken.

The rite of baptism was celebrated without the church, in a building called the baptistery, which was generally very large, and often used as a place of instruction for the catechumens,—the font, or pool of water, wherein persons were immersed, being within it. This also was large, for as the stated periods of baptism recurred but seldom, vast numbers usually presented themselves for baptism at the same time. There were two parts in a baptistery,—the porch or ante-room, where the catechumens made their profession of faith; and the inner room where the ceremony of baptism was performed. Originally there was but one baptistery in a city, and that at the bishop's church. Libraries and schools seem to have been attached to the churches as early as the third century. Alexander, bishop of Jerusalem, built a library for the service of that church; and Eusebius, the historian, tells us that he found there the greater part of the materials from which he composed his history.

Whether churches were consecrated by any peculiar ceremonies in the first three centuries is not certain, though it is probable that some solemn prayers and thanksgivings were customary, not only because the practice was in use among the Jews, but because it was the constant habit of the Christians to consecrate even their daily food by thanksgiving and prayer. After the time of Constantine, the consecration of churches seems to have been universal. The Church of Jerusalem, built by that emperor over our Saviour's sepulchre, was consecrated in a full synod of all the bishops of the East. The sacred buildings were often chosen as the best places for private devotion and prayer upon extraordinary occasions; and many were so built as to have private cells or recesses, into which persons might retire for private reading of the Scriptures, meditation, and prayer.

The rite of baptism, being that by which admission into the Church was obtained, held a most important position, in the eyes of Christians, from the first preaching of the Gospel. Heretics rejected or corrupted it, but their doctrines were confuted and denied by the most influential writers of the period.

Irenæus charges the followers of the heretic, Valentinus, with rejecting baptism; and Tertullian brings a similar accusation against Quintilla, a woman-preacher at Carthage, who, a little before his time, began to deny baptism with water as useless; pleading that faith alone was sufficient to save men, as it did Abraham, who pleased God without any other sacrament but the sacrament of faith.

Although the baptism of infants is plainly recognised by early writers, yet the main body of baptized persons in those days were adults, who were previously catechised, and trained in the principles of Christianity. These catechumens were admitted to the state of preparation by imposition of hands and prayer, and were signed with the sign of the Cross. No general rule existed as to the length of time during which they should remain catechumens, but three years is known to have been sometimes considered necessary. During this period they were never allowed to see baptism administered, still less the Holy Eucharist, these rites being considered too sacred for them until after their preparation. At the commencement of their instruction, they were taught the doctrine of repentance, and remission of sins, the necessity of good works, and the nature and use of baptism, after which followed an explanation of the several articles of the Creed. The catechumens were allowed to read some portions of the Scriptures ;—the historical books, and those containing special moral and religious instruction, being thought most proper at first for their instruction. At the approach of the time appointed for the administration of the sacred rite, it was usual, for the Competentes, or candidates, to give their names, and send in their petition for admission to the bishop ; and these names, together with those of the sponsors, were registered in the books of the church. Examination followed, and the candidates, if approved, were sometimes called Electi, or chosen. For twenty days after this, they were ordered to practise abstinence and fasting, to confess their sins—sometimes publicly, sometimes privately—and to undergo what was termed exorcism, which consisted of certain forms, such as imposition of hands, breathing upon them, and signing them with the sign of the Cross; but chiefly of prayers, taken from the Holy Scriptures, beseeching God to save them from the dominion of Satan. The competentes were also, at this time, taught the words of the Creed, which they were obliged to learn, and repeat to the bishop at their last examination before baptism. The Thursday in the Holy Week was especially appointed for this examination and repetition. That this creed was a rule of faith, handed down from the time of the apostles, is apparent, when we remark the various references made to it by the writers of the Early Church. Irenæus speaks of such a creed having been received from the apostles and their disciples, and dispersed over the whole world. Tertullian describes it as having come down from the beginning of the Gospel; and although the precise terms used in what is now called the Apostles' Creed are not repeated, yet the substance of them is given in the references made to this standing rule of faith. Thus, for instance, Tertullian says, "There is one rule of faith only, which admits of no change or alteration, that which teaches us to believe in one God Almighty, the Maker of the world, and in Jesus Christ, His Son, who was born of the Virgin Mary, crucified under Pontius Pilate, the third day arose again from the dead, was received into Heaven, and sitteth now at the Right Hand of God, Who shall come again to judge both the quick and the dead, by the resurrection of the flesh." The creed, indeed, seems to have formed the most important part of the instruction given to the catechumens; but the precise words were probably not committed to writing during the times of persecution, from reasons of reverence and caution; the Christians being unwilling to expose subjects so sacred to the scoffs of unbelievers. Having learnt the Creed, the competentes were made to repeat the Lord's Prayer, which was not ordinarily allowed to the catechumens till immediately before their baptism. "For this prayer was usually called the prayer of the faithful, as being peculiarly used only by persons baptized, who were made sons of God by regeneration, and had title, as such, to address God under the denomination of their Father which is in Heaven, which catechumens could not so properly do." Together with the Creed, the catechumens were also instructed how to make their proper responses in baptism, and especially they were taught what related to the renunciation of the devil, and enter-

30*

ing into covenant with Christ. These engage-
ments they actually entered into, not only at their
baptism, but previous to it, the renunciation being
solemnly made to the bishop on the preceding day,
in the words, " I renounce Satan, and his works, and
his pomps, and his service, and his angels, and his
inventions, and all things that belong to him, or are
subject to him ; " after which followed the act of
self-dedication : " I give myself to Thee, O Christ,
to be governed by Thy Laws." At this time
also the catechumens were questioned by the
bishop as to their knowledge of the Christian
faith. It was customary for the competentes to go
with their faces covered some days before baptism,
in order, it is supposed, that their attention might
not be diverted by outward objects from the sacred
duty before them. In the early days of the Church,
the rite of baptism was administered at all seasons,
but at the period when Tertullian wrote, it began to
be limited to stated periods—Easter, and Whitsuntide, and the days between those festivals. Easter
even was especially set apart for the purpose. So
also, when Christianity was first preached, baptism
was administered at any place where there was
water, though always as near as possible to the
place of public worship. Afterwards, when bap-
tisteries were built adjoining the church, a rule
was made that the Sacrament should never be administered elsewhere, except in cases of necessity,
such as sickness and imprisonment. Some persons
had a superstitious wish to be baptized in a particular spot, as at Jerusalem, or in the river Jordan,
and therefore deferred their baptism till they could
conveniently reach the destined place. In reference to this, Tertullian warns his people that
" there is no difference between those whom John

baptized in Jordan and those whom Peter baptized in the Tiber." Baptism was also sometimes deferred for other reasons. Those who loved the world, and were unwilling to give up its pleasures, deceived themselves by thinking that they could indulge themselves till the last moment, and then receive cleansing and forgiveness by baptism ; and others there were who professed to be afraid of falling into sin, after being admitted to the sacred rite. There was, they knew, no second baptism to regenerate them again. Whereas, if they were baptized at the hour of death, Heaven, they imagined, would be immediately open to them, and they might enter it pure and undefiled. With regard to the danger of dying before baptism, they flattered themselves that God would accept the will for the deed, and the desire of baptism for baptism itself. Constantine the Great was amongst the number who thus deferred his baptism till a very late period of life, and it is one of the most startling inconsistencies in his history; for, as an ancient writer remarks, " for an unbaptized man to think he is baptized in the sight of God, whilst he depends upon His mercy in the neglect of baptism; or to imagine himself in the Kingdom of Heaven without doing the things that belong to the Kingdom of Heaven, is but a false hope, bewitching the soul with false appearances and pretensions."

The catechumens having been carefully prepared for baptism, in the manner before mentioned, were brought at the appointed time to the entrance of the baptistery, and here the renunciation, covenant, and profession which they had made on the preceding day to the bishop, were required of them again ; though they appear now to have been made in the form of question and answer, very much as is the present custom in the English Church.

One sponsor was required for each person ; but in the case of adults, the only business of the sponsor was to be the instructor of the catechumen before baptism, and the guardian of his spiritual life afterwards. Upon this account, deaconesses were usually employed in the private instruction of women, to teach them how to make their responses in baptism.

The sponsors for infants, who were generally their parents, were of course called upon to answer the questions put before baptism ;—the children being unable to make the required profession for themselves.

The terms of the covenant, having been thus far fulfilled, the person to be baptized was anointed with the sign of the Cross on his forehead, and the unction was then applied to other parts of his body, his hands, feet, &c., oil being considered symbolical of the Holy Spirit. This practice is not, however, considered to belong to the very earliest days, as there is no mention of it before the time of Tertullian. The bishop or priest then proceeded to consecrate the water, pouring in some of the holy oil in a manner representing the sign of the Cross, and pronouncing a prayer of thanksgiving, an ancient form of which ends with this solemn petition : " Look down, O Lord, from Heaven, and sanctify this water, give it grace and power, that he that is baptized therein, according to the command of Christ, may be crucified with Him ; and die with Him, and be buried with Him, and rise again with Him to that adoption which comes by Him ; that, dying unto sin, he may live unto righteousness."

The act of immersion followed this prayer. It was performed three times. Women were either baptized apart, or at separate times from the men, and the deaconesses of the Church attended upon them.

The form of words used in the administration of the rite appears never to have altered. Our Lord commanded His disciples to baptize in " the Name of the Father, and of the Son, and of the Holy Ghost ; " and the same sacred words were from the beginning deemed necessary to the right administration of the sacrament; so necessary, indeed, that Athanasius, and many other writers of those times, speak of any baptism which shall be otherwise performed as being of no effect; whilst the main argument for admitting the baptism of heretics lay in the fact, that even amongst them the rite was usually administered with the form of words commanded by Christ. The baptized person being come up out of the waters, a white garment was put upon him, with this charge, or one resembling it : " Receive the white and immaculate garment, and bring it forth without spot before the tribunal of our Lord, Jesus Christ, that thou mayest have eternal life. Amen." From the custom of wearing these white garments, Pentecost (which was one of the chief seasons for baptism) was called Whitsunday. It was usual to wear the white dress for a week after baptism. It was then taken off and laid up in the church, that it might be brought forward as an evidence against those who corrupted or denied the faith which they had professed on their admission into the Church. Another ceremony used as a form of congratulation to the newly baptized was the kiss of peace, and it was also usual to give them a little taste of milk and honey, in allusion to the food of children, and to signify their being born into the family of God.

In those early days confirmation generally followed immediately upon baptism, the newly-made Christians being brought to the bishop, if he was present, in order that they might receive his benediction, which was a solemn prayer for the descent of the Holy Ghost. To this prayer there was usually joined the ceremony of a second anointing and imposition of hands, and the sign of the Cross. But if the bishop was absent, confirmation was deferred until the next convenient opportunity. It is supposed to have been the practice for the catechumens to subscribe their profession of faith in the register of the Church; but although there are allusions to this custom, there are no certain records of it. Although the imposition of hands was not considered necessary for salvation, yet its neglect was punished by public censure, such persons as had voluntarily omitted it being ordinarily denied admittance to holy orders. Infants as well as adults were considered fit for confirmation. Immediately after the baptism in Easter Week, a series of instructions on the Eucharist was given to the neophytes or new-made Christians. Heretics and schismatics who had been baptized in infancy out of the Church, were received by imposition of hands, or confirmation, when they returned to it.

The ordinary public services of the early Christians appear to have varied according to the condition of the Church. Although assemblies for religious services were held at first every day, the most solemn meetings were on the first day of the week. Not long, however, after the time of Justin Martyr, it was customary to meet for especial worship on Wednesdays and Fridays, which were called the stationary days, because the services were continued till three o'clock in the afternoon, the Communion being always celebrated on these occasions. It seems probable that during these lengthened services time was left for meditation and private prayer. Athanasius mentions religious assemblies on the Saturday or seventh day, but the writers who precede him are silent about it.

The service was always performed in the language of the country, and there are distinct traces of set forms from the very foundation of the Church, especially in the celebration of the Eucharist, which was the great service to which all that went before was but an introduction. In later times, reference is made by many writers, but especially by St. Cyprian, to the very words used in the Communion Service of the English Church.

The service appears to have begun with the salutation of the bishop or priest, "The Lord be with you," followed by the reading of the Scriptures, both of the Old and New Testament; but at first there appears to have been no settled portion, the meetings of the Christians being often disturbed by the heathen. Both Justin Martyr and Tertullian own that only so much was chosen as the condition of the times permitted. Afterwards regular lessons, suited to the Church seasons, were appointed. Origen tells us that the Book of Job was read during Passion Week, because the sufferings of Job were considered typical of the sufferings of the Redeemer. The writings of men eminent for piety were also read on these occasions. The Epistle of Clemens Romanus was amongst the number, and also the book called "The Shepherd," written by Hermas. Persons not regularly ordained were allowed to exercise the office of reader. Psalms and hymns formed a considerable portion of the service. Whilst the gift of inspiration lasted, the hymns were often extempore, at other times they were either taken from the Holy Scriptures or composed by private persons. There is reason to believe that the psalms were sung alternately. Ignatius is said to have introduced the custom, in consequence of having in a vision heard the angels praising the Holy Trinity with alternate hymns. The reading of the Gospel succeeded the psalms, and the bishop or priest then preached a sermon, generally an exposition of the portion of Scripture which had just been read. Sometimes there were two or three sermons or addresses during the same service, the presbyters first exhorting the people, who stood to listen, and the bishop following them. Prayers for the catechumens, energumens, and penitents came afterwards, and when they were ended, it was customary in the Greek churches for the deacon to cry aloud, " Those that are catechumens depart." The form in the Latin or Roman churches was " Ite missa est." " Depart ; there is a dismission of you." This is the origin of the term " Mass," applied to the principal service in the Roman Catholic Church.

In the early days the whole of the public services, from the commencement till the time that the catechumens were dismissed, was called " Missa catechumenorum," the mass or service of the catechumens ; whilst that which followed was termed " Missa fidelium," the mass or service of the faithful.

The forms observed in the celebration of the Eucharist must, as we gather from ancient liturgies and from reference to various writers, have resembled greatly those now in use in the English Church,—some few exceptions may be noticed. The bishops and the priests at the altar were accustomed to wash their hands before commencing the service, thus signifying the purity of heart required of those who draw nigh to God; and this action was followed by the kiss of peace. Prayers for the Church in general succeeded, together with forms of salutation and thanksgiving for the great mercies of Redemption. After this the people made their offerings, and the elements were consecrated by the bishop, who, having devoutly received them himself, delivered them to the people in both kinds. A prayer of thanksgiving concluded the liturgy, and the congregation departed after receiving from the bishop the salutation, " Peace be with you," to which they replied, " And with thy spirit."

Justin Martyr and Irenæus tell us that the sacramental elements were, after consecration, sent to persons who had been compelled to be absent from the service; and in times of persecution those who were anxious to communicate sometimes carried back a portion of the Eucharist to their homes, and partook of it every day in private. Infants also were permitted to receive it, and the practice was continued for many centuries. It appears to have been discontinued in the Western Churches from the consideration that by baptism children are admitted into covenant with God, and so, through His mercy, placed in a state of salvation; and that they cannot rightly partake of the Eucharist until they are of an age to understand that they do so in remembrance of Christ. It is probable that the first Christians communicated every day; but forms of morning and evening service

31

were used apart from the celebration of the Eucharist; and a second, or Evening Service, was always provided for the Lord's Day.

The offerings brought by the people, and from which the elements were taken for consecration, were originally provided for the Agapæ, or Love Feasts, held in the church, sometimes before the Communion, sometimes after, or in the evening. Portions of the bread thus offered were blessed by the bishop, and sent as a sign of fellowship to the catechumens and others who had no right to partake of the Eucharist. It was usual, in many places, to rehearse the names of such as offered, and to offer prayers and praises for them.

Another mention of individuals was sometimes made after the salutation of the kiss of peace;—the names of eminent saints and martyrs, written in books called diptychs, because they were folded together,—being read aloud; partly to celebrate their memory as still living, although in another state of existence; and partly to excite those present to follow their holy lives.

The practice of turning to the east in prayer appears to have begun in the earliest times. Clement and Tertullian say that this was because the east was considered the type of Christ, as being the quarter from which light sprang. The usual posture of the early Christians, when engaged in prayer, was kneeling, and it was not unusual to spread out the hands so as to shadow out an image of the Cross. On the Lord's Day they were accustomed to pray standing. An ancient writer says upon this subject: "That for six days we pray upon our knees, is in token of our fall from sin; but that on the Lord's Day we do not bow the knee, does symbolically represent our resurrection,

by which, through the grace of God, we are delivered from our sins and the power of death."

The custom of hallowing the day on which our
Blessed Saviour rose from the dead, dates from
the time of the Apostles. All lawsuits were forbidden on this day, and all worldly employments,
except such as men were called upon to undertake,
either by charity or necessity. Constantine obliged
those of his soliders who were Christians to attend
the services of the Church, and directed the
heathens to repair to the open fields, and there,
having laid aside their arms, upon a signal given,
to address their supplications to God, the Supreme
King of all ; and for this purpose he is said to have
given them a prayer of his own composing. Fasting was especially prohibited on the Lord's Day,
which, in memory of the resurrection of Christ,
was always considered a day of peculiar joyfulness.
Next to the Lord's Day, the Saturday, or Sabbath,
was held in veneration ; this feeling being of course
derived from the Jews. In the Eastern Churches
it appears to have been kept as a festival, but in
the Western as a fast.

Easter, Whitsuntide, Christmas, and Epiphany
were the other great festivals, the two latter being
often comprehended under the general name of
Epiphany. The first traces of the celebration of
Christmas are said to be found in the second century, and a sad illustration of the fact of its observance is stated to have occurred in the time of
the Diocletian persecution. The Christians of
Nicomedia, being met together to commemorate
their Saviour's Nativity, Diocletian, who then kept
his court in the city, commanded the church doors
to be closed and the building to be set on fire, and,
in a short time, the congregation and the church

were reduced to ashes. The whole period from Easter to Pentecost is often called Pentecost by early writers, and in many churches it was considered unlawful at that time to worship publicly, kneeling. Ascension Day appears to have been early considered a day of special rejoicing.

The anniversaries of those days on which the chief martyrs died, were also solemnly but joyfully remembered in the early Church, and the preceding night was observed as a vigil, being spent in psalmody and prayers till the dawn of morning. "We keep," says an ancient writer, "the memories of the saints, of our ancestors, and friends that die in the faith, both rejoicing in that rest which they have obtained, and begging for ourselves a pious consummation in the faith. And we celebrate, not the day of their nativity, as being the inlet to sorrow and temptation, but of their deaths, as the end of their miseries, and that which sets them beyond the reach of temptation. And this we do, both clergy and people meeting together, inviting the poor and needy, and refreshing the widows and orphans, that so our festival may be—both in respect of them whom we commemorate, the memorial of that happy rest which their departed souls do enjoy,—and in respect of us, the odour of a sweet smell in the sight of God." The festival of the Holy Innocents, kept in memory of the children slain by Herod, at the time of our Saviour's birth, is likewise of very ancient date.

At first the solemnities on the anniversaries of the martyrs' deaths were observed at their tombs, which usually were in the cemeteries, apart from the places of public worship; but as Christianity spread, churches were built on these spots, in remembrance of those who were buried there.

The fasts of the early Christians were of two kinds, weekly and annual. The weekly fasts were kept upon Wednesdays and Fridays, in remembrance of the betrayal and the crucifixion of our Redeemer. Sometimes they were called stations, in allusion to the watchful guard maintained by the soldiers at the military stations. They lasted till three o'clock in the afternoon, public prayers and services being the employment of the people until that hour, when the Eucharist was administered and they returned home.[*]

The great annual fast was that of Lent. It appears to have been originally kept for forty hours, as a time of mourning between the death of our Lord and His Resurrection; but it is certain that in the time of Irenæus and Tertullian the appointed period had increased beyond this, though the full term of forty days was appointed at a much later date. The object of the fast doubtless was to recall men from their worldly occupation, and force them to examine their hearts, and repent of their sins; whilst they were especially required to join in prayer with those who were about to present themselves at Easter to receive either baptism or absolution; Lent being always most strictly observed by catechumens and penitents.

The usual mode of observing this fast amongst persons religiously disposed was to abstain from all food until the evening. Then a supper was allowed, in which food of any kind might be taken in moderation.

What was thus saved from their own personal indulgence was given to the poor, for Lent was considered a time for exercising especial works of

* Bingham's Antiquities, book xxi. chap. iii. sect. 3.

31*

charity, visiting and feeding those who were destitute, or suffering, or in prison; and striving to promote peace amongst such as were at variance. These duties were thought to be especially binding on such persons as from sickness and infirmity of body were not able to observe a strict fast.

Religious assemblies for prayer and preaching were usually every day in Lent. The festivals of martyrs do not appear to have been in general observed at this time; but the Lord's Day was still considered a festival with which nothing could interfere. The week before Easter was kept with extraordinary strictness, some persons going without food for many days together. Charity to the poor was also exercised with increased liberality. Easter Eve was, by the whole Church, observed as a fast not only till evening, but till cock-crowing in the morning, which was the supposed time of our Saviour's Resurrection. The preceding hours of the night were spent in a vigil, when the people assembled for solemn services of devotion, singing psalms, reading the Scriptures, praying, and preaching. Easter Eve was also a celebrated time for baptism. It was a tradition amongst the Jews that Christ would come at midnight, and from this it is supposed, a custom arose, even during the time of the Apostles, not to dismiss the people on the vigil of Easter until midnight, after which the Church believed itself secure and at liberty to keep the festival. In the time of Constantine, the vigil of Easter was observed with great pomp. Lofty pillars of wax were set up to burn as torches all over the city, and lamps lighted in all places.

The fast in the Ember weeks appears to have dated from a later period than the reign of Constantine, as at first there were no certain times of ordination in the Church, the rite being administered at any time, as necessity might require.

Besides these set times for solemn services, the Christians, as early as the second century had set hours for private prayer during the day. Clemens Alexandrinus, Cyprian, and others refer to this fact. The third, sixth, and ninth hours, answering to our nine and twelve in the morning, and three in the afternoon, appear to have been particularly set apart for devotional purposes, and we are told that at midnight likewise they were wont to rise, pray, and sing hymns to God,—a custom which probably originated in the times of persecution, when their religious assemblies were always held at night.

The common actions of the early Christians were also hallowed by religious observances. Tertullian says they signed themselves with the sign of the Cross " at their going out and coming in, at their going to a bath, or to bed, or to meals, or whatever their employment or occasion called them to." They were accustomed to use a form of prayer before meals, and to sing psalms during dinner,—a practice which Clemens Alexandrinus commends, " as being very suitable to Christians, and as a modest and decent way of praising God, whilst we are partaking of His creatures." Prayer and thanksgiving also followed the meal.

In their domestic life the Christians were careful to avoid the vain pomp and show so much sought after by the heathen. " Stately palaces, costly furniture, rich hangings, fine tables, curious beds, vessels of gold and silver," as Clemens Alexandrinus says, " create envy.   Will not a knife cut as well," he adds, " though it have not an ivory handle, or be not garnished with silver ? Will not an earthen basin serve to wash the hands ?   Will not the table hold our provisions, unless its feet be made of ivory ? or the lamp give its light, although made by a potter, as well as if it were the work of the goldsmith ? May not a man sleep as well upon a mean couch, as upon a bed of ivory ? upon a goat-skin, as well as upon a purple or Phœnician carpet ? Our Lord ate His meat out of a common dish, and made His followers sit upon the grass, and washed His disciples' feet, without ever fetching down a silver bowl from Heaven ; He took the water which the Samaritaness had drawn in an earthen pitcher, not requiring one of gold, showing how easy it was to quench His thirst. For He respected the use, not the vain and superfluous state of things."

In their dress the first Christians avoided singularity, yet, at the same time, they were exceedingly careful to give up all unnecessary ornament or finery. Justin Martyr, when giving an account of the Christians to a friend, tells him that " they are not in any thing affected or fantastic ; but inhabiting partly amongst Greeks, partly in barbarous cities, as every one's lot is fallen, they follow the customs of their country, both in clothes and diet, and all other affairs of outward life." " The garment that we should wear," says Clemens Alexandrinus, " ought to be mean and frugal, not curiously wrought with divers colours, but white, to denote our embracing and professing simplicity and truth. Our outward clothing is an indication of the temper of our minds. That is true simplicity of habit, which takes away what is vain and superfluous ; that the best and most solid garment which is furthest from art and curiosity, and most apt to preserve and keep warm the body."

But although this was the rule, yet it must be

owned there were exceptions to it, especially amongst women. Christian ladies, in those times, as in the present, were apt to bestow far too much attention and money upon outward adornment. Their absurdities are thus described by Tertullian, who, having a tendency himself towards the severities of the Montanists, was particularly keen in his satire upon such follies : " A great estate," he says, " is drawn out of a little pocket. It is nothing to expend many thousand pounds upon one string of pearls ; a weak, tender neck can make a shift to carry about whole woods and lordships. Vast sums of money, borrowed of the banker, and noted in his account-book, to be repaid every month with interest, are weighed at the beam of a thin, slender ear. So great is the strength of pride and ambition, that even the weak, feeble body of one woman shall be able to carry the weight and substance of so many pounds taken at usury." Clemens Alexandrinus condemns the offence more gravely, and declares that although gluttony and intemperance are great vices, they are not to be compared to extravagance in dress. Most probably, he means from its insatiable and unbounded nature ; for he adds, " where there is an affectation of finery, of gold, purple, or jewels, there not the treasures of the creation, not what is above or under ground, not the spoils of the Tyrian Sea, not the freights from India or Ethiopia,—no, nor Pactolus, with his golden streams,—would suffice ; nay, such persons, though as rich as Midas, would not yet think themselves rich or fine enough." He compares women who adorn their bodies but neglect their souls, to the Egyptian temples. " Look upon their outside, and they are most magnificent, encompassed with groves, built with large entries and stately porticoes, surrounded with several rows of pillars, the walls both within and without set off with stones of several countries, curiously wrought and carved; the temples themselves garnished with gold, silver, amber, and all the glittering and precious stones that India or Ethiopia can afford. But enter within them, and enquire for the deity that is there worshipped—and you shall be gravely shown, behind a curtain, a cat, or a crocodile, or a serpent of that country, or some such ill-favoured beast, which is the tutelary deity of that place. And just such," he says, " do those women seem to me, who trim themselves with gold, and are taken up in curling their hair, painting their faces, blacking their eyes, colouring their locks, and other undue acts of softness and luxury, beautifying the outward rail and fence. But if a man look within the veil and covering of the temple for what is under all this gayness and finery, he shall be so far from meeting what is truly beautiful, that it will excite his horror and aversion. He shall not find the Image of God dwelling there, as might reasonably be expected; but instead thereof, some filthy and treacherous beast, that possesses the most inward recesses of the soul; or that crafty serpent, that devours the understanding of a man, and turns his soul into a nest or den, full of most deadly venom, and the poison of his error and deceit."

Temperance in eating and drinking was a duty as much enforced as neatness and sobriety in dress. " Many," says Clemens Alexandrinus, " like brute beasts, live only that they may eat; but, for us, we are commanded to eat that we may live. Food and pleasure are not the work and design for which we live in the world; our residence here being in order to an incorruptible life, and, therefore, our nourishment ought to be easy and simple, and such as is subservient to the two main ends of life, health and strength."

This strictness and purity of life was encouraged not only by the general example, but by the discipline exercised upon all who were guilty of notorious offences. Excommunication, or suspension from communion with the Church, was inflicted according to the nature of the offence—for two, three, ten, fifteen, twenty, or thirty years, and sometimes for the whole life. If the person offending had received holy orders, he forfeited his ministry; and, though upon repentance he was admitted to Communion, yet it was only as a lay person; he was never restored to the dignity of his office.

The sentence of excommunication appears to have been passed at public assemblies, and from that time the offenders were prohibited from joining with others in any offices of religion. During the period of their penance, they dressed in mourning garments, and, at the time of public service stood at the church doors to entreat the prayers of those who entered; and at these times they made open confession of their faults, without which their repentance was accounted unreal.

The time of penance being expired, they offered their petition for absolution, and if found, upon enquiry, to be sincerely repentant, they were openly re-admitted into the Church, each penitent kneeling before the bishop,—or, in his absence, the presbyter,—who, laying his hand upon his head, solemnly blessed and absolved him.

Whilst the number of Christians was small the bishops were able to perform these and other offices required of them, without assistance ; but about the time of the Decian persecution, when the number of the lapsed was unhappily so great, it was deemed desirable to appoint a public penitentiary, whose office it was to receive the confession of all great offenders and restore them to the Church ; and this office continued for many years after, but was at length abolished on account of its abuses. The martyrs in prison were also accustomed, as it has been shown before, to exercise a somewhat similar power. Amongst the crimes especially incurring the sentence of excommunication, idolatry was naturally considered one of the most heinous, as involving not only its own guilt, but that of other sins connected with it. The horror which the early Christians entertained for all which, even indirectly, tended to this sin, may be seen from the care taken to prevent its being, in the slightest degree, encouraged by those who professed themselves Christians. Persons who had been actors or stage players, who fought as gladiators, or drove the chariots in the public games, were compelled, when they became Christians, to quit these practices, since all, more or less, contributed to the maintenance of the idolatry which accompanied them. If they persisted in them, they became liable to the sentence of excommunication. Idol makers, artificers who erected idol altars or shrines, merchants who sold frankincense for the heathen temples, or sold the animals used for sacrifice, were not admitted to baptism without renouncing their trade. Attendance at a heathen temple was, of course, most strictly forbidden ; but a great difference was made between frequenting from curiosity or going thither from a call of duty or necessity. " It were to be wished," says Tertullian, " that we could live without seeing those things which we cannot lawfully practise; but, because idolatry has so filled the world with evils, a man may be present in some cases where duty binds him to the man, and not to the idol. If I am called to a priesthood or a sacrifice, I will not go, for that is the proper office or service of the idol, neither will I contribute by my counsel, or my expense, or my labour, to any such thing. If, when I am called to a sacrifice, I go and assist, I am partaker of the idolatry; but if any other cause joins me to the sacrifice, I am only a spectator of the sacrifice." Tertullian applies this rule particularly to slaves waiting on their heathen masters, and children or clients on their parents or patrons, and officers on governors and judges. He gives the same direction in some other instances which might occur in domestic life, such as a marriage, or the setting a slave free by giving him a new name, or the solemnity, common amongst the Romans, of conferring upon a youth the " Toga virilis," or dress of a man. These things were innocent in themselves, and, though idolatrous rites were usually mixed with them, yet a man might be present without joining in such ceremonies.

Of the government of the early Church before the reign of Constantine, little is to be said, except what has before been stated in speaking of the times of the Apostles. The bishop was the head of his diocese, and all matters of dispute were referred to him. In cases of difficulty, he assembled a council of his clergy; and debated with them the question requiring to be settled. When controversies arose between several bishops; reference was made to the bishop of the metropolitan city of the province. These metropolitan bishops held frequent intercourse by letters, and sought each other's advice in important cases ; and when a person was elected to any of the greater sees, it was the custom for him to send a confession of his faith to the metropolitan bishops, and to receive in return congratulatory letters, but no one bishop exercised control over the whole Church.

Traces of the superiority of metropolitan bishops are thought by some to be found as far back as the time of the Apostles. Some early writers state that Titus had the superintendence of all the Churches in Crete, and that Timothy was entrusted with the government of the Church in the whole region or province in which Ephesus was situated ; and it is certain that such superiority had been known long before the Council of Nice, for when questions of government were brought before that synod, the following canon or law was made :—

" Let.the ancient customs be continued, that the Bishop of Alexandria have power over those that are in Egypt, Libya, and Pentapolis, because such also is the custom of the Bishop of Rome. And in Antioch and in other provinces let the privileges be preserved to the churches."

The bishops of the three great sees here mentioned were, after the Council of Nice, called Patriarchs, and their power extended over more than one province. The number of patriarchs increased in succeeding ages.

Dioceses, it may be remarked, were first formed by the union of several country churches with a church in a city. After a time, they included not only the city in which the bishop resided, but a territory adjoining it, of the same extent as that which in civil affairs was under the authority of the Roman magistrate. In like manner, the provinces were marked out according to the divisions of the Roman government.

Many of these ecclesiastical arrangements naturally grew out of the circumstances of different ages, but it is evident that the Apostles themselves organised the Church from the beginning, in a definite form, and, as we have every reason to believe, in obedience to instructions given by their Blessed Lord.

The separate offices of the bishops, priests, and deacons, recognised from the first ages of the Church, are clearly defined when brought before us in history. The three orders are continually referred to by early writers, and it is uniformly affirmed that in order to make their titles of value, they must represent a clergy who had derived their authority by uninterrupted succession from the Apostles; and that, wanting this, they wanted every thing which constituted the outward call. Deacons were not ordained before the age of five and twenty. The rite of ordination was performed by the bishop alone, who, laying his hands upon the person kneeling before him, prayed that "God would make His Face to shine upon that, His servant, who was then chosen to the office of a deacon, and fill him with His Holy Spirit and power as He did Stephen the Martyr; that he, behaving himself acceptably, and uniformly, and unblamably in his office, might be thought worthy of a higher degree."

The deacons were expected to assist the bishop and presbyters in the service of the altar, taking care of the Holy Table, and all that belonged to it. They received and presented the offerings of the people, and rehearsed the names of the givers. In many churches they were called upon to read the Gospel in the service for the day, and they always assisted in administering the hallowed elements in the Eucharist, but were not permitted to consecrate them. Another office of the deacons was to direct the people in their public devotions, for which purpose they made use of certain known forms of words to give notice when each part of the service began. Remains of this custom are to be found in the exhortation, " Let us pray," used in the Prayer Book of the English Church. The deacons also warned the catechumens, penitents, and energumens, when to come up and make their prayers, and when to depart ; and in several prayers they repeated the words before them, to teach them what they were to pray for. They were also expected to rebuke persons who behaved in a disorderly manner during the time of Divine service. After obtaining the bishop's license, deacons might both preach and baptize, and in case of extreme necessity they were allowed to receive penitents into the Church. The alms of the Church were distributed through their hands, and they were appointed to make particular enquiry into the state of the poor, and also into the general conduct of the people ; for which reason they were usually styled the eyes, ears, mouth, right hand, and heart of the bishop ; because, through them, he was enabled to overlook his charge. Deacons were expected to pay great reverence to the bishops and presbyters, being forbidden to sit down before them in the public assemblies.

The ordination of a priest differed from that of a deacon, both in its form and in the powers conferred by it. The ordination of a deacon might be performed by the bishop alone, but in some churches, when a presbyter was ordained, the other presbyters who were present were required to join in the imposition of hands, as is the custom in the English Church at the present day. The same ceremony, it has been thought, is alluded to by St. Paul, when he says to Timothy, " Neglect not the gift which was given thee by prophecy, with the laying on of the hands of the presbytery." The dignity of presbyters was much greater than that of deacon. They were accustomed to sit in a semicircle, on each side of the bishop, whilst the deacons stood by their side ; and this honour was shown them because they were looked upon as the bishop's ecclesiastical council, without whose advice he would not decide any question of importance. They might baptize, preach, consecrate, and administer the Eucharist in the bishop's absence, or in his presence, if he so authorized them. They might also reconcile penitents, and grant them absolution, and in certain extreme cases they appear to have been permitted to confirm, when especially authorised by the bishop.

The power of the bishops included the whole authority and discipline of the Church. Every bishop could form his own liturgy, express the meaning of the universal creed in his own words, and appoint particular days of fasting in his own church, and, indeed, act in every way independently, so long as he did not corrupt the doctrines of the Catholic Church.

A bishop was not usually ordained until he was thirty years of age, and he was not considered qualified unless he had been previously one of the Church over which he was to rule. He was required to pass through the office of a deacon, and generally, but not always, through that of a priest. There are instances of exceptions also to

32*

the former rule. The bishops of the province were called upon to be present, if possible, at the ordination. In case of necessary absence, they were expected to send their consent in writing, but three bishops, having the consent of the metropolitan, were considered a sufficient number to perform the ceremony of consecration. By the laws of the Church, every bishop was consecrated in his own church, in the presence of his own people. At the time of consecration, the book of the Gospel was held over him by two bishops, who pronounced the prayer of consecration, whilst the rest of the bishops present laid their hands upon his head; but there were variations in this part of the ceremony, according to the customs of different Churches.

The consecration being ended, the bishops present conducted the newly ordained bishop to his chair or throne, and placing him in it, saluted him with the kiss of peace. The Scriptures were then read, according to custom, as part of the daily service; after which the new bishop made a discourse or exposition upon the appointed portion.

It appears to have been a general rule of the Church, from the beginning, that there should be but one bishop in a diocese, though, in case of age or illness, a coadjutor or assistant was sometimes allowed, who was to succeed to the see after the bishop's death. As the dioceses were enlarged by the conversion of the heathen, other assistants, called chorepiscopi, or country bishops, were also placed by the chief bishops in distant parts of their dioceses, and, being regularly consecrated, were allowed to exercise the episcopal office.

Bishops appear to have been elected by the joint consent of the clergy and people. No bishop was intruded on a people holding the Catholic faith without their agreement, which was expressed sometimes by general acclamation, when they exclaimed, with one voice, " Dignus," He is worthy; and sometimes in writing, when they subscribed the decree of election. If the bishop proposed was thought unworthy, public accusations were brought forward against him,—a practice which occasionally was the cause of great tumults. In some instances, the people being anxious for the appointment of a particular individual, famed for his sanctity, seized and compelled him to accept the office, even against his own inclination. It should be remembered that the title of Papa or Pope, signifying " father," now assumed particularly by the bishop of Rome, was originally given to all bishops, and is still retained in the Greek Church. Presbyters and deacons were chosen by the bishops and clergy, yet not without the agreement of the people.   Exceptions were to be found to this rule when the greater part of the people of the diocese were heretics or schismatics, or when a bishop was ordained for a very distant or heathen country. In neither of these instances could the consent of the people be either asked or obtained.

The maintenance of the clergy, including bishops, presbyters, and deacons, certainly depended at first upon the voluntary offerings of the people. Of these, it has been thought, there were two kinds. One was the weekly or daily oblation, made at the altar ; when, at the time of the celebration of the Eucharist, every rich communicant presented not only bread and wine, but also other necessaries, together with money for the maintenance of the Church and the relief of the poor. The other was a monthly oblation, given to the treasury, but the amount of which depended entirely on the will of the contributor. Another source of revenue for the clergy existed in the lands and possessions which, in very early days, were given to the Church. Not, indeed, that these were always kept as lands, for in the midst of the persecutions to which the Christians were exposed, such possessions were always in danger of confiscation. The Church of Rome, when offerings of this kind were made, directed them to be sold, and the price to be divided into three parts, one devoted to the maintenance of the Church, another given to the bishop, and a third to the rest of the clergy. But other Churches kept their property, and often preserved it in the times of persecution, and even received it again after it had been taken away.

First-fruits are also frequently alluded to by primitive writers, as forming a portion of the Church revenues; Irenæus and Origen both mention them.

These sources of income were all placed in the hands of the bishop, who, with the advice and consent of the senate of presbyters, distributed them as the necessities of the Church required. In order to avoid suspicion, and prevent mismanagement, an account of the administration of the revenue was given in a synod of the province, and the bishop, at his election, was called upon to give a list of his own goods, in order that such things as belonged to him might be distinguished from those that belonged to God and the Church. A certain portion of the revenue, generally either a third or a fourth, was allotted to the relief of the poor and sick, to martyrs and confessors in prison, strangers, and to the virgins and widows of the Church. At Rome, in the time of Cornelius, the contemporary of St. Cyprian, there were 1500 persons provided for in this way.

The clergy often lived with the bishop, forming but one household, and originally they were all considered as belonging to the mother or cathedral church, and not to any particular congregation; the various churches in the diocese being served indifferently by presbyters or deacons connected with the mother church.

It does not appear that, in the primitive days, there was any distinction of dress, on ordinary occasions, between the clergy and the people. During times of persecution, any difference of attire would have been attended with danger, and the bishops and presbyters were little likely to make their appearance in public in a distinct dress, whilst their enemies were diligently searching for them to put them to death. But particular dresses, worn during the time of ministering in Divine service, are known to have been in use in the beginning of the fourth century.

Marriages were celebrated in a manner similar, in many respects, to the customs of the present day. Christians were obliged to acquaint the bishop of the church with their intention beforehand, in order that, if any obstacle suggested itself, they might be dissuaded from their purpose, and they were especially forbidden to intermarry with heathens. The practice of giving a ring was usually observed at the ceremony of the espousals, when a contract was entered into which it was considered unlawful to break.

The marriage was celebrated with religious rites, and, when the service was ended, it was usual to crown the bride and bridegroom with crowns or garlands.

The heathens were accustomed to burn the bodies of the dead; but the Christians abhorred this practice, and either buried them in the ground, or embalmed and laid them in the catacombs. The heathens performed their funeral rites at night, fearing the pollution which, according to their superstition, might be incurred by attendance upon them; but the Christians knew no such fear. The bodies of their brethren, whether alive or dead, were the members of Christ, they were but sleeping for a time in preparation for the Day of Resurrection; and with this thought in their hearts, as soon as they were freed from the terrors of persecution, they bore them to their graves in the light of day, with psalms and thanksgivings; those only being denied this honour who were excommunicated, or had been guilty of suicide.

In the first ages the poor were buried at the common expense and care of their brethren; afterwards, two orders of men, called Parabolani and Fossarii, were appointed, whose particular business it was to attend to the sick, and to do all that was necessary to provide for the decent interment of the poor.

The regular service of the Church was usually performed at a funeral, the Eucharist being celebrated if it took place in the morning; and psalms and prayers forming the service in the afternoon. At this time thanksgivings were offered to God, by the bishop, for the triumphant warfare of him who had died in Christ; and the deacon read such portions of Scripture as contained the promise of a resurrection; a hymn to the same purpose being afterwards sung. Then the catechumens were dismissed, and the chief deacon made a commemoration of departed saints, and exhorted all present to follow the example of their brother, and to entreat God for a happy end. The bishop finally offered a prayer for the deceased,—"that God would pardon him whatsoever he had willingly or unwillingly sinned against Him, that He would grant him favourable angels, and place him in the bosom of patriarchs, prophets, and apostles,—where there is no sorrow, grief, or trouble, but a place of rest for the godly, and a land of quietness for the upright, and for all those who therein see the glory of Christ."*

Then were the early Christians laid to rest, and the rude monuments discovered in the catacombs, where, for the first three hundred years, so many found a shelter in life and a home in death, bear witness, like their prayers, to the earnestness and sincerity of their faith.

The monumental inscriptions of pagan Rome, and the collected inscriptions gathered from the catacombs, are now placed confronting each other in the long corridors of the Vatican. One amongst the many heathen gravestones thus records the feelings of a mother mourning for her child: "O relentless Fortune! who delightest in cruel death, why is Maximus so suddenly snatched from me?"

A Christian says, "In Christ, Alexander is not dead, but lives beyond the stars. His body rests in the tomb."

---

* Bingham's Antiquities, quoted from the Apostolic Constitutions, book xxiii. chap. iii. section 13.

THE END.

9 783744 704595